DEMANDING SEX: CRITICAL REFLECTIONS ON THE REGULATION OF PROSTITUTION

AF755148

Demanding Sex: Critical Reflections on the Regulation of Prostitution

Edited by

VANESSA E. MUNRO
University of Nottingham, UK

MARINA DELLA GIUSTA
University of Reading, UK

Routledge
Taylor & Francis Group
LONDON AND NEW YORK

First published 2008 by Ashgate Publishing

Published 2016 by Routledge
2 Park Square, Milton Park, Abingdon, Oxfordshire OX14 4RN
711 Third Avenue, New York, NY 10017, USA

First issued in paperback 2016

Routledge is an imprint of the Taylor & Francis Group, an informa business

Copyright © Vanessa E. Munro and Marina Della Giusta 2008

Vanessa E. Munro and Marina Della Giusta have asserted their rights under the Copyright, Designs and Patents Act, 1988, to be identified as the editors of this work.

All rights reserved. No part of this book may be reprinted or reproduced or utilised in any form or by any electronic, mechanical, or other means, now known or hereafter invented, including photocopying and recording, or in any information storage or retrieval system, without permission in writing from the publishers

Notice:
Product or corporate names may be trademarks or registered trademarks, and are used only for identification and explanation without intent to infringe.

British Library Cataloguing in Publication Data
Demanding sex : critical reflections on the regulation of
prostitution
1. Prostitution - Great Britain 2. Prostitution - Social
aspects 3. Prostitution - Psychological aspects
I. Munro, Vanessa II. Della Giusta, Marina, 1970-
344.4'10544

Library of Congress Cataloging-in-Publication Data
Munro, Vanessa.
Demanding sex : critical reflections on the regulation of prostitution / by Vanessa Munro and Marina Della Giusta.
p. cm.
Includes index.
ISBN 978-0-7546-7150-3
1. Prostitution--Great Britain. 2. Prostitution--Social aspects. 3. Prostitution--Psychological aspects. I. Della Giusta, Marina, 1970- II. Title.

KD8077.M87 2008
306.740941--dc22

2008010699

ISBN 13: 978-1-138-27551-5 (pbk)
ISBN 13: 978-0-7546-7150-3 (hbk)

Contents

List of Contributors

Gill Allwood is a Reader in Gender Politics at Nottingham Trent University. She is author of *Women and Politics in France* (Routledge, 2000) and *French Feminisms: Gender and Violence in Contemporary Theory* (UCL Press, 1998). She has published widely on feminism and political representation and her current research interests involve the relationship between prostitution policy, citizenship and national identity.

David Archard is Professor of Philosophy and Public Policy at Lancaster University. He is author of various works in applied ethics. He has published the book, *Sexual Consent* (Westview, 1998), as well as several articles and chapters on the topics of consent and equality as these apply to sexual practices, both commercial and non-commercial.

Rosie Campbell is Chair of the UK Network of Sex Work Projects (UKNSWP). She is co-editor (with Maggie O'Neill) of *Sex Work Now* (Willan, 2005) and has been carrying out applied policy research on prostitution since 1995. As Chair of the UKNSWP, she works with sex work projects throughout the UK and is involved with strategic development and interventions.

Alan Collins is a Professor of Economics at the University of Portsmouth. He is co-author of *Playing the Love Market: Dating, Romance and the Real World* (Free Association Books, 2000) and a past guest editor of *Urban Studies* ('Sex and the City: Social and Economic Explorations in Urban Sexuality', August 2004).

Madeleine Coy is a Research Fellow at the Child and Woman Abuse Studies Unit (CWASU), based at London Metropolitan University. She has previously worked as an outreach and support worker, and completed her PhD on the links between sex work and local authority care in 2007. She is co-author of a recent CWASU report on the narratives of men who pay for commercial sex.

Sophie Day is a Professor of Anthropology at Goldsmith's College London. She is author of *On the Game: Women and Sex Work* (Pluto, 2007) and co-editor (with Helen Ward) of *Sex Work, Mobility and Health in Europe* (Routledge, 2004). In addition, she has recently conducted studies examining sex work in London (funded by the Wellcome Trust) and HIV prevention among prostitutes (funded by the European Commission).

Marina Della Giusta is Senior Lecturer in Economics at the University of Reading. She has co-authored *Sex Markets: A Denied Industry* (Routledge, 2008) and her research spans across development and institutional economics. Her main publications are in economics of trust, social capital and development, gender and development and the economics of prostitution. She has had research grants from the ESRC, the British Academy, and internationally from the MIUR and has been involved in the evaluation of international development projects and of government policy in the UK.

Sharron A. FitzGerald is a Research Fellow at the Research Institute for Law, Politics and Justice, based at Keele University. She has conducted previous research on cultural geography, postcolonial theory and identity formation. Her recent work focuses on human trafficking and prostitution debates as they relate to issues of migration, border control and cultural politics in the European Union. She has produced a formal response to the Home Office's consultation document on a National Anti-Trafficking Action Plan on behalf of the Centre for Law, Gender and Sexuality (Keele).

Guy Judge is Deputy Head of the Department of Economics at the University of Portsmouth. He is a specialist in quantitative economics and has been working with Alan Collins to investigate the economics of client participation in the sex industry, working from a platform of rational choice theory and risk modelling.

Vanessa E. Munro is Professor of Socio-Legal Studies at the University of Nottingham. She is author of *Law and Politics at the Perimeter* (Hart, 2008) and co-editor of *Sexuality and the Law: Feminist Engagements*. She has published widely on feminist theory and sexual consent, conducted research on sex trafficking (funded by the Nuffield Foundation) and was appointed as advisor to the Parliamentary Joint Committee on Human Rights in its Report on Human Trafficking.

Maggie O'Neill is a Senior Lecturer in Criminology and Social Policy at Loughborough University. She has published widely on social theory, and in particular on sex work and the impact upon local communities of street sex markets. Amongst other works in this area, she is author of *Prostitution and Feminism* (Polity, 2001), co-editor (with Roger Matthews) of *Prostitution: A Reader* (Ashgate, 2002) and, more recently, co-editor (with Rosie Campbell) of *Sex Work Now* (Willan, 2005).

Jo Phoenix is a Reader in the School of Applied Social Science at Durham University. She is author of *Making Sense of Prostitution* (Palgrave, 2001) and co-author of *Illicit and Illegal: Sex, Regulation and Social Control* (Willan, 2005). In addition, she has published a number of articles and book chapters on the topic of prostitution – focusing in particular on regulatory responses to sex work and on the nature of young people's involvement in commercial sex.

Teela Sanders is a Senior Lecturer in the School of Sociology and Social Policy at the University of Leeds. She is author of *Sex Work: A Risky Business* (Willan, 2005) and *Paying for Pleasure: Men Who Buy Sex* (Willan, 2008). She is currently working (with Maggie O'Neill and Jane Pitcher) on a textbook on *Prostitution, Policy and Practice* (Sage, 2009). She is Chair of the Board of Trustees at Genesis (an outreach project for sex workers) and a Board Member of the UK Network of Sex Work Projects (UKNSWP).

Jane Scoular is a Reader in Law at the University of Strathclyde. She has recently completed a large study (funded by the Joseph Rowntree Foundation) into UK street sex work and the community. She is a member of the Scottish Parliament's Expert Panel on Prostitution, and has published widely on prostitutes' experiences of violence, social exclusion and legal regulation. She is currently completing a monograph entitled *The Subject of Prostitution* (Routledge-Cavendish, forthcoming).

Acknowledgements

The chapters contained in this collection emerged out of a series of workshops, held at King's College London and at the University of Reading in 2005/06, and funded by the Economic and Social Research Council and the British Academy. The editors would like to acknowledge their considerable gratitude to these funding bodies for their support of this inter-disciplinary project. They would also particularly like to thank not only those who contributed the chapters that follow, but also those invited discussants who attended the workshops and who contributed so productively there.

Editors' Introduction

The Regulation of Prostitution: Contemporary Contexts and Comparative Perspectives

Vanessa E. Munro and Marina Della Giusta

It is often said that prostitution is 'the oldest profession', but what exactly we are to make of this claim is far from clear. Some take this to reflect the inevitability of prostitution as a social practice and draw upon this to suggest the futility of efforts designed at its eradication in the modern world. By contrast, in a context in which the majority of prostitutes are female and their clients are heterosexual men, others take this to illustrate the complex inter-relation between prostitution and male domination: since patriarchy is the oldest form of social organisation, it is no accident that prostitution has been so resilient, but this, it is submitted, tells us nothing about its future in a world of genuine equality and empowerment for women.

The question of how to conceptualise, and accordingly of how to regulate, prostitution has long been a focus of attention. Diverse agendas about gender equality, the regulation of sexuality, personal self-determination, state protectionism, public nuisance and socio-economic disparity have come together in debates on prostitution policy – often fusing and/or clashing with one another in complex, unpredictable and controversial ways. In addition, particularly in modern times, debates over prostitution policy have intensified, fuelled by the development of a number of high profile, and markedly diverse, legal and policy responses at national state level. These responses range from regulative regimes for legalisation of the sex industry, to less interventionist models of decriminalisation of sex work, through to proactive efforts at its eradication through the criminalisation of the purchase of sex. The exact parameters of, and rationales for, these responses raise a number of crucial questions about our conceptualisation of the sex industry, as well as about how these policy level imperatives are being translated, or failing to be translated, into practice.

The deconstruction of sex work as legitimate labour has led to the legalisation/regulation of prostitution in several countries. Although the exact detail of the regulation approach varies across national jurisdictions, its basic starting point is that both indoor and outdoor prostitution are legal, so long as they are conducted in accordance with specific requirements. In the Netherlands, since the lifting of the ban on brothels in 2000, prostitution is permitted in licensed brothels, in toleration zones, and in other places that cause no disturbance to public law and order. Similarly, in Germany, a change to the Civil Code in 2002 means that prostitution is no longer classified as 'an offence against good morals', and selling sex both on and off street is now legal – subject to compliance with local authority regulations designed to limit the areas and conditions in which prostitution takes place. Under this regulation approach, then, sex work is officially recognised and dealt with as a legitimate occupation: sex workers are entitled to a number of employment-related protections under the law and local authorities are required to ensure that brothels are suitably licensed, and operating in accordance with relevant health and safety requirements.

This legalisation model can be contrasted against the related but distinct decriminalisation approach adopted most recently in New Zealand. Prior to the passing of the Prostitution Reform Act 2003, prostitution itself was not illegal in New Zealand, but there were a range of related offences – soliciting, brothel-keeping, procuring intercourse, and breaches of the Massage Parlours Act – that could be committed. Now, these activities associated with prostitution have a decriminalised status. Brothels are not subjected to any specific state licensing system, but are governed by the usual employment and health regulations that apply to other businesses. Soliciting has been decriminalised and there are no legal impediments to recruiting clients in public bars or hotels. In passing these reforms, the New Zealand government emphasised that its aim was not to legitimise prostitution but to offer to those who worked in the industry an improved level of protection and to eradicate the barriers to women's exiting prostitution, which may be created by a criminal conviction.

Though sharing this desire to facilitate 'exit', the abolitionist approach – most closely associated with, but not unique to, Sweden – adopts a somewhat different model. In Sweden, it is now an offence, punishable by a fine or imprisonment for up to six months, to obtain a casual sexual relationship for payment. Both outdoor and indoor prostitution are prohibited, although only the clients will be criminalised. As a result, the spotlight here shines squarely on the purchaser of commercial sex, and on criminalising his role in creating demand for the sex industry. A key rationale behind this is that prostitution is a central manifestation of male violence against women, which in turn means that those who sell sex should not themselves be punished, since they are victims rather than criminals. True gender equality, it is argued, is attainable only when men are no longer permitted to buy, sell and exploit women in prostitution, and the Swedish government has coupled this legislative initiative with a number of outreach programmes designed to assist women who wish to leave the industry.

These divergent modes of responding to prostitution, which have been developed and defended by different countries, have in turn become increasingly bound up with national identity. Regional and international discussions on sex industry regulation have been punctuated by episodes of posturing on the part of delegates from nations that adopt divergent perspectives – as if their state's response to this activity provides some kind of index, or measure, of their cultural ethos and 'civilisation'. Notably, thrown into the mix here is not just impassioned faith that each regime has secured access to the 'truth' of prostitution – a 'truth' that is denied or obscured in the alternatives – but also a sense of national pride at their own achievement, and of frustration at the resistance that is encountered from others.

In support of the legalisation model, it has been argued that women working in toleration zones or regulated brothels (in the Netherlands or Germany, for example) are now less marginalised and better off (both personally and financially) than they were previously. Commentators have suggested that the ability of these sex workers to avail themselves of the collective bargaining of trade unions represents a significant improvement. At the same time, though, critics have pointed out that many sex workers in Germany remain unregistered – often for tax reasons – and that experience in the Netherlands suggests that the transition to a license-based regime has had negative side-effects: in particular, establishing regulatory systems and policing toleration zones has imposed hefty demands on state agencies and it has been suggested that the most vulnerable women (for example, those with irregular migration status or drug addictions) have been pushed into illegal sectors where there is no protection. There have been problems in finding a suitable location for toleration zones, and it has been argued that many men who purchase sex – preferring to remain anonymous – will be reluctant to frequent more visible areas, creating inevitable demand for unregulated arenas. In addition, moreover, concerns have been expressed by critics that this type of response focuses too little attention on the societal impact of prostitution, and on devising schemes that would provide effective assistance to those sex workers who are seeking routes out of the industry.

Some of these shortcomings might, of course, be usefully remedied by a decriminalisation approach. Indeed, the regulation/legalisation model was explicitly rejected by New Zealand on the basis that a licensing regime would need extensive administrative and enforcement resources, and risked the creation of a two-tier industry, in which the legal side of the market would come under the control of big business and the illegal side would be populated by sex workers who are most vulnerable to exploitation. While offering the benefits associated with the reduction of sex work stigma and the greater visibility of sex workers (which is thought to render them less vulnerable to abuse), it has been argued that decriminalisation may offer the added advantage of limiting state intrusion into the private lives of sex workers, and permitting them greater flexibility in their working practices. As critics point out, however, the downside of this flexibility remains that a lack of regulation may permit abuses to go unchecked. In addition, mirroring the critique of legalisation discussed above, some have argued that the hands-off ethos of decriminalisation avoids difficult ideological questions about the status of prostitution as a form of condoned labour only at the cost of selective blindness to the harms that are inherent in the sale of sex.

For many of these critics, it seems that the most acceptable response to prostitution lies in the abolitionist model. Supporters of this approach have pointed to the importance of the message sent out about the status of women, and have drawn upon the narratives of women who express gratitude for a legislative framework that gave them the added incentive to leave prostitution. A number of commentators have also highlighted the practical, and positive, impact of this response in quashing demand. It is argued that there has been a marked decline in the number of prostitutes working on Swedish streets. But critics point out that street prostitution had been in decline in advance of this policy, triggered by changing market conditions and the increased use of technology to recruit clients. In addition, critics point to a lack of information about off-street prostitution in Sweden and suggest that abolitionism may have simply forced a relocation to less visible sites in which sex workers may be at increased risk of abuse, or drawn into a more competitive market in which they have to cut prices or offer riskier services to secure the business of a decreasing client base.

Compounding the controversy in these inter-national debates are ideological disagreements over whether to respond to the individual experience of involvement in prostitution or the structural significance of men's commodification and consumption of female sexuality. In addition, there are significant methodological difficulties generated by the lack of reliable data about the scale and operation of this often illicit industry, as well as by the resultant dependency of researchers on case study evidence that renders systematic evaluation of the comparative merits and demerits of regulatory responses extremely difficult. Added to this are political conflicts arising from wider disputes about the acceptability of state paternalism, the scope of free movement imperatives, the impact of globalisation, the relevance of moral authoritarianism and the legitimacy of governmental intervention into what makes for 'good' work and/or sex. In addition, in a contemporary context in which patterns of (female) migration – both regular and irregular – have been linked to prostitution, these discussions have been increasingly marked by an imperative to identify victims of 'sex trafficking' as distinct from those persons (migrant or not) that 'freely' provide sexual services. These developments continue to beg important questions, however, not least since their focus on autonomy and self-determination requires engagement with the terrain of agency in circumstances in which social and economic constraints restrict the freedom to choose any viable alternative. Despite this, the spectre of trafficking, and its relation to sex work, has been a key feature of modern prostitution policy.

While the response to prostitution in England and Wales has not undergone the kind of dramatic legislative overhaul that has been witnessed over the past decade in some other jurisdictions, there is little doubt that this has also been a period of significant reflection and flux. The formal position on prostitution in England and Wales remains largely as proposed by the Wolfenden Committee Report in the late 1950s. Prostitution itself is not illegal, although many of the activities that facilitate or flow from both its street and off-street manifestations (including soliciting, kerb-crawling, controlling prostitution for gain and so on) are criminalised. Notably absent from the reform initiative that preceded the passing of the Sexual Offences Act 2003 in England and Wales, the issue of (non-trafficked) prostitution became the focus for dedicated consideration in the *Paying the Price* consultation, which was produced by the government in 2004. While this document presented itself as open to wholesale reform on the regulation of prostitution – putting legalisation, decriminalisation and abolitionist frameworks out for consideration – the outcomes of this exercise have been regarded by many as profoundly disappointing. The resultant response, produced by the government in 2006, declines to align itself wholeheartedly with any of these regulatory models. It is, however, clearly sympathetic to abolitionism – at least as far as street sex work is concerned – and reflects a complex narrative comprised of a concern to protect communities from prostitution-related nuisance, to 'crack down' on the organised criminal networks that are bound up with the sex industry, to provide avenues for exiting to all those who are prostituted, and in particular to rescue those whose involvement is coerced. Although an undertone of moral disapprobation of sex work can still be identified, the response emphasises the harms that are deemed to be inherent in prostitution and insists that those who sell sex should be seen primarily as victims – unless and until they fall foul of this categorisation by refusing assistance to 'exit' and opting instead (whether by choice or circumstance) to continue to sell sex. In addition, it clearly shares the abolitionist conviction that reduction of women's involvement in sex work can usefully be achieved by efforts to quash demand, in particular by stricter enforcement of kerb-crawling laws that target clients.

The failure of this consultation to embrace more deep-seated reform of the UK domestic response to prostitution, by making a clear and wholehearted commitment to any of the competing models on the table, has rendered it a target for critique. It has been suggested that the consultation failed to do enough to take on board the lessons available from other country's responses to the sex industry. While this may be true, and the nature of these lessons will emerge as a recurring theme in the ensuing chapters, it is important to bear in mind the following two caveats. First, while the outcomes of the consultation have not yielded wholesale reform, they have provided a window into a shifting frame for prostitution policy in England and Wales, and have given rise to a number of changes in enforcement practice that require no statutory intervention (whether these changes are for the better is, of course, another question – and one that will be examined from a range of perspectives in the following chapters). Second, the dangers of adopting a simplistic 'transplant model' for prostitution reform – though perhaps not the driving force behind the UK government's lack of ambition – are significant. The assumption that we can take up a model from one jurisdiction and predict the consequences of transplanting it into another, which has tended to animate much of the contemporary discussion on comparative prostitution policy, is problematic – at least to the extent that it tends to ignore or trivialise the peculiarity of the cultural environment of comparator countries. To assume that legislative change will – in and of itself – bring about attendant social change, let alone predictable social change that can be mapped from experience in another socio-spatial context, places far too much faith in the power of law as a reformist institution. Historical state/civil society relations, distributive patterns of gender power, attitudes towards sexuality and consumption, and diversity in the forms, scale and operation of commercial sex transactions, all contribute towards the creation of a unique national cultural context within which regulatory responses to prostitution will produce divergent, and often unpredictable, practical outcomes. To deny this reality in preference for a simplistic transplant model would be both disappointing and misleading.

Charting the Terrain of Feminist Debate: The Relevance of Terminology and Ideology

These disagreements over regulatory responses to prostitution are, of course, grounded in and informed by the significant ideological debates between feminist scholars and activists, not just over women's scope for legitimate autonomy in this arena, but also over the most appropriate mechanisms for redressing the vulnerability and marginalisation that sex work can bring. While some have argued for protective legislation that would improve the working conditions of prostitutes and decrease their social stigmatisation, others have argued that, since the violence within prostitution is not incidental to the conditions in which it is conducted but endemic within a structure that promotes women's sexuality as a commodity to be purchased by men, prostitution must be abolished.

Within the context of these prostitution debates, it is clear that one's choice of terminology has assumed a perceived relevance, often acting as a shorthand identifier of a substantive position. Thus, the language of 'prostitute' and 'prostitution' have been closely aligned with abolitionist perspectives that see the sale of sex as entailing women's exploitation and objectification, both by those who manage and create the opportunity for the sexual transaction as well as by those clients who make the purchase and maintain the demand. By contrast, the language of 'sex workers' and 'sex work' has typically been preferred by those who emphasise women's agency in entering into commercial sex transactions (albeit perhaps under conditions of constraint) and who call for the regulation of the sale of sex as akin to the sale of non-sexual labour or services.

It is the view of the editors, and one of the driving inspirations behind this collection, that each of these polarised perspectives proves problematic, in different ways, when presented as an abstract position that claims universal applicability to all women and all commercial sex. Despite their heated disagreement, each of these positions falls into a significant epistemic pitfall by presuming the existence of a unitary truth, not only of the practice of prostitution but also of female (and, indeed, male) sexuality itself. There is a tendency in these accounts both to disengage from the diversity of sex markets (and the sexual services they encompass) and to artificially abstract the licit/illicit industry dichotomy from the messiness of its operation in the global (capital) economy. In addition, the threat of essentialism looms large here, as other forms of discrimination (race, age, class and so on) that may also feature in the commercial sex transaction are 'trumped' by the preoccupation with gender/sex difference.

At the same time, however, in concrete contexts in which the narratives of individual women who sell sex are themselves complex, multi-faceted, fluctuating and contradictory, and in which there is considerable diversity in the terrain of transactions across different sex markets, it seems that neither of these analyses can be wholly rejected. On that basis, and in an effort to reflect a conscious but not dispassionate ambivalence about these frameworks, this edited collection seeks to bring together a range of voices and perspectives on prostitution. Terminology fluctuates between chapters and a conscious decision has been made to allow these points of divergence to stand. Often, language choice does indeed betray greater allegiance to one perspective than another, but rarely should this be read as indicative of unqualified endorsement of the universal applicability of any one ideological standpoint.

In focusing upon the notion of supply/demand, this collection applies what – at first sight – may appear as a straightforwardly economic analysis in which prostitution emerges as a form of labour, subject to the same forces that animate many other capitalist forums. It is certainly true that several contributors to the collection do – to varying degrees and with varying levels of qualification – advocate this approach. At the same time, however, it is not the aim of this collection to provide an uncontested ideological platform for one or other side of the prostitution debate. As a result, there are also several contributions in which authors – despite on some occasions invoking terminology more akin to the market model – continue to express concern about the legitimacy of women's choice in entering sex work, about the exploitation that may be not only incidental to, but also inherent within the sex industry, and about the broader social implications for women of living in a society in which sex is commodified and served for male consumption. The improvements that may be offered by regulation – specifically in terms of security and non-stigmatisation for individual women – are evaluated in this collection against the risks associated with recognising prostitutes as sellers in the sexual economy (which include normalising sexual alienation, creating illegal sectors where exploitation proliferates, or losing impetus to support 'exit' from prostitution for vulnerable women).

Although this collection focuses on the issue of supply/demand, it is not its aim to provide an uncritical endorsement of sex work or an instruction manual for its regulation as a market economy. The emphasis on supply/demand does not entail a restricted focus on the market model, but a broader engagement with sociological and psychoanalytical factors that also inform this dynamic in the context of prostitution. By interrogating supply/demand from an inter- and multi-disciplinary perspective, the chapters in this collection aim to broaden engagement beyond the routine analysis of the locus of violence in prostitution and the validity of the prostitute's consent. A focus on the supply/demand dynamic, whilst not excluding these concerns, brings into play a range of other societal, economic and psychological factors, including but not restricted to the social construction of sexuality, the viability of alternative choices for prostitutes and clients, and the impact of internal and external regulatory regimes on the provision of sexual services. In addition, a focus on supply/demand entails studying not just the factors that underlie each component of the dyad (for example, questions of access to, and the nature of, alternative employment opportunities that underpin supply, or of the role of personal characteristics and socio-economic standing in shaping client demand), but also a critical examination of their dynamic interrelation. This is important, since it is this interaction that determines the existence of many different types of prostitution, each of which poses its own questions and produces its own responses to the divergent regulatory regimes.

There is a large amount of literature available on the issue of prostitution, but this has often come from the discipline of sociology, which operates with its own paradigms and modes of analysis. This edited collection links these insights to perspectives from a range of other disciplines, namely economics, law, political and social theory, philosophy, human geography and anthropology. Each of these disciplines has vital contributions to make to the field of prostitution discourse yet they have often been overshadowed by the dominance of sociological perspectives. Drawing these disciplinary engagements in from the margins and submitting their key claims to scrutiny both across and within disciplines, this project seeks to move discussion beyond the dichotomous conflict between 'pro-sex work' and 'abolitionist' positions that has too frequently paralysed sustained engagement. Moreover, by consciously infusing the analysis with perspectives and methodologies from disciplines, such as economics and law, which characteristically have a high level of engagement with policy, this collection interrogates prescriptions that build on the core ideological engagements rehearsed in sociological work. In so doing, it aims – amongst other things – to draw attention to the tensions that arise between social policy, practical enforcement and resultant outcomes in a world in which routes into and out of prostitution (as a client and sex worker) are diverse, and in which the sex industry displays both considerable fluidity and resilience.

Review of the Chapters

The first four chapters in this collection share the concerns raised above over the failure of much current prostitution policy, in both the UK and elsewhere, to acknowledge the complexities involved in the exchange of commercial sex, and critically consider the consequences that derive from this failure in terms of social justice. Across these chapters, the authors' engagement with the perceived shortfalls of current regulatory approaches is marked by different disciplinary perspectives, but is simultaneously united by a commitment to feminist critique, and by an attendant desire to enliven their theoretical analyses with grounded and evidence-based claims, as well as with positive suggestions for future praxis.

Scoular and O'Neill open the collection with a critical assessment of the growing influence of abolitionism, reflected in recent legislative efforts to challenge the supply/demand nexus in prostitution. They convincingly demonstrate the limitations of programmes and techniques designed to criminalise and responsibilise the buyers and sellers of sex, both from a practical and an ideological point of view. More specifically, they argue that the form of 'social inclusion' that is offered here is premised on a subject's victim identity and that this – in turn – perpetuates the exclusion of those who do not fit the normative paradigm, whilst re-affirming a narrow and unchallenging vision of citizenship. As an alternative, they argue for an ethics of inclusion, rooted in a feminist approach, which challenges socio-sexual inequalities and advocates the recognition of sex workers as citizens in issues of governance.

Phoenix traces a trajectory of change in UK prostitution laws since the 1990s, reflecting, she argues, a shift away from public nuisance concerns and towards an agenda for eradicating male violence and economic exploitation. This chapter reflects on the ways in which, despite a raft of local and national level policy initiatives, punitive and coercive measures continue to affect disproportionately the more economically and socially marginalised street based sex workers, and draws attention to the negative impact of these regulatory responses, particularly upon grass-roots agencies that were originally mandated to support and represent those women. Building on this, Phoenix examines the acute dilemmas that the new regulatory regime, especially when coupled with a child protection agenda that imposes an obligation to 'rescue' young persons engaged in prostitution, has presented to those involved in sex industry outreach projects, and highlights their paralysing effects.

Like Scoular, O'Neill and Phoenix, Day also looks at recent developments in UK prostitution policy, and is similarly sceptical about the sentiment of the current regulatory regime. She argues, however, that the traditional coexistence within the sex industry of both formal and informal politics may, even in the context of this new repressive environment, offer productive potential to the sex workers' movement. Set against the backdrop of the fiftieth anniversary of the Wolfenden Report, her chapter provides a careful evaluation of British abolitionism, intersected with an historical overview of the *modus operandi* of sex worker movements in their engagement with the state on issues of rights, recognition and representation. At the heart of Day's analysis of prostitution policy is a concern with women's representation and their lived (as well as symbolic) empowerment. These are issues that animate a number of the chapters in this collection, albeit that in other contributions, what counts as ('real') empowerment may be approached from a rather different perspective.

Offering a valuable moment for some comparative insight, Allwood's chapter provides an informed and rich engagement with the evolution of policies towards prostitution in France over the last ten years, examining in particular the ways in which prostitutes, clients and the relationship between them has been constructed and contested. She illustrates how current policies are contradictory in their efforts to incorporate an abolitionist (the traditional approach in French policy), anti-trafficking and anti-immigration agenda. Notwithstanding calls for more support of those who want to leave the industry, current service providers receive very little funding. By contrast, the new right-wing government agenda, as of 2002, has included prostitution in its Domestic Security Law, creating a serious offence of passive soliciting, and simultaneously representing prostitutes both as victims of vicious trafficking rings who need to be saved and as criminals who should be fined heavily, imprisoned and, if foreign, deported. A distinction has been drawn, Allwood suggests, between 'traditional' (French) prostitutes, fondly represented as part of the national heritage, and victims of sex trafficking/illegal immigrants, who were designated as the real targets of the new measures. The client, ignored for many years by the law, is increasingly present in these debates, and is even criminalised in the case of prostitutes who are under 18 (2002) or are 'particularly vulnerable' (2003). However, echoing the concerns of previous contributors, Allwood notes that these debates, which are situated within a broader security discourse, concerned at the local level with preserving public order and at the national level with controlling immigration, only address street prostitution. This means, amongst other things, that middle-class men, who are increasingly turning to other forms of less visible prostitution, are unlikely to be affected.

Continuing to develop this focus on the theoretical instruments deployed in the construction of discourses surrounding prostitution and trafficking, the chapters by Munro and FitzGerald situate these national policy initiatives in the inter-national context. Munro illustrates how the concept of exploitation has been (mis)understood in debates on sex and labour trafficking, reflecting upon the ways in which the malleability of the concept has been deployed to preserve (explicitly or otherwise) dubious victim hierarchies in national, regional and international legal responses. In particular, she draws attention to inconsistencies in the use of exploitation across the labour and sex variants of people trafficking, and examines the implications of this for prostitution policy. Drawing on exploitation and consent theory, she argues that situations may exist in which, although the background conditions of full and free choice are not met, it is possible to exercise a meaningful degree of agency in entering into transactions, and that although these arrangements may be rightly recognised as exploitative, they may nonetheless bring about a level of advantage to both parties. Unpicking the meaning and significance of exploitation claims in the context of prostitution, she argues for a more careful and candid approach, and dedicates her chapter to exploring avenues for further examination that might transcend some of the polarities of the pre-existing debates.

FitzGerald discusses the background to feminist campaigning on trafficking from the perspective of feminist cultural and post-colonial geography, highlighting the similarities with imperial rhetoric about the female 'Other' and the 'fallen woman'. Her chapter usefully deconstructs contemporary discourses around women's agency in prostitution and in particular the agency of non-Western women. In addition, through a careful analysis of the lobbying undertaken at the European level in recent sex trafficking debates, FitzGerald links her discussion to broader issues of women's political representation, and examines the risks associated with adopting a feminist perspective that aligns itself too closely to a conservative anti-immigration agenda that, in turn, threatens to restrict female mobility and behaviour.

The chapters by Della Giusta, and Collins and Judge, provide a new disciplinary angle to the discussion by considering regulatory regimes from an economic perspective, focusing in particular on the likelihood that policy-makers might switch regimes (Della Giusta) and the effect of different enforcement on the spatial interaction between supply and demand (Collins and Judge).

Della Giusta introduces an economic approach to studying prostitution, critically assessing the current limitations of economists' contributions to this important policy debate and illustrating the relative merits of economic modelling for policy design. Central to her approach is the recognition of the role of social stigma in determining the configuration of the exchange of paid sex, and the way in which this is, in turn, both understood and influenced by policy. The discussion begins with an illustration of the main ideas underpinning the economic model, which is then enlarged to illustrate the choice of policy regimes by policy-makers. To choose between policy options – if we assume a rational action approach – an evaluation of the costs and benefits in welfare terms of different regulatory regimes would have to be conducted. In the absence of such calculations, Della Giusta uses stylised facts from the sex trade to advocate liberal policies that maximise public welfare by lifting the stigma associated with the sector, and illustrates the conditions (for example, a concern about voting or re-election) under which policy-makers may nonetheless fail to adopt them.

Collins and Judge, though continuing to utilise the economic lens, turn attention to a slightly different issue, namely client participation and behaviour in paid sex markets. After examining the economic literature that has explored the demand side of the market, the authors consider the likely impact on consumers of alternative regulatory models. Having done so, they then move on to explore the likely effects of enforcement level variability on client behaviour within any given regime, concluding that it is likely to lead to the consumption of commercial sex being subject to spatial displacement.

The final three chapters continue this focus upon the client, but turn their attention more directly to the question of how to respond to the purchase of commercial sex by examining – amongst other things – the call to criminalise clients of prostitutes, and the claim to the objectification of women in prostitution on which this is based. Archard explores the case for prosecuting men who unknowingly use trafficked prostitutes and reflects specifically upon the jurisprudential problems arising from the proposal to consider them guilty of the offence of rape. Subjecting clients to sanction in this way poses, he suggests, a number of interrelated problems, particularly in terms of the legitimacy of extending the criminal law to new domains. His discussion centres specifically on the difficulties associated with presuming clients' knowledge as to the prostitutes' circumstances, and questions the extent to which such a presumption can be enlarged to the general circumstances surrounding prostitution – or to analogous situations of client/consumer responsibility towards the providers of a service or good.

Sanders and Campbell share this focus on recent policy shifts in the UK that 'tackle client demand', but they situate this discussion in the broader context of radical feminist lobbying, which typically sees sex work as inherently violent, inevitably involuntary, and a prolific generator of the objectification of women. More specifically, they observe that although this approach may appeal to policy-makers, it does little to address the complexities of the sex industry, and, more importantly, fails to address the negative impact of such policies on sex workers themselves – as their rights, social inclusion and safety are weakened through the creation of an even more risky and illicit industry. Together, Sanders and Campbell argue for regulation of a legal industry, which would ensure rights for sex workers and leave scarce policing resources to focus upon exploitative practices. They ask also that more consideration be given by policy-makers to existing research on men who pay for sex in order to produce evidence-based policies.

Coy, in her chapter, however, takes a quite different perspective, grounded upon her empirical work as a feminist researcher with a background in outreach projects involving sexually exploited girls and young women, as well as adult women in prostitution. She discusses the role of notions of objectification and commodification in the construction of commercial sex by both clients and prostitutes, and places this in the context of the wider (and, in her view, problematic) socio-cultural context in which there is an increasing mainstreaming and normalisation of the sex industry. She holds the perspective that prostitution constitutes not only a significant barrier to gender equality but also a form of violence against women, and accordingly argues for policies that support exit, alongside the provision of mechanisms for effective intervention to prevent women and girls from being coerced into either entering or continuing in prostitution.

Concluding Remarks

This is a collection that brings together a range of perspectives on prostitution, framed and communicated across a diversity of disciplinary contexts. Our aim in bringing these contributors together has not been to try to impose any kind of strict coherence upon this multiplicity, but instead to present a series of commentaries that constructively underscore the complexity and ambiguity of contemporary engagement with, and regulation of, supply/demand dynamics in the commercial sex context. As part of this project, it has been vital to understand how different theoretical perspectives can help to illuminate (as well as obfuscate) the positions that are represented in current debates and policies on prostitution. At the same time, this collection emphasises the importance of rendering policy-makers alert to the evidence emerging from empirical studies conducted in different fields of enquiry, in the hope of moving beyond polarity and politics at the local, national and international level.

A key sub-theme here is the role of consumerism in shaping the sex industry, in terms of both the construction of the client–prostitute exchange and the increasingly globalised and normalised nature of its operation. The role of the market – its positive and negative potential – emerges as an important issue which merits further research, not least since it often plays an under-theorised role in feminist debates, with protagonists pointing to both the inclusion *and* the exclusion of commercial sex from the market economy in order to account for the continuation of gender discrimination. On the one hand, it is true, of course, that supply and demand are theoretical constructs that make sense only when one accepts that the exchange taking place happens in a market (however informal or formal this may be). But on the other hand, as many commentators have convincingly argued, the language of the market – much like the language of the law – makes a pretence at neutrality, and as a result, using the market as a metaphor for what is happening in the exchange of paid sex may risk implicit acceptance and, even validation, of the extant power structures and inequalities. Unpicking the dilemmas associated with supply/demand entails a critical exploration of micro- and macro-level power relations, as well as of the dyadic relationship between the two. It requires an account of what forms of consumption and commodification are intolerable, and equally important, it demands that we subject the intuitions we conjure up by posing that question to sustained and critical scrutiny. In so doing, it may offer vital and valuable potential, in the context of prostitution policy, for some fresh thinking around the politics of sexuality, the practices of patriarchy, the feminisation of poverty and the suppression of vice – all of which impinge directly upon the forms and freedoms of the contemporary economies of commercial sex.

*****

Between the submission of this manuscript and its coming to press, the UK Criminal Justice and Immigration Bill 2007, to which a number of the authors in this collection make reference, was enacted. In its original form, the Bill envisaged the removal of the term 'common prostitute' from the statute books and the introduction of special rehabilitation measures for those convicted of loitering or soliciting for prostitution. At a relatively late stage in the debates, however, the Government opted to remove these provisions, apparently concerned that objections raised at the House of Lords in regard to the 'piecemeal' nature of this reform effort would delay the Bill's progress in a context in which its other clauses were seen to be a more pressing priority. The forms of governance reflected in the Home Office's *Coordinated Prostitution Strategy* clearly support these initiatives, and their removal from the Bill was coupled with an express statement of intent to re-visit and re-introduce them – possibly as part of a more far-reaching reform proposal, pursuant upon a further study on client demand – in the next Parliamentary session. To this extent, the shifts in the framing of, and responses to, prostitution that these clauses illustrate remain highly pertinent, and the evaluations provided by contributors in this regard are thus of considerable value.

Chapter 1

Legal Incursions into Supply/Demand: Criminalising and Responsibilising the Buyers and Sellers of Sex in the UK

Jane Scoular and Maggie O'Neill

The aim of this chapter is to assess critically contemporary legal reforms that operate according to an abolitionist vision: one which understands prostitution as paradigmatic of a system of male power and seeks its elimination by removing both the supply and demand of sexual services. This schema has influenced a number of legal reforms including international law's position on trafficking[1] and domestic laws, such as those in Sweden and the UK, which combine increased punitive sanctions for clients with efforts to exit women from prostitution. While recognising the urgent need to address the many harms experienced by those involved in selling sex and understanding the desire to offer a coherent political resistance to what is often considered to be a 'global sex trade', we urge critical caution as we highlight both the ideological and practical limitations of abolitionist approaches. We consider the myopic approach to power inherent in domination theories, which we argue often robs feminism of its dynamism and instead co-opts it into systems of governance. We cite the current strategic focus on exiting as a prime example of such a process as we highlight the way in which efforts to free women from harmful aspects of sex work become so easily translated into techniques of advanced liberal governance and control. Interventions which are intended to help women only do so within the confines of New Labour's narrow responsibilisation agenda, which sustains the binaries between good and bad, deserving and undeserving women, so that only those who responsibly exit, who fit dominant forms of citizenship and resume normal lifestyles and relationships are socially included, leaving those outside increasingly marginalised.

It is not our intention to offer a nihilistic critique. Rather we use this analysis to develop and inform an alternative approach to the politics of prostitution and to social justice – one that recognises the material insights offered by a political economy of sex but seeks to move beyond its identitarian logic.[2] In focusing upon

1 This chapter will primarily consider domestic laws that attempt to advance abolitionist aims. The issue of trafficking is more fully discussed in Chapters 5 and 6.

2 Identity thinking is a concept emerging from critical theory. It refers to the way unlike things are made to appear as equivalent. For example, the way that sexist stereotypes identify an equivalence between women that serves to sustain inequalities through both discourse

a politics of inclusion we hope to offer a more critical and holistic understanding of a social justice that coalesces around discourses of rights, redistribution and recognition (Fraser 1997; Scoular and O'Neill 2007; O'Neill 2007a).

We begin by tracing the growing influence of abolitionist doctrine in legislative efforts to challenge the supply/demand nexus in prostitution. We go on to show that the practical limitations of such models, which typically rely on the criminalisation of clients and measures to help women as victims, stem from a problematic ideological grounding. The form of 'social inclusion' they offer is premised on a subject's victim identity. This not only continues the exclusion of those who do not fit the normative paradigm, it also perpetrates narrow and unchallenging visions of citizenship, serving to undermine a broader ethics of inclusion that we have been involved in supporting for some years (O'Neill 2001, 2008; Scoular 2004a, 2004b; Scoular and O'Neill 2007). We suggest, instead, an ethics of inclusion that is necessarily rooted in a feminist approach and challenges sexual and social inequalities in order to promote a more complex understanding of women and young people's lived experience. We also advocate for the inclusion of sex workers as citizens in issues of governance. Where recent policy initiatives seek to remove sex workers, or to offer them only limited accommodation, our aim is to bring them back in to the theoretical discursive frame. We also seek to open up the possibilities for dialogue and discussion that acknowledge the unsettled, unfinished elements of progressive governance (as well as the state's attempts to centralise and control) for it is in the spaces created for participation and inclusion that we may develop resistance and challenges that can lead to social change and social justice.

Abolitionism Today

> Sweden has given notice to the world that it regards prostitution as a serious form of oppression against women, and that efforts must be made to combat it (Swedish Government, *Prostitution and Trafficking in Women Fact Sheet*, April 2003).
>
> One of the key objectives that came out of the *Coordinated Prostitution Strategy* was the importance of tackling the demand and to challenge the existence of street-based sex markets, along with the commonly held view that they are inevitable and here to stay (Home Office 2007b).

These quotes signify the increasing influence of abolitionism in a number of legal systems' efforts to tackle prostitution.[3] Heavily influenced by radical feminism, this

---

and symbolic re-presentations. This drive for equivalence can be found in the identification between 'prostitutes' and disease/dirt or the equivalence between women selling sex and a victim role. 'Non-identity thinking interrogates such easy assumptions of identity and equivalence' (see O'Neill 2007b, 120–35; O'Neill 2001).

3 We do not mean to imply this is a new phenomenon nor that it is universal, as there are of course a number of alternative models operating in comparative systems. What we are highlighting is the increased salience of abolitionism in specific political contexts, looking at both the conditions and implications of this resurgence. Mirroring earlier feminist work (Walkowitz 1980; Self 2003) we seek to demonstrate the way in which contemporary feminist

approach is characterised by an understanding of commercial sexual relations as the epitome of male power. Prostitution is consistently characterised as a predetermined system constituted by an inherently abusive demand by men for the sexual services of a group of perpetually victimised women. Challenges to this system take the form of appeals for state disruption of the supply/demand nexus of power, specifically via criminal sanctions designed to cut off demand by clients, as well as for increased social interventions designed to reduce women's victimisation by assisting them to exit from sex work and re-enter 'normal' society.

We begin by considering these central tenets in abolitionist doctrine and highlight what we consider to be the fundamental problems with its ideology and its translation into practice before going on to offer a way forward based upon a politics of inclusion.

Prostitution as a System of Gender Oppression

> Prostitution remains morally undesirable ... because it is one of those most graphic examples of men's domination over women (Pateman 1983, 561).

While feminists in general have highlighted the harms experienced by women involved in prostitution, a number of writers have, during the last 40 years, sought to locate and theorise these harms within a radical analysis of the state and sexuality (Millet 1975; Barry 1979, 1995; Pateman 1983; MacKinnon 1982, 1989; Dworkin 1987, 1989). In this body of work, prostitution is regarded as the epitome of the female condition under patriarchy.[4] Violence is described not only in the practice of prostitution but as being fundamental to the very idea of 'buying sex', which is so inextricably linked to a system of heterosexuality and male power that it represents 'the absolute embodiment of patriarchal male privilege' (Kesler 2002).

It is clear that within this schema, sexuality is considered to be the primary dynamic in the ordering of society. Sex is to radical feminism 'what work is to Marxism' (MacKinnon 1982, 515) and prostitution, by analogy, is frequently cited as a 'class condition':

> My study of sex as power ... inevitably, continually, unrelentingly returns me to prostitution ... one cannot mobilize against a class condition of oppression unless one knows its fullest dimensions. Thus my work has been to study and expose sexual power in its most severe, global, institutionalised, and crystallized forms ... Prostitution – the cornerstone of all sexual exploitation (Barry 1995, 9).

Thus prostitution is not simply an example of women's oppression but is regarded as 'a foundational idea that pre-determines it' (Scoular 2004a). 'Choice', therefore, is

---

efforts to prohibit prostitution frequently converge in unhelpful ways with regimes of power; as we look in particular at the way in which radical feminist concerns coalesce with a system of neo-liberal governance (Halley et al. 2006; Scoular and O'Neill 2007).

4 Paradigmatic of women's social, sexual and economic subordination, prostitution is also linked to other forms sexual abuse, for example Dworkin states: 'Incest is boot camp [for prostitution]' (Dworkin 1997).

a misnomer, as radical feminists dispute that autonomy can be exercised in a system that is fundamentally oppressive (Jeffries 1997; Raymond 2003). Any political or legal recognition of 'sex work' (via decriminalisation or legalisation) is thought to both sanction a culture in which men purchase women for sexual gratification and to normalise violence and sexual abuse. Radical feminists seek to challenge the apparent reification of prostitution and to highlight the prevalence of a political economy of sex in which 'men create the demand and women are the supply' (Hughes 2000, 635). Abolitionism is their goal and the role of law is to make incursions into this supply/demand dynamic by criminalising the purchasers of sex and by dealing with women as victims of what is regarded as a contemporary form of sexual slavery.

Thus, contemporary campaigns by radical feminists frame all prostitution as a violation of women's human rights. Through the Campaign Against Trafficking in Women (CATW) a number of prominent radical feminists focus attention on trafficking, citing it as a graphic example of the wider sexual slavery inherent in the prostitution of women and children. By collapsing trafficking with prostitution, this group intends to explode what it regards as 'the false distinction between forced and voluntary prostitution' (Jeffries 1997, 10). By rendering choice irrelevant, they seek to stymie demand by rendering the purchasing of all sex as a criminal act. This position has gained some recognition in some domestic systems.

In Sweden, for example, radical feminism played a key role in influencing a particular hegemonic form of state feminism (Scoular 2004b) which was, in part, responsible for the 1998 law which prohibits the purchasing of sexual services.[5] Commentators describe the impact of other factors such as a national anxiety over entry into the European Union and a perceived need to assert a coherent national identity against a growing migration and perceived permissiveness in Europe (Gould 2001; Kulick 2003). However, the role of radical feminist ideology and, in particular, the way in which its construction of 'state' and 'subject' coalesced with conservative social policy norms cannot be underestimated (Scoular 2004a). In describing the reasoning behind the Swedish law, Sven-Axel Månsson notes:

> The law presuppos[es] that a real change in gender relations calls for a radical reconsideration of men's responsibility in prostitution. The basis of such a reconsideration is that prostitution must be defined as a male issue; that prostitution is about men's sexuality, not women's (Månsson 2002).

Thus, apparent equality is achieved by moving from criminalising women in prostitution to penalising men's role as purchasers. This change in focus is also evident in the intensification of surveillance and arrest of clients in the United States and Canada (McElroy 1998) and the emergence of 're-education' programmes in these jurisdictions.[6]

---

5 The Prohibition of the Purchase of Sexual Services Act 1998, 408 states: 'A person who obtains a casual sexual relation in return for payment will be sentenced – unless the act is punishable under the penal code – for the purchase of sexual services to a fine or a term of imprisonment not exceeding six months.'

6 Although it is questionable to what extent increasing men's criminalisation actually reduces women's. For reasons explained below, using criminal law as a means of seeking

Recent reforms in the UK similarly rely on abolitionist configurations of supply and demand, seeking to challenge this dynamic via the increased criminalisation of clients while promoting women's rehabilitation (via social-welfare exit programmes) from prostitution (Home Office 2004, 2006; Prostitution (Public Places) (Scotland) Act 2007). For example, a recent Home Office briefing outlines the rationale behind the proposed 'new' approach:

> The aim is to reduce the demand for street prostitution and bring to justice those who contribute to the vicious cycle of prostitution. Targeting those who create that demand can be highly effective at disrupting the market, provided that the full range of enforcement measures and sentencing options are used … (Home Office 2007a).

Thus (certain) purchasers, notably kerb-crawlers, have been the subject of increased policing and stigmatising. Kerb-crawling has recently been made a criminal offence in Scotland (Prostitution (Public Places) (Scotland) Act 2007), despite adequate common law powers to deal with any nuisance. In England and Wales, where it is already a summary offence (s71 Criminal Justice and Police Act 2001), 'naming and shaming' now features at the centre of the government's approach (Home Office 2007b) and pressure to criminalise further the purchasing of sexual services mounts as the Criminal Justice and Immigration Bill 2007 passes through Parliament.[7]

The increased criminalisation of clients runs alongside the efforts to 'empower' those involved in selling sex by recognising their victimisation and facilitating their exit:

> Most women involved in street-based prostitution are not there through choice. They are amongst the most vulnerable people in society. Nearly all are addicted to heroin or crack or both. Many come from abused childhoods and many are homeless. And many become involved before they reach 18. Kerb crawlers on the other hand do have a choice in the matter and we want to send the message that kerb crawling will not be tolerated. Men who choose to pay for sex on-street are indirectly supporting drug-dealers and abusers whilst perpetuating a market fraught with violence and abuse (Home Office 2007a).

Thus, in order to disrupt the 'market', recent reforms seek to create a climate of zero tolerance primarily in relation to street sex workers,[8] to be achieved via increased enforcement (especially against kerb-crawling), the use of Anti-Social Behaviour

---

political recognition and redistribution simply shifts criminal status and sanctions to men. By maintaining the agents and rationalities of control, criminalisation will remain for women who persist in sex work (Scoular et al. 2007).

7 For example Harry Cohen's amendment seeks to make rehabilitation compulsory for those who pay for the sexual services of those who have been trafficked. If knowledge is required then the provision will be of little practical use, yet the rhetoric is often considered more important. See also Chapter 9 in this collection for further discussion.

8 Street sex work has been the major focus of government attention. Indoor work, which represents a far greater section of the sex industry, is almost ignored – perhaps because indoor sex work is considered to present a more complex account of women's agency beyond apparent victimhood, thus making the impetus to 'save' and control less immediate and self-evidently justified.

Orders, the promotion of prevention and support for women to exit prostitution. The latter is to be achieved via a four-staged approach which begins with voluntary referral to services and increases along a continuum to prosecution (Home Office 2006, 39). Central to this is the introduction of a rehabilitative order, proposed in Part 6, clause 72 of the Criminal Justice and Immigration Bill 2007, which seeks to impose compulsory drug and alcohol rehabilitation courses on pain of 72 hours' detention if those referred fail to attend three sessions with a 'supervisor'. These orders will apply to women who are found to be persistently soliciting, with persistence now defined as soliciting on two or more occasions over a period of three months. This is a significant extension from the previous requirement of two or more occasions in one day. Thus, in order to 'protect', the net of control has been widened to include a larger group of women who are now subject to compulsory rehabilitation.

Before embarking on a critique of these measures (particularly on their limited understanding of the supply/demand dynamic and their problematic use of law, which operates to reduce agency while increasing control), we want first to acknowledge the importance of radical feminist work, which has provided a vital articulation of the harms that women have experienced, and continue to experience, 'under' eroticised power relations. We have argued before that this can be overlooked in some critiques which dismiss such perspectives out of hand:

> An uncompromised account of domination does offer opportunities for action in the face of the seeming nihilism of more abstract post-modern theories and the de-politicisation created by the normalisation of heterosexual power differentials and the apparent market inevitability of their commodification (Scoular 2004a).

We recognise the efforts made to raise awareness of the harms that overwhelmingly impact upon women and to tie this to an understanding of the gendered nature of the state. By linking prostitution to other forms of sexual subordination, radical feminists attempt to provide a platform for solidarity and offer the kind of political coherence necessary for claims to law. Yet it is this coherence that is problematic. As we argue below, the political consensus offered by the construction of the prostitute subject as a victim of gendered power is achieved by overlooking the complexities and contradictions inherent in prostitution, which point to wider structures, including law, which intersect to create its marginal status. It is also achieved at the expense of a recognition of women's agency. Preferring to advocate a rhetoric of victimhood, these discourses may actually consolidate and legitimise law's power over women's bodies, foreclosing any discussion of forms of rights or recognition which could support counter-hegemonic challenges.

Our critique is motivated by a concern to preserve feminism's counter-hegemonic challenge whilst also arguing for an acknowledgement of women's agency in order to loosen the uni-directional account of women as victims who need to be made responsible and/or saved. Through a politics of inclusion we want to hear the voices of women who sell sex both on and off street in debates and dialogue and also to work across the binary divide between radical and regulatory feminisms on this issue.

Critiquing Abolitionism

While the highly gendered nature of commercial sex appears to offer a graphic example of a system of male domination, exercised through the medium of sexuality, there are a number of problems with such an account.

First, it assumes that commercial sex has the same, stable meaning across both time and space (Zatz 1997; Scoular 2004a). By over-determining gendered power-dynamics, domination theory does not fully recognise the importance of other structures which also determine its marginal status. Developed to capture the all-pervasiveness of male power, the unified, transhistorical, global reach of patriarchy, domination theory suggests that power is identical across diverse historical and cultural states and relegates class and race as subordinate to gender. Thus, while gender and sexuality clearly play important structuring roles in prostitution, by reducing the phenomenon to a single trait, radical work does not fully capture the importance of other structures such as money, culture and race (Zatz 1997, 279). In considering the contradictions and discrepancies in the history of modern prostitution, Donna Guy notes that these tensions, rather than needing to be resolved around a single axis, offer instead:

> … a dynamic perspective on the private lives of women as well as the public functioning of medicine, patriarchy and the nation state and emphasises the need to understand how gender and sexuality are interrelated inextricably to race, cultural diversity and economic circumstances (Guy 1995, 182).

Thus, we argue that it is vital to comprehend the dense network of structures and processes that combine to understand 'prostitution' better with a view to developing policy and practice that is based on social justice and inclusion.

Second, by defining prostitution as inherently abusive (across time and space) some radical scholars attribute a particular value to sex, which is then used to argue against its commodification (Oerton and Phoenix 2001, 387). In doing so, this reifies the dominant norms of sex that they seek to destabilise. In her radical critique of prostitution, Pateman, for example, defines the difference between paid sex and loving sex as:

> … [the] difference between the reciprocal expression of desire and unilateral subjection to sexual acts with the consolation of payment, it is the difference for women between freedom and subjection (Pateman 1988, 204).

Barry echoes this when she notes, 'when sex is not explicitly treated as genuine human interaction, it dehumanises the experience and thereby dominates women' (1995, 28). This fails to recognise the contested nature of sex itself and confirms current normative understandings of 'genuine' sex as in some way outside power. Moreover, it accepts the culturally specific processes that separate work from relationships of intimacy (Olsen 1983, 1497; Zatz 1997, 303), missing the more complex and potentially challenging relationship that sex/work has to gender hierarchy. Described by Zatz as a 'bifurcated event', prostitution is an act that cannot be identified as singularly a market transaction or the realisation of private desire

(1997, 303). Its failure to adhere to one realm fuels the whore stigma (Pheterson 1989) which can be read as an expression of deeply felt anxieties about women trespassing the boundaries between private and public (McClintock 1992, 73). This also motivates criminalisation, which attempts to force back public elements of prostitution into the realm of private sexuality, thus keeping the economy and sexuality 'symbolically separated', maintaining the boundary between the forms of affective labour routinely assigned to and expected of women and those practices recognised as work (Zatz 1997, 287).

Finally, by uncritically appealing to law, the abolitionist approach understates the vital role of law in structuring the marginal position of sex work. A careful consideration of the role of law helps to provide a more complex picture of sex work's relationship to gender hierarchy. It also recognises the extent to which law actively helps to maintain the sex/work boundary and the ways that criminalisation itself becomes a 'trapping' factor (Sanders 2007).

Taken together, these three strands of analysis illustrate that abolitionist and radical feminist approaches fail to move outside the hetero-normative order which separates work from sex. By naturalising men's power and women's victimhood, domination theory also inadvertently augments the on-going hegemonic moral and political regulation of sex workers. For these reasons, reforms which seek to support an abolitionist agenda should be subject to thorough critical analysis.

Breaking the System: Legal Incursions into Supply/Demand – Criminalising Demand?

Of course, law and policy in prostitution has been discriminatory, focusing almost exclusively on the female role while largely ignoring the position of the male client. However, the supposition that the criminal law is the best medium to redress this injustice or to achieve 'equality', or even that the criminal frame offers a sufficient lens through which to view male behaviour in the context of commercial sex, is much more questionable.

The issues that sustain prostitution as a marginal and dangerous activity do not translate into the narrow lens of criminal law. The complex aetiology that explains the purchase of sex within a cultural, gendered and economic context (Brooks-Gordon and Gelsthorpe 2003, 438) is brutally simplified in the necessarily rigid definition of criminal responsibility, which 'divides the world into victims and victimizers' (Bernstein 2001, 389). In critiquing the Swedish system, it has been argued:

> By utilising a male disciplinary model, it is likely that any success will be limited to shifting the whore stigma to a new deviant group. Responsibility becomes increasingly narrowed to client motives and individual sexual ethics, which are pathologised rather than explained in relation to their historical specificity and to the social and economic institutions that themselves structure the relations of gender domination (Scoular 2004b).

Deviant identities become the focus for law reform rather than the social factors that construct these identities in the first place. Models that have emerged that seek to tackle demand by focusing on criminal law 'abstract prostitution from its systemic and structural roots and treat it merely as a question of individual morality' (O'Connell Davidson 1998, 199). The appeal to criminal law as a means of seeking political recognition and redistribution simply shifts criminal status and sanctions to men. In so doing, it simply individualises control over a perceived 'risky' group of purchasers. Indeed evaluations show that state interventions against clients achieve little more than the criminalisation of a typically lower tier of male heterosexual practices such as kerb-crawling (Fischer et al. 2002) and 'the re-gendering of sexual stigma in certain middle-class factions' (Bernstein 2001). Thus the productive relations that determine the dynamics of commercial sex, while they may be inverted in certain areas, are left largely untouched and are never transformed (Scoular 2004b).

Moreover, as we go on to show in the next section, increasing men's criminalisation may not lead to a corresponding reduction in women's punishment. For that to be the case would assume that the criminal and welfare systems operate according to a zero sum logic: that the increase in A's criminalisation leads to a reduction in B's. However, the rationalities and imperatives of both crime and welfare control are far more complex and would suggest an ongoing preference for maintaining systems and rationalities of control that continue to exclude those women who persist in sex work (Scoular et al. 2007).

Breaking the System: Legal Incursions into Supply/Demand – Empowering Victims?

> We now have practical experience of what works so we can reach out and protect those trapped in prostitution and offer them exit routes ... We in this century must do what Josephine Butler attempted over 100 years ago, in a very different era and in a very different way (Home Secretary, the *Guardian*, 30 December 2003).

While at first glance efforts to exit women may seem like an important move in recognising the harm and social marginalisation experienced by women involved in sex work, our recent work shows that such 'social inclusion', when premised on responsibilition to exit, may be more rhetorical than real (Scoular and O'Neill 2007). Crucially, the Home Office approach fails to address root causes and may lead to an overly simplistic view of the complexities involved, in both sex work and politics. We caution against notions of supply and demand that are too prescriptive, un-reflexive, and fail to recognise women's agency within complex lived relations; as well as the intersections of gender, capitalism, consumerism and trans-nationalism.

As we argue in an earlier paper (Scoular and O'Neill 2007) premising social inclusion on exiting renders sex work incompatible with norms of citizenship and inclusion. Not only does this reinforce a particular and hegemonic version of citizenship that casts those involved in sex work as in some way outside 'society' but it simultaneously removes the state from any role in this exclusion. Rather, it is recast as the protective force against a demonised, distant and organised 'sex trade', the reformer of what will in effect be only a small section of clients and the facilitator of exit and support to those sex workers re-classified as victims. By prioritising their 'exiting' as the primary means of facilitating social inclusion, inclusion becomes a tool of individualised risk assessment facilitating 'rehabilitation' according to unchanged dominant norms. The underlying structures of the state, market and family remain and indeed are reified. Structural factors (poverty, homelessness) are mentioned but are subject to individualised application as they are used to identify those most at risk and most in need of support. The result is that material realities and structural exclusions recede from official attention, which becomes focused upon individual needs and protecting women from risk, rather than supporting processes of social justice for women that incorporate their inclusion into dialogue and debate on these issues. Thus, by appealing to law for protection as victims rather than seeking political recognition of structural harms and rights, abolitionist measures which seek to exit women serve to legitimise the individualising tendencies of neo-liberal forms of power. In this way, radical feminist concerns have been translated into techniques of control in recent programmes to criminalise and responsibilise the buyers and sellers of sex.

What is most disturbing is the way that the current politics of prostitution reform conflates the subject herself with her own oppression. Indeed, the current focus on saving women and criminalising men is an example of identity thinking in practice.[9] What she does becomes who she is, her identity is fixed along a victim trajectory that has little room for her agency and more complex account of identities and subjecthood (O'Neill 2001). As highlighted above, abolitionist approaches which centre on the victimhood of women who sell sex actually legitimise many of the familiar modes of control – of both criminalisation and apparent 'benevolent' interventions (Agustín 2007).

In this way, contemporary legal reforms mirror an old paradigm of welfare responses that focus on 'saving' and 'responsibilising' fallen women (Walkowitz 1980; Mcleod 1982; Mahood 1990; Agustín 2005) but utilise increasingly sophisticated techniques of risk management to legitimise new forms of behavioural regulation and control. Moreover, radical feminist concerns are being co-opted and translated into techniques of control. Described by some writers as an example of governance feminism (Halley et al. 2006), these strategies are, according to Wendy Brown (1995), based on 'ressentiment' (that is, demands to the state for redress of injured identity), which can end up re-inscribing, rather than neutralising, the injured identity itself, as stated earlier in this chapter. Brown suggests that we should be even more cautious about attempts to protect women sexually:

> ... such appeals for protection ... involve seeking protection from masculinist institution against men, a move more in keeping with the politics of feudalism than freedom. Indeed, to be 'protected' by the same power whose violation one fears perpetuates the very modality of dependence and powerlessness marking much of women's experience across widely diverse cultures and epochs (1995, 65).

---

9 A further critique of identitarian logic in operation can be found in the works of Agustín (2007) and O'Connell Davidson (2006) where we find critical feminist analysis of the conflation of discourses of migration and trafficking that totalise the experiences of all migrants working in the sex industry along a trajectory that is constituted by 'victim of trafficking'. This also serves to silence the women who become defined as 'perpetually underprivileged and marginalised' (Kapur 2001, 866).

The Way Forward: Rights, Recognition and Redistribution

The failure to engage with the complexity of the phenomenon of prostitution (highlighted above) is reflected very clearly in a model of victimisation linked to responsibilisation. Moreover, exclusion from public spaces, through an abolitionist informed focus upon supply/demand that promotes responsibilisation to exit, symbolises a retreat from social justice for women selling sex. This is especially the case for those who refuse the victim identity (and the option of being rehabilitated to exit) who will remain subject to criminal sanctions.

By contrast, we argue that there is a need to develop an alternative approach to social justice – one that recognises the material insights offered by a political economy of sex but seeks to move beyond its identitarian logic. In focusing upon a politics of inclusion, we offer a more critical and holistic understanding of a social justice that coalesces around discourses of rights, redistribution and recognition (Fraser 1997; Bauman 2001) whilst also acknowledging the structures and processes of the global capitalist economy.

We argue that any strategic response to this issue should first focus upon the complexity of sex work. Second, it should be grounded in the multiple standpoints and experiences and realities of the women, men and young people involved. And third, it should be underpinned by principles of inclusion, rights, recognition, respect and redistribution (O'Neill 2007a, 2008). This invokes a women-centred response that creates the space for women's voices by using inclusive research methodologies, such as participatory action research and biographical, ethnographic methods, in order to create safe spaces for dialogue and research *with* sex workers.[10] Ultimately, what we are suggesting here is a politics of inclusion (Newman 2003) informed by a politics of feeling (O'Neill 2001, 2007c).[11] This brushes against the grain of the new punitiveness and moral authoritarianism, and re-connects with radical feminist perspectives on violence against women from the perspective of women's lived experience – not government agendas – and includes both rights (through *redistribution*) and *recognition* (Fraser 2000).

In the Home Office strategy, the identity of 'the prostitute' is fixed along a victim trajectory that ignores the wealth of research documenting the subjecthood of female and male sex workers. Recognition is thus based upon assuming a victim identity. This constitutes mis-recognition. On the other hand, sex worker rights and

---

10 A range of ethnographic women and young person centred research of this ilk exists – see research by Margaret Melrose (2002); Jenny Pearce et al. (2002); Teela Sanders (2004); Rosie Campbell and Kinnell (2001) (to name but a few).

11 A politics of feeling is defined by O'Neill (2001) as the exploration of the politics of everyday life through women's narratives, through their inclusion in the research process via ethnographic participatory research. A politics of feeling privileges emotions, feelings and meanings in accessing 'lived experiences' or 'lived cultures', and explores experiences, meanings, practices through the tension or mediation between feeling and reason involved in critical interpretive ethnography. A politics of feeling – draws upon 'feeling forms' (Witkin 1974) such as art, life story narratives, film and dance to re-tell, re-present the multiple stories generated through interpretive ethnographic research. This process is captured also in O'Neill's concept of 'ethno-mimesis'.

unionisation are a key step on the road to recognition of the sex worker as a worker. In abolitionist discourses, the rights of sex workers to work on street are contested but, more than this, claims to redistribution and analysis of the material/structural realities that foster routes in and help to sustain women in sex work are displaced by recognition claims – the woman accepts her victim status and responsibly exits.

We argue here that the tension *between* recognition and redistribution (highlighted by Fraser)[12] can be reconciled. In current discourses around sex as crime versus sex as work, redistribution is displaced by identity politics (recognition claims). We need to work across this divide and challenge sexual and social inequalities with respect to both. Fraser goes on to suggest that instead of treating (mis-)recognition through group identity (in our example – sex worker or victim status) the status of the group members should be as full and equal partners in social interaction and their status not reduced to group identity. To be mis-recognised (*as victim*) is to be denied the status of full partner in social interaction 'unworthy of respect and esteem' (Fraser 2000, 114). Fraser argues that it is important to conceptualise:

> … struggles for recognition so that they can be integrated with struggles for redistribution, rather than displacing and undermining them. It also means developing an account of recognition that can accommodate the full complexity of social identities, instead of one that promotes reification and separatism (2000, 109).

In the section that follows we offer an alternative reading of the recent Home Office *Co-ordinated Strategy*, published in 2006, highlighting what can be gained by moving from an abolitionist reading of supply/demand to one which seeks to challenge these dynamics with an approach based on a politics of recognition, redistribution and inclusion.

A Co-ordinated Strategy?

Current critiques of the Home Office strategy argue that the complexity of the issue has been missed in an attempt to manage public space, and protect communities and sex workers by promoting a zero tolerance approach to street work (Scoular et al. 2007; Phoenix 2007). These interventions do little to address structural factors and, as Boynton and Cusick argue, 'will not, therefore, tackle genuine areas of vulnerability and exploitation' (Boynton and Cusick 2006, 191). Focusing upon routes out, the Home Office strategy ignores routes in and the structural basis for entry into selling sex (Melrose 2006, 19). For many women and men, economic need is the bottom line for entry into sex work (Roberts et al. 2007; Roberts 2007; O'Neill 2001). Thus, a key issue for us is promoting forms of solidarity that can challenge and change these structural conditions whilst recognising the multiple subject positions and lived experiences of the women involved.

Hence, our focus and the challenge for feminist politics in this area is to advance a politics of solidarity, which recognises the need to address structural inequalities and

---

12 Fraser (2000) argues that currently claims for *recognition* (identity politics) are displacing claims for *redistribution* and that this has serious consequences.

the ideologies that underpin their sexual manifestations, but is *not* based on victim identities. For some feminists, sex worker support projects and sex worker activists, responding to this 'Othering' of sex workers requires a focus upon the *recognition* (identity politics) of women (and men) as workers (Bindman and Doezema 1997). Radical feminists, on the other hand, as articulated above, focus upon the need to prioritise the human *rights* of women selling sex and the endemic nature of male violence against sex workers in particular. Additionally, research over a number of decades, indeed centuries, has articulated the important issue of *redistribution* and established that 'routes in' and sustained involvement is based largely upon economic need, with poverty and homelessness as the key conditions for entry into sex work. The socio-economic disadvantages experienced by sex workers clearly foster processes of social exclusion (Campbell and Kinnell 2001; Pearce et al. 2002; O'Connell Davidson 1998).

We suggest that one way out of the impasse and binary divide between abolitionism, with its uni-directional focus on supply/demand, and de-criminalisation/regulatory arguments would be to develop collaborative work across the abolitionist/regulatory divide. This work must be conducted *with* sex workers and could focus upon safety and violence as the basis for collaborative work that 'engages and works with complexity and promotes social justice in contrast to that which re-creates binaries/ liminality and the illusion of justice (however well intentioned)' (O'Neill 2008).

Towards a Politics of Inclusion

How might we proceed? The first task is to unpack the rhetoric around the victimhood of women who sell sex in order to develop work with women as being of equal status to ourselves – basically to engage in a process of de-'Othering!' Walklate (2005) has recently written about the rhetoric of victimhood as a source of oppression and this, we argue above, is exactly the process at work in the current politics of prostitution reform. Such reform displays a blinkered focus on addressing supply and demand, and on the development of a culture of control underpinned by zero tolerance and the drive to facilitate exit. Sex workers are symbolised as perpetrators of criminal acts/immoral subjects as well as victims. This is an example of identity thinking in operation supported by an abolitionist approach that, as we argue above, revolves around a single organising principle – the domination of women by men within a patriarchal system. The very act of selling sex makes victims of the women involved. However, if we loosen up this analysis and introduce the complex contexts in which sex is bought and sold cross-nationally then a different picture emerges. Through ethnographic work – immersion and identification in the lived cultures of individuals and groups – followed by subsequent commentary and criticism, we can see that economic need, a lack of other viable options, poverty and conflict, as well as environmental and natural disasters can create the motivating agents for entry into sex work. And, moreover, that the women who sell sex do not always experience themselves as victims. As a respondent (migrant in Spain) talking to Agustín tells her:

> No one brought me here or deceived me and I never had bad experiences ... I take care of myself, I have a private insurance policy and social security. My work life has been tranquil, in flats. I'm not proud of what I do but it's a job. It's the fastest way to make money (Colombian woman in Spain 2007, 74).

In a similar vein, in a 2007 paper, Ron Roberts published results of a pilot study conducted across two British universities and concluded, 'available evidence suggests that changes in the funding of higher education have led to some students entering the sex industry in order to make ends meet' (2007, 323).

The marginal and abusive status of commercial sex is not consistent across time and space. In a global capitalist economy, for the migrant in Spain and some students in UK universities, the economic gains of selling sex outweigh the associated stigma and risks. Thus, people make choices but not always in conditions of their own choosing (Giddens 1986).

Second, we do need to recognise the harms that impact overwhelmingly upon women selling sex. Violence against sex workers is endemic and radical feminists have for decades drawn attention to the sexual and social inequalities that lead to the violence and abuse of women. However, seeking to re-dress endemic violence against sex workers through an abolitionist discourse that promotes rehabilitation and responsibilisation towards exit and denies women agency serves to undercut the radical nature of feminism. Feminism is a practice, a politics as well as an intellectual movement (Gray 1998; O'Neill 2001, 183). As we stated earlier in this chapter, promising inclusion for those who responsibly exit, and threatening further exclusion and criminalisation for those who do not, sustains binaries between good/bad women, and deserving/undeserving victims. This supports ideological thinking (the promotion of sectional interests as universal), sustains binary distinctions and works against the feminist project of envisioning transformations in sexual, social and cultural inequalities.

Third, the current politics of prostitution reform should be challenged by the feminist agenda, not supported. As we identify in our previous joint and separate work, the Home Office *Coordinated Prostitution Strategy* has at its centre a lack – the absence of the voices of the women who sell sex, who make choices, who experience violence, who manage 'whore stigma'. The focus of the strategy is upon disrupting demand, protecting communities, preventing routes in and promoting routes out. There is also a focus upon partnerships, the co-ordination of welfarist policing and the enforcement of the law to divert, deter and rehabilitate those women who do not choose to exit as the most 'responsible' option. As we argue earlier, the identity of 'the prostitute' is fixed along a victim trajectory. Moreover, the image and re-presentation of 'the prostitute' as an 'Other' is apparent in government policy, rhetoric, media representations and inevitably the public imagination. Indeed, the activities of the state through progressive governance, depend upon what Newman (2003) calls systems of co-arrangements that include co-steering, collaboration and co-operation that in turn depend upon new systems of patronage. What emerges in our critique of New Labour (progressive) governance in this area is that prostitution reform is indicative of broader shifts to intolerance and greater punitiveness in Western societies and the operation of the moral forces of authoritarianism (Phoenix and Oerton 2005). This state of affairs is deeply problematic for both the women involved in selling sex and feminist debates, policy and practice.

In order to counter these hegemonic tendencies, we need critical criminological work to problematise and critique dominant discourses *and* imagery, as well as research and policies that are sensitive to complexity. Women's (and men's) multiple subject positions must be recognised and space needs to be made for dialogue and for women's (and other's) voices to speak and be heard. Hence, we argue in this chapter for a renewed research agenda[13] that, in focusing upon a politics of inclusion, both theorises and seeks to produce social justice as praxis (purposeful knowledge) and is radically different from the research agenda the Home Office currently employs.

As highlighted above, for us, social justice is defined as being constituted by the inter-relation of cultural justice (issues of recognition), distributive justice (equality of opportunity, that is, redistribution), and associational justice (patterns of association and inclusion, which include networking and participation) (see O'Neill et al. 2004; O'Neill 2007a). The latter includes a recognition of the importance of what Woods identifies as 'interlocking democratic rationalities' defined as: decisional (involvement in decision-making), discursive (participation in debate and dialogue), therapeutic (enhanced self esteem through involvement) and ethical (aspiration to truth and meaning integral to authentic participation) (Woods 2003, 157).

We argue for new forms of consolidation and solidarity around inclusion and social justice and we support the need for a radical democratic imaginary[14] as a dialectical/constellational project rather than one that deals in binaries. Critical and cultural criminologists argue that the combination of social research and cultural analysis can provide a richer, more sensuous understanding of society and lived experience with a view to social change/transformation (O'Neill 2004; Presdee 2004; Ferrell et al. 2004). This knowledge can help us to avoid identitarian thinking and feeling, and help us to re-imagine relationships between lived experience, social regulation, the culture of control, and policies for real social inclusion and justice.

What is clear from our analysis is that the abolitionist approach is an insufficient base on which to build law and social policy because subject positions and politics are seen as 'settled' and do not include the realities of contradiction and struggle in the lives of those involved in selling and buying sex. The political space in which we (radical and regulatory feminists and policy-makers) may meet is where understanding and allegiances to human rights, social justice and the safety of sex workers could emerge as defining aims on which to build solidarity, to address

---

13 A renewed research agenda is motivated by our commitment to feminist critical theory/criminology and our involvement in empirical research in the context of various forms of governance, and varying 'social justice' outcomes.

14 'Laclau and Mouffe contend that radical democracy is the best route towards progressive social change for the Left today. Radical democracy embraces many aspects of the socialist tradition ... appropriates the most progressive moments of the liberal democratic, anti-racist, anti-homophobic and environmentalist traditions ... The ability of the oppressed to imagine the complete overthrow of their oppressors depends upon the circulation, radicalization and institutionalization of democratic discourse' (Smith 1998, 6–7). Thus, 'democratization is understood not as a set of superficial reforms, but as the struggle to institutionalise a radical pluralist imaginary' (1998, 5).

structural inequalities, and to seek rights and recognition through constellational *not* binary thinking. Our task as critical theorists is to take responsibility for catalysing 'dialogic understanding in the general public, to opening up and keeping open spaces for critical discourse' (Bauman 1995, 242), and to bring into being what Laclau (2004) calls 'radical democracy'.

Laclau argues that radical democracy 'is the result of a pluralisation of social struggles anchored in the new structures of contemporary capitalism' (2004, 183). So, in building solidarity across the feminist divide we need to discard essentialist ideas of identity and uni-directional binaries that talk about prostitution as abuse or work. In moving towards a better understanding of social justice in this area we must acknowledge the associational, cultural and distributive aspects of justice for women. Thus, we need to establish a 'chain of equivalence among the different democratic struggles so as to create an equivalent articulation[15] between the demands of women, blacks, workers, gays, and others' (Mouffe 1995, 318). Thus, researchers, activists, feminists across the work/abuse trajectory, sex workers and sex work support projects could direct attention at the priorities and commitments that drive us, and identify the points of intersection – the spaces where solidarity would count.

What might these points of intersection be? Social justice and human rights? Violence and safety? Sexual and social inequalities? Specific examples might include inequalities of income, education, welfare and health, employment and training opportunities, the feminisation of poverty, the loss of student grants and the introduction of fees that see young people leave university with debts in the region of £24,000 for a first degree, the activities of the state including the development, operation and interpretation of the criminal and civil law. We might start by recognising each others' perspectives, acknowledging the paradoxes and contradictions, the similarities and differences and the possibilities for consensus and equivalence.

Establishing chains of equivalence will further help to realise the counter hegemonic role of feminism(s) through dialogue, practice and politics. Indeed, this could provide the political and practical space for a renewed research agenda that uses social justice and cultural citizenship as the leverage on which to base a radical democratic approach to prostitution reform (O'Neill 2008).

Our vision is of a research agenda that works with (not on or for) sex workers through participatory methodologies and through constellational thinking that acknowledges the full complexity of selling sex without reducing it to supply and demand – a further example of binary thinking in operation.[16] Research methodologies which incorporate the voices of citizens through scholarly/civic research as participatory research can not only serve to enlighten and raise our awareness of certain issues

---

15 Articulation is defined in Smith 1998 as a contingent link – a 'family resemblance' partially fixed through the creation of nodal points.

16 An example of participatory approaches that create the space for the voices of sex workers to speak and be heard (including a report and images) can be found at <www.safetysopbox.co.uk>. Here transformative change through dialogue, participatory and visual methodologies emerged through research undertaken with the very women who are the current subject-objects of reform as well as residents living in areas of street sex work.

but also produce critical reflexive texts which may help to mobilise social change (O'Neill 2007c, 216), especially the ideological effects of policy, practice and re-presentations that mark sex workers out as 'Other' and/or 'victim'.

In conclusion, feminism is the struggle against the multiple forms in which the category 'woman' is constructed in subordination – not only those linked to gender. This allows us to understand how 'the subject is constructed through different discourses and subject positions' and enables us to avoid the reduction of 'our identity to one single position – be it class or race or gender' (Smith 1998, 329) or, in this context, stigmatised victim – 'Other' – prostitute.

Our argument stresses the need 'to grasp the diversity of ways in which relations of power are constructed and helps to reveal the forms of exclusion present in all pretensions to universalism and in claims to have found the true essence of rationality' (Smith 1998). It insists, moreover, that the critique of essentialist arguments is the condition of feminism's possibility (Mouffe 1995). In this sense, our critique of the current politics of prostitution reform provides the context for the possibility of re-imagining the governance of sex work. It does so via what we call a politics of inclusion that deals with the unfinished, unsettled aspects of state power, in the context of capitalism, consumerism and the realities and lived experiences of those people involved in both the demand and supply of sex for sale.

Rather than seeking justice in terms of victimhood and effecting the removal of sex workers, we seek an alternative vision of social justice based on including women in dialogue, debate, research and praxis. This demands a renewed research agenda that focuses on complexity in subject positions, in lived realities and recognises the sheer complexity of the contemporary sex trade within the context of global capitalism. To this end, we call for academics, policy-makers, sex workers and sex work projects to transgress the divisions that currently exist between abolitionist and regulatory approaches in order to work together to create 'chains of equivalence', in order to address the sexual and social inequalities experienced by women and men who sell sex, and in the process to facilitate the production of social justice via a politics of inclusion.

References

Agustín, L. (2005), 'Migrants in the Mistress's House: Other Voices in the "Trafficking" Debate', *Social Politics* 12:1, 96–117.

Agustín, L. (2007), *Sex at the Margins* (London: Zed Books).

Barry, K. (1979), *Female Sexual Slavery* (Englewood Cliffs, NJ: Prentice-Hall).

Barry, K. (1995), *The Prostitution of Sexuality* (New York: New York University Press).

Bauman, Z. (1995), *Life in Fragments: Essays in Postmodern Morality* (Oxford: Blackwell).

Bauman, Z. (2001), *Community Seeking Safety in an Insecure World* (Cambridge: Polity).

Bernstein, E. (2001), 'The Meaning of the Purchase: Desire, Demand and the Commerce of Sex', *Ethnography* 2:3, 389–420.

Bindman, J. and J. Doezema (1997), *Redefining Prostitution as Sex work on the International Agenda*, available at <http://www.walnet.org/csis/papers/redefining.html#1>.

Boynton, P. and L. Cusik (2006), 'Sex Workers to Pay the Price', *British Medical Journal* 332, 190–91.

Brooks-Gordon, B. and L. Gelsthorpe (2003), 'Prostitutes' Clients, Ken Livingstone and a New Trojan Horse', *The Howard Journal* 437–51.

Brown, W. (1995), *States of Injury: Power and Freedom in Late Modernity* (Princeton, NJ: Princeton University Press).

Campbell, R. and H. Kinnell (2001), 'We Shouldn't Have to Put Up With This: Sex Workers and Violence', *Criminal Justice Matters* 42, 12–13.

Davis, N. (1993), *Prostitution: An International Handbook on Trends, Problems and Policies* (Westport, CT: Greenwood Press).

Doezema, J. (2001), 'Ouch! Western Feminists' "Wounded Attachment" to the Third World Prostitute', *Feminist Review* 67:1, 16–38.

Dworkin, A. (1987), *Intercourse* (New York: Free Press).

Dworkin, A. (1989), *Pornography, Men Possessing Women* (New York: Plume).

Dworkin, A. (1997), 'Prostitution and Male Supremacy' in *Life and Death* (New York: Free Press).

Ferrell, J., K. Hayward, W. Morrison and M. Presdee (eds) (2004), *Cultural Criminology Unleashed* (London: Routledge-Cavendish).

Fischer, B., S. Wortley, C. Webster and M. Kirst (2002), 'The Socio-Legal Dynamics and Implications of "Diversion": The Case Study of the Toronto "John School" Diversion Programme for Prostitution Offenders', *Criminal Justice* 2:4, 385–410.

Fraser, N. (1997), *Justice Interruptus: Rethinking Key Concepts of a Post-socialist Age* (New York: Routledge).

Fraser, N. (2000), 'Rethinking Recognition', *New Left Review* 3, 107–20.

Giddens, A. (1986), *The Constitution of Society: Outline of the Theory of Structuration* (Cambridge: Polity).

Gould, A. (2001), 'The Criminalisation of Buying Sex', *Journal of Social Policy* 30:3, 437–56.

Gray, A. (1998), 'Learning from Experience: Cultural Studies and Feminism' in J. Mcguigan (ed.), *Cultural Methodologies* (London: Sage).

The *Guardian*, 30 December 2003.

Guy, D. (1995), *Sex and Danger in Buenos Aires: Prostitution, Family and the Nation in Argentina* (Lincoln, NE: University of Nebraska Press).

Halley, J., P. Kotiswaran, H. Shamir and C. Thomas (2006), 'From the International to the Local in Feminist Legal Responses to Rape, Prostitution/Sex Work, and Sex Trafficking: Four Studies in Contemporary Governance Feminism', *Harvard Journal of Law and Gender* 29, 336–419.

Home Office (2004), *Paying the Price: A Consultation Paper on Prostitution* (London: HMSO).

Home Office (2006), *A Coordinated Prostitution Strategy*, <http://www.homeoffice.gov.uk/documents/cons-paying-the-price/ProstitutionStrategy.pdf?view=Binary>.

Home Office (2007a), *Crime Reduction Briefing, Prostitution*, <http://www.homeoffice.gov.uk/crime-victims/reducing-crime/prostitution/>.

Home Office (2007b), *Campaign to Deter Kerb-Crawling*, <http://www.homeoffice.gov.uk/documents/kerb-crawling-marketing-material/>.

Hughes, D. (2000), 'The "Natasha" Trade: The Transnational Shadow Market of Trafficking in Women', *Journal of International Affairs* 53:2, 625–51.

Jeffries, S. (1997), *The Idea of Prostitution* (Melbourne: Spinifex Press).

Kampadoo, K. and J. Doezema (eds) (1998), *Global Sex Workers: Rights, Resistance, and Redefinition* (London: Routledge).

Kapur, R. (2001), 'Post-Colonial Economies of Desire: Legal Representations of the Sexual Subaltern', *Denver University Law Review* 78, 855–85.

Kesler, K. (2002), 'Is a Feminist Stance in Support of Prostitution Possible? An Exploration of Current Trends', *Sexualities* 5:2, 219–35.

Kilvington, J., S. Day and H. Ward (2001), 'Prostitution Policy in Europe: A Time of Change?', *Feminist Review* 67, 78–93.

Kulick, D. (2003), 'Sex in the New Europe: The Criminalization of Clients and Swedish Fear of Penetration', *Anthropological Theory* 3:2, 199–218.

Laclau, E. (2004), 'Ethics, Normativity, and the Heteronomy of the Law' in S. Cheng (ed.), *Law, Justice and Power, Between Reason and Will* (Stanford, CA: Stanford University Press).

MacKinnon, C. (1982), 'Feminism, Marxism, Method and the State', *Signs* 7:3, 515–44.

MacKinnon, C. (1987), *Feminism Unmodified: Discourses on Life and Law* (Cambridge, MA: Harvard University Press).

MacKinnon, C. (1989), *Toward a Feminist Theory of the State* (Cambridge, MA: Harvard University Press).

Mahood, L. (1990), *The Magdalenes: Prostitution in the Nineteenth Century* (London: Routledge).

Månsson S.A. (2002), 'Men's Practices in Prostitution: The Case of Sweden' in B. Pease and K. Pringle (eds), *A Man's World: Changing Men's Practices in a Globalised World* (London: Zed Books).

Matthews, R. (2005), 'Policing Prostitution Ten Years On', *British Journal of Criminology* 45, 877–95.

McClintock, A. (1992), 'Screwing the System: Sexwork, Race and the Law', *Boundary* 19, 70–95.

McElroy, W. (1998), 'Prostitutes, Anti-pros Feminists and the Economic Associates of Whores' in N. Elias (ed.), *Whores, Hustlers and Johns* (New York: Prometheus Press).

Mcleod, E. (1982), *Women Working: Prostitution Now* (London: Croom Helm).

Melrose, M. (2002), 'Labour Pains: Some Considerations on the Difficulties of Researching Juvenile Prostitution', *International Journal of Social Research Methodology* 5:4, 333–51.

Melrose, M. (2006), 'Trying to Make a Silk Purse from a Sow's Ear? A Comment on the Government's Prostitution Strategy', *Community Safety Journal* 5:2, 4–13.

Millet, K. (1975), *The Prostitution Papers* (St Albans: Paladin).

Mouffe, C. (1995), 'Post-Marxism, Democracy and Identity', *Environment and Planning, Society and Space* 13:3, 259–65.

Newman, J. (2003), 'New Labour, Governance and the Politics of Diversity' in J. Barry, M. Dent and M. O'Neill (eds), *Gender and the Public Sector, Professionals and Managerial Change* (London: Routledge).

O'Connell Davidson, J. (1998), *Prostitution, Power and Freedom* (Cambridge: Polity).

O'Connell Davidson, J. (2006), 'Will the Real Sex Slave Please Stand Up?', *Feminist Review* 83, 4–22.

O'Neill, M. (2001), *Prostitution and Feminism: Towards a Politics of Feeling* (Cambridge: Polity).

O'Neill, M. (2004), 'Crime, Culture and Visual Methodologies: Ethno-Mimesis as Performative Praxis' in J. Ferrell, K. Hayward, W. Morrison and M. Presdee (eds), *Cultural Criminology Unleashed* (London: Glasshouse Press).

O'Neill, M. (2007a), 'Community Safety, Rights and Recognition: Towards a Coordinated Prostitution Strategy?', *Community Safety Journal* 6:1, 45–52.

O'Neill, M. (2007b), 'Theodor Adorno' in R. Stones, *Key Sociological Thinkers* (London: Palgrave Macmillan).

O'Neill, M. (2007c), 'Feminist Knowledge and Social–Cultural Research: Ethno-mimesis, Feminist Praxis and the Visual Turn' in T. Edwards (ed.), *Cultural Theory* (London: Sage).

O'Neill, M. (2008), 'Sex, Violence and Work: Transgressing Binaries and the Vital Role of Services to Sex Workers Public Policy Reform' in G. Letherby, P. Birch, M. Cain and K. Williams (eds), *Sex as Violence* (Cullompton: Willan).

O'Neill, M., R. Campbell, P. Hubbard, J. Pitcher and J. Scoular (2008), 'Living with the Other: Street Sex Work, Contingent Communities and Degrees of Tolerance', *Journal of Crime, Media and Culture* 4:1, 73–93.

O'Neill, M., P. Woods and M. Webster (2004), 'New Arrivals, Participatory Action Research, Imagined Communities and Social Justice', *Journal of Social Justice* 32:1, 75–89.

Oerton, S. and J. Phoenix (2001), 'Sex/Body Work: Discourses and Practices' *Sexualities: Studies in Culture and Society* 4:4, 387–412.

Oliver, M. and M. Travis (2003), 'Victorian Reformer Inspired Blunkett', the *Guardian*, 30 December 2003, 2.

Olsen, F. (1983), 'The Family and the Market: A Study of Ideology and Legal Reform', *Harvard Law Review* 96:7, 1497–507.

Pateman, C. (1983), 'Defending Prostitution: Charges against Ericsson', *Ethics* 93, 561–5.

Pateman, C. (1988), *The Sexual Contract* (Cambridge: Polity).

Pearce, J., M. Williams and C. Galvin (2002), *It's Someone Taking a Part of You: A Study of Sexual Exploitation* (London: National Children's Bureau Enterprises Ltd).

Pheterson, G. (1989), *A Vindication of the Rights of Whores: International Struggles for Prostitutes' Rights* (Seattle, WA: Seal Press).

Phoenix, J. (2007), 'Regulating Prostitution: Different Problems, Different Solutions, Same Old Story Policy', *Community Safety Journal* (Special edition on the Home Office Prostitution Strategy) 6:1, 7–11.

Phoenix, J. and S. Oerton (2005), *Illicit and Illegal: Sex, Regulation and Social Control* (Cullompton: Willan).

Presdee, M. (2004), 'Cultural Criminology: The Long and Winding Road', *Theoretical Criminology* 8:3, 275–85.

Prohibition of the Purchase of Sexual Services Act 1998, 408.

Prostitution (Public Places) (Scotland) Act 2007, <http://www.opsi.gov.uk/legislation/scotland/acts2007/20070011.htm>.

Raymond, J. (2003), '10 Reasons for Not Legalizing Prostitution', Coalition Against Trafficking in Women International Resources, March 25, <http://action.web.ca/home/catw/readingroom.shtml?x=32972>.

Roberts, R. (2007), 'Sex Work and Students: An Exploratory Study', *Journal of Further and Higher Education* 31:4, 323–34.

Roberts, R., S. Bergstro and D. La Rooy (2007), 'UK Students and Sex Work: Current Knowledge and Research Issues', *Journal of Community Applied Social Psychology* 17, 141–6.

Sanders, T. (2004), *Sex Work: A Risky Business* (Cullompton: Willan).

Sanders, T. (2007), 'Becoming an Ex-Sex Worker: Making Transitions out of a Deviant Career', *Feminist Criminology* 2:1, 74–95.

Scoular, J. (2004a), 'The "Subject" of Prostitution: Interpreting the Discursive, Symbolic and Material Position of Sex/Work in Feminist Theory', *Feminist Theory* 5:3, 343–55.

Scoular, J. (2004b), 'Criminalising "Punters": Evaluating the Swedish Position on Prostitution', *Journal of Social Welfare and Family Law* 26, 195–210.

Scoular, J. and J. Nicholson (2002), *Background Noise: Mapping the Policy Context of the Routes Out of Prostitution Social Inclusion Partnership* (Edinburgh: Scottish Executive).

Scoular, J. and M. O'Neill (2007), 'Regulating Prostitution: Social Inclusion, Responsibilisation and the Politics of Prostitution Reform', *British Journal of Criminology* 47:5, 764–78.

Scoular, J., J. Pitcher, R. Campbell, P. Hubbard and M. O'Neill (2007), 'What's Anti-Social About Sex Work?: Governance, Discourse and the Changing Representation of Prostitution's Incivility', *Community Safety Journal* (Special edition on the Home Office Prostitution Strategy) 6:1, 11–18.

Self, H. (2003), *Prostitution, Women and Misuse of the Law: The Fallen Daughters of Eve* (London and New York: Routledge).

Smith, A-M. (1998), *Laclau and Mouffe: The Radical Democratic Imaginary* (London: Routledge).

Walklate, S. (2005), 'Imagining the Victim of Crime', *Social Justice* 32:1, 89–100.

Walkowitz, J. (1980), *Prostitution and Victorian Society: Women, Class and the State* (Cambridge: Cambridge University Press).

Witkin, R. (1974), *The Intelligence of Feeling* (London: Heinemann).

Woods, P. (2003), 'Building on Weber to Understand Governance: Exploring the Links Between Identity, Democracy and "Inner Distance"', *Sociology* 37:1, 143–63.

Zatz, N. (1997) 'Sex Work/Sex Act: Law, Labor and Desire in Constructions of Prostitution' *Signs*, 277–308.

Chapter 2

Be Helped or Else! Economic Exploitation, Male Violence and Prostitution Policy in the UK

Jo Phoenix

Introduction

The last 15 years has been a tumultuous time in regards to prostitution policy in the UK. The 1990s witnessed growing concern about men's violence, victimisation and exploitation of women, young people and children in prostitution, as well as about the ability of the UK's long-standing prostitution laws to deal adequately with the problems of sex work. The main problems, it was claimed, were that the policies did not limit the nuisance caused by sex work to neighbourhoods and residents any more than they addressed the social, political and welfare difficulties of those in prostitution, or adequately policed or punished those men who exploited, victimised or coerced individuals who sell sex. By the end of the 1990s prostitution policy was seen to have failed in many key respects.

Following these concerns and since the late 1990s there has been a proliferation of piecemeal changes to prostitution-related legislation, including measures to protect children and young people from internet sexual exploitation and grooming, and – with adults – from trafficking for prostitution. New provisions have also prohibited adults from paying for sex from a child, from facilitating, causing, inciting or arranging child prostitution or the commercial sexual exploitation of children, and from exploiting, coercing or controlling children or adults for the purposes of commercial sexual exploitation or trafficking. In addition to legislative changes, successive guidance documents, reviews and strategies published by central governmental agencies have generated a veritable explosion of national, regional and local strategies on street prostitution, young people and prostitution, drugs and prostitution, housing and prostitution, and indoor prostitution. Accompanying these policies and strategies has been a concomitant series of service-level agreements between local authorities, relevant voluntary agencies and other statutory agencies.

This chapter takes as its object of analysis the regulation of prostitution in the UK at the beginning of the twenty-first century. The basic argument is that this most recent flurry of policy activity signifies an important shift in the official discourses of prostitution – or more precisely a gradual erosion of the dominance of the discourse of public nuisance. Paradoxically, however, this shift has not been accompanied by any change in the regulation and governance of prostitution. As will be demonstrated below, the burden of punitive and coercive regulation continues to fall on the more economically and socially marginalised street-based sex workers. What has changed is that current policy reforms operate to govern not just the sex workers, but also the agencies working with and often providing a political voice for them.

To make my argument, the first section of the chapter reminds readers of some of the largely unchanged lived realities of involvement in prostitution – focusing specifically on street-based sex work. The second section examines shifting discourses of prostitution and their effects subsequent to the growing awareness both of HIV/AIDS and of children and young people's involvement in prostitution. The final section focuses on the recent national strategy on prostitution.

The Lived Realities of Selling Sex

Studies of prostitution demonstrate that the empirical realities of engagement in prostitution have remained fairly stable in recent history. For most sex workers, selling sex is above all else an economic activity. As McLeod (1982) argued, women's decisions to enter prostitution are shaped by broader economic push and pull factors not limited to whether and how much money women can earn through paid employment. Support for childcare, unequal distribution of familial resources, access to social security benefits, and access to housing all impact on women's decisions to sell sex. Notwithstanding the claim that the drive for social equality for women in the last 50 years in the UK has allegedly freed women from economic dependency on male relatives, increased their economic opportunities and permitted a life not based on domesticity and familialism, empirical evidence also indicates that women's lives are still circumscribed by dynamics of gendered inequality. The Annual Survey for Hours and Earnings confirms that although hourly pay differentials between men and women have narrowed, there still exists a median gap of 12.6 per cent which widens to 26 per cent when patterns of work (that is, full or part time) were included in the analysis (Office for National Statistics ASHE 2006). Women's economic stability relative to men's is further reduced because women's patterns of employment tend to be discontinuous and part-time, meaning that they are often excluded from the full range of financial benefits accrued through employment (pensions, social security benefits, sick pay and the like). So while pay differentials have been falling over the past three decades, women's pattern of employment activity means that, for many women, economic security is nevertheless still mediated by and through their relationships with men. To put it another way, independence from men often contains with it the risk of economic insecurity, and for working-class (or young) women with limited education and training and few marketable skills, that risk translates to poverty and periods of their life spent relying on state benefits.

Empirical studies detailing the lived experiences of women in prostitution – particularly street-based sex workers – have catalogued the contradictory social and economic forces at play. Many women come from backgrounds marked by profound poverty, homelessness, social insecurity, limited opportunities for meaningful paid employment, as well as histories of abuse within the family and from partners, and growing up in Local Authority Care. For them, prostitution represents a means of gaining independence (from state benefits, from violence or abusive partners) and of securing a more stable financial future for themselves and any dependents they may have. The women in these studies are like many other working-class women in that they face the risks of poverty (and violence) and make choices in their struggle to survive. Some of the choices are commonplace, such as claiming benefits, whereas others are more extraordinary, such as engaging in prostitution (Phoenix 2001; O'Neill 2001; Sanders 2005).

But contemporary ethnographic studies of women's involvement in prostitution also tell another tale. They document the complex relationships between violence, drugs, criminalisation, financial security and poverty that many of the UK's sex workers experience. These tales highlight the many ways in which the very poor working conditions of street-based sex work coalesce in ways to lock women within prostitution. So, for instance, since the late 1980s problematic drug use has been particularly associated with street prostitution (Church et al. 2001; Taylor 2003). By the early 1990s some researchers were claiming that drug suppliers were the 'new pimps' (Faugier and Sargeant 1997) with crack cocaine coming to dominate the street sex market in the last few years (May and Hunter 2006). Some women cite drug problems as driving their involvement in prostitution whilst others comment that they only acquired their drug problems in response to the working conditions they experienced as street-based sex workers. The issue of poverty and economic dependency on violent, exploitative men is similarly complex. Whilst street prostitution might well provide women with a strategy to survive the shattering effects of poverty and abuse from men, it also exposes them to risks that further entrap them in that poverty and exacerbate the violence and abuse for which prostitution was seen as a solution (Barnardos 1998; Phoenix 2001). Recent qualitative research has described the way in which working in prostitution leads to even greater levels of dependency on men, and through economic exploitation, greater levels of poverty, homelessness and violence (Kinnell 2006).

Research has also indicated that regulating prostitution through criminal justice has a profoundly negative impact on many women's lives (especially those working from the street). The Street Offences Act 1959 formalised a means of regulating prostitution which (i) placed the responsibility for regulating prostitution in the realm of criminal justice (as opposed to welfare services, employment or health, for instance); (ii) focused almost exclusively on the prostituting activities of the women selling sex rather than the men purchasing it; and (iii) intensively regulated the activities of street-based sex workers, as opposed to indoor workers. To put it simply, for the better part of the twentieth century, policing prostitution translated into arresting, prosecuting and punishing (by fining) street-based sex workers for soliciting or loitering in a public place for the purposes of prostitution. There is an obvious impact that such a practice has of creating a revolving door – women go back to prostitution to earn the money to pay their fines. But there are also less obvious impacts. High policing activities tend to displace women from familiar areas of work to unknown parts of the city or other cities (Hester and Westmarland 2004). The fear of arrest impacts directly on the time women take to negotiate with potential clients (Kinnell 2006). Finally, in an atmosphere where the police regularly target particular areas and women for criminalisation, when serious crimes do occur against the women, they are less likely to report such events to the police or cooperate with the police in arresting and prosecuting the offenders (Kinnell 2006). In this respect, research has told a very important tale about the interconnections between criminalisation, poor working conditions and women's continued involvement in prostitution.

Social and economic changes in relation to young people have also had a direct impact on prostitution. There are now few or no social benefits that the young can claim: entrance into the legitimate labour force and the provision of social security benefits are all age-restricted (Hill and Tisdall 1997). The practice of informal school exclusions has meant that many young women effectively leave school long before the official leaving age. In this context, it should come as no surprise, therefore, that adult and young women report that selling sex provides them with a means to acquire money to buy things that they cannot otherwise afford (such as consumables), to fund drug and alcohol problems (both their own and their partner's) and as a means of supporting themselves and any dependents they may have whilst avoiding begging or other criminogenic activities which attract (up to now) much harsher and higher levels of punishment. In short, younger women are often turning to sex work for much the same reasons as older women – rather than as a result of exploitation and coercion.

In summary, empirical research on women's involvement in prostitution demonstrates that prostitution is a gendered survival strategy often used by poor women trying to create a better future for themselves and their dependents. However, such security and independence are often illusory because involvement in prostitution is also a form of gendered victimisation: those self-same women are exposed to the regularity of sexual violence, even greater levels of poverty, economic dependency on men who exploit them and further degradation of their financial and social well-being and security.

Shifting Forms of Regulation: The 'Golden Decade' of the 1990s

Throughout the 1980s and 1990s, and in response to worries about the spread of HIV/AIDS, concern grew about the impact of prostitution (and sex workers) on the population. Within popular discourse, street-based, drug-addicted sex workers themselves were identified as a bridge between the undeserving and diseased few and the healthy, moral many. Many of these fears were based on constructions of sex workers as being always and already potential reservoirs of disease – constructions which long predated HIV/AIDS. Witness the Contagious Diseases Acts of 1864, 1866 and 1869, which targeted sex workers for forced medical examinations to establish whether they were 'diseased'. But the climate of the 1980s and early 1990s was especially vituperative. In the UK, such was the climate of hostility towards women in prostitution that several commentators accused the media of conducting and fuelling a witch hunt (Roberts 1992; O'Neill 2001; ECP 1997). For instance, in 1992, the *Sunday Express* reported that the police in London's King's Cross alleged that three-quarters of the women working in the area were infected with the

AIDS virus. The allegation was found to be untrue and based only on the opinion of various arresting officers as to whether individual women might be infected (ECP 1997). By the early 1990s, medical researchers had created entire taxonomies of 'risky' behaviour in an endeavour to understand the epidemiology of HIV/AIDS. This resulted in a shift in the focus of anxiety from sex workers *per se* to the specific behaviours and lifestyles that they shared. Largely as a result of this burgeoning field of knowledge, a plethora of services were developed with the specific aim of minimising the potential risks of sex work by adopting a public health approach and a harm-minimisation, supportive method of intervention.

At a pragmatic level, considerable financial resources were made available throughout the 1990s to genito-urinary clinics and sexual health outreach projects from the Department of Health to work with women in prostitution (McKeganey and Barnard 1996; Ward and Day 1997; O'Neill and Campbell 2001). Whilst early projects sought to educate women about 'high-risk' behaviours and in particular sought to provide advice, services and help for women in order that they could do sex work in more healthy ways, the agenda rapidly moved beyond sexual health to general support (EUROPAP 1994; UKNSWP 2004). In order to achieve their aims, most sexual health outreach projects adopted a multi-agency approach in which everything from general and sexual health concerns, drug and alcohol abuse and misuse, housing and homelessness and domestic violence were addressed. Women were brought into the service either by referral from another agency or through personal contact. Involvement with sexual health outreach projects was voluntary and anonymous.

The success of this agenda *vis-à-vis* street-based sex work was such that it provided the conditions for a reconfiguration of the relationship between these support services, the police and the women.[1] This change started as outreach projects, identified violence as being a key threat to the health of sex workers, and sought to liaise with local police about the arrest and prosecution of violent punters and local men who were exploiting women. For example, during the 1990s, the SAFE Project in Birmingham provided sexual health education, gave women condoms, took them to the genito-urinary clinic, helped them access other multi-agency projects and services, and went with the women to court, but they also pioneered the 'Ugly Mugs Scheme' in which identifying information about violent and dangerous punters was passed from police to deal with a vociferous vigilante movement against street-working women (the Streetwatch and Care Association). In doing so, the SAFE Project created a template for intervention in which the police were drawn upon not to prosecute the women but rather to protect them against the violent and exploitative activities of others. This template was copied across many of the major cities in the UK and by the end of the 1990s most UK cities had their own sexual health and multi-agency outreach projects.

The growth of support services for sex workers changed the way prostitution was governed (see also Matthews 2005). By 1999, the police scaled down their direct

1 The plethora of support agencies that sprang up in the 1990s did not work exclusively with street-based sex workers, although this group formed the base of their client-group. Many organisations established contacts with indoor workers and home workers.

regulation of prostitution across the country and instead worked in conjunction with the outreach projects to help produce a more 'manageable' street trade without resort to coercive, punitive hard-line policing, arrest and conviction. This shift is reflected in the remarkable decrease in the number of women being arrested and convicted for loitering or soliciting in public for the purposes of prostitution. In 1989, there were over 15,739 women cautioned or convicted for soliciting. By 2002, this number had fallen to 4,102. By 2003, the number had fallen still further to just under 3,000 (Criminal Justice Reform Group, Home Office). The most significant drop in arrest rates occurred precisely in the last half of the 1990s – just as sexual health outreach services were expanding throughout the country.

To summarise, in the 1980s and 1990s concerns about how prostitution might threaten public sexual health in the UK resulted in the growth and establishment of sexual health outreach projects. These projects played an important role in shifting the mode of regulation. Instead of policing prostitution through arrest and punishment of sex workers, local support agencies worked with the women and the police to both provide support for the women. Crucially, many of these projects provided important mediation services between vociferous communities, the police and the women in ways that fostered a climate of tolerance (Hester and Westmarland 2004). As a result, coercive state-centred responses were displaced as formal criminal justice interventions gave way to a public health and welfare agenda.

One of the unintended consequences of the growth of this benevolent regulation was an explosion in the amount of information that was being compiled on the UK's sex workers. Part of the work that sexual health and other multi-agency organisations undertook was to research the difficulties experienced by working women in their localities. As required by their funders, most projects collected information about the ages and experiences of the women they encountered and of the various ways in which the projects were (or were not) able to support the women. This information was collected in order to identify the needs of the women, identify gaps in provision, justify funding and, importantly, apply for additional funds from both the state and charities. More than anything else, sexual health and other projects working with women in prostitution became one of the key political voices for sex workers and sources of information about the lived realities of involvement in prostitution in the UK at the latter end of the twentieth century. The activities of POW (Prostitute Outreach Workers) provide a good exemplar. The organisation was launched in 1990 when funding was secured from the World Health Organization and Nottingham Health Authority. This funding paid for a group of local sex workers to be trained as volunteer researchers to assess the health and intervention needs of sex workers in one area of Nottingham. The result of this research was both the identification of gaps in provision for sex workers as well as a baseline from which to design an outreach and referral service. Nearly two decades later, POW is an independent charity and is seen as an authoritative source of information about the health and welfare needs and services for sex workers and other socially excluded people.

The generation of such massive amounts of information across the UK meant a greater awareness of the issue of young people's involvement in prostitution and of the sheer level and realities of the drug dependency, violence and exploitation that many women experienced – especially those working from the streets. The irony that will be detailed below is that, by recognising the abuse and violence endemic to prostitution in the UK, local agencies created the imperative for state-centred action which has in turn created the conditions for a curtailment of the benevolent potential of such agencies and the reentrechment of criminal justice responses to prostitution.

The Return to Criminal Justice 'for' Sex Workers: Violence, Exploitation and Deeper Regulations in the Name of Protection

From Youth Prostitution to Commercially Sexually Exploited Children

By the turn of the millennium, concern about young people being involved in prostitution created the impetus for some of the first formal reforms to prostitution policy in the UK since the Street Offences Act 1959. The major UK children's charities ran campaigns calling for a change in the way in which girls in prostitution were treated. They claimed that not only was the practice of charging and convicting girls under the age of sexual consent for prostitution-related offences a legal anomaly (Lee and O'Brien 1995), but most girls in prostitution were the victims of exploitation and child abuse (Van Meeuwan et al. 1998). Pressure culminated and eventually the Department of Health and the Home Office issued a guidance document in May 2000, entitled *Safeguarding Children Involved in Prostitution.* This guidance directed all individuals working with young people in prostitution to treat them as victims rather than potential (prostitution-related) offenders. The importance of this guidance document should not be underestimated for two reasons. Firstly, it created a legal requirement for agencies – including the same supporting agencies that pioneered the benevolent interventions of the 1990s – to deal with young people in prostitution differently than adults and differently than they had been dealing with them to date. Secondly, it was shaped by and within a different discourse of prostitution than had been operationalised through the state before. Specifically, *Safeguarding Children Involved in Prostitution* formally created a new category of sex workers (children abused through prostitution) and singled them out for a very different type of treatment.

The central claim of *Safeguarding* was that no child (legally defined as anyone under the age of 18 years old) could consent to being involved in prostitution, that most young people are coerced into prostitution and that at any rate the men who entrap them in prostitution or buy sex from them are child sexual abusers and should be prosecuted:

> The Government recognises that the vast majority of children do not voluntarily enter prostitution. They are coerced, enticed or utterly desperate. We need to ensure that local agencies act quickly and sensitively in the best interests of the children concerned ... They should treat such children as children in need, who may be suffering, or may be likely to suffer significant harm (Department of Health/Home Office 2000, 3).

The introduction of these changes was based on a line of demarcation drawn between young victims in prostitution, adult sex workers and criminal, abusive men. Quite simply, *Safeguarding Children Involved in Prostitution* rested on an age based distinction between different categories of sex workers and then inscribed characteristics, motivations and entire social circumstances to those individuals who were younger than 18 years old. Unlike their adult counterparts, children in prostitution were *victims* and should not be punished for their involvement in prostitution.[2] Instead, these children and young people should be treated as victims of child abuse and sexual abuse and offered support and care through statutory child protection procedures and services. At the risk of repetition, *Safeguarding* established the practice of distinguishing between groups of sex workers, not on the grounds of 'visibility' (as had been the case with the Wolfenden Report), but on an assessment of their status as victims.

This line of demarcation has had the unintended effect of expanding the state-based institutional sites through which prostitution is governed and has paradoxically strengthened the criminal justice response. Sexual health outreach programmes continued to work with adult women and provided general welfare and health services, but reported difficulties in sustaining their work with anyone under the age of 18 years, as the involvement in prostitution of such people had been redefined as a child protection issue. In practice, this meant that sexual health and other non-state organisations could no longer offer the degree of confidentiality that they had enjoyed previously (see Phoenix 2002 for a fuller explanation). Instead, a plethora of multi-agency teams grew to meet the needs of these young people. These multi-agency teams frequently were little more than constellations of local police, existing statutory child protection social services and voluntary children's services, and were oriented to traditional child protection methods of work and intervention. Importantly, this includes the capacity to incarcerate young people 'for their own protection'.

Using existing social services, voluntary organisations and the police to regulate young people's involvement in prostitution is not without difficulty. Voluntary organisations and social services now have a legal obligation to get young people out of prostitution, often without extra funding. Perhaps more importantly, though, the complex needs of young people are not easily accommodated by child protection methods of working. Many agencies report that they can offer little more than 'working with where the young person is at' through self-esteem work, counselling and advocacy. In the seven years since the introduction of this guidance, more coercive forms of regulation have emerged as many young women in prostitution have ended up incarcerated in secure units – not as a punishment for their involvement in prostitution, but as a means to limit the liability of the organisation and the individual professional when girls continue to sell sex.

Safeguarding has also acted to challenge the dominance and progressive agenda of non-judgmental support. New language has entered policy documents and practitioners' discussions. Instead of young people or children in prostitution, the concern is now for the sexual exploitation of children (that is anyone under

2 I am not challenging the veracity of claims about the victimisation of young people and children who sell sex. Rather, I am pointing to the difficulties inherent in reducing their social experiences and existence to their status as victims.

the age of 18 years). Barnardos in particular has been instrumental in expanding the term of reference such that any sexual abuse of children which involves some pecuniary gain is now treated and thought of as the same. The point here is that such a change creates a very different landscape for regulation and practice. The non-judgmental approaches of supporting agencies, within such a landscape, are located as supporting and condoning child abuse. At a practical level, this meant that these organisations found themselves engaged with statutory social services and police whose child protection trump card forced changes to the way the support organisations worked. So, for instance, early research into the implementation of *Safeguarding* revealed that a constant complaint from the voluntary sector about the involvement of the police was that, although the one or two officers that had had the most sustained and regular contact through the multi-agency forum were 'good', 'helpful' and 'engaged', the message and approach had not spread throughout the organisation locally. This was especially clear in relation to the regulation of young people in prostitution wherein both 'vice' police and child protection police teams threatened voluntary organisation workers if and when the workers attempted to ensure the confidentiality of their clients. The point that emerges out of this critique, then, is that those state agencies with statutory powers are always and already able to shift the terrain of regulation in their favour (Phoenix 2002).

One of the more controversial clauses within *Safeguarding Children Involved in Prostitution*, which has come to be known as the 'persistent returners clause', retained the possibility of criminal justice interventions against the very young. By drawing such a sharp line of demarcation between child *victims* of prostitution and sex workers, *Safeguarding* foreclosed the possibility that young people could be victimised within prostitution but nevertheless also voluntarily engage in prostituting activities. Simply, according to the constructions underpinning *Safeguarding*, young people either are or are not victims. When they are victims, help, support and assistance through child protection is offered – even if that means incarceration for welfare reasons. However, when they are not victims, then the full force of criminal justice can be warranted:

> However it would be wrong to say that a boy or girl under 18 *never* freely chooses to continue to solicit, loiter or importune … and does not knowingly break the law … The criminal justice process should only be considered if the child persistently and voluntarily continues to solicit, loiter or importune for the purposes of prostitution (Department of Health/Home Office 2000, 27–8: original emphasis).

There are two significant consequences of the persistent returners' clause. Firstly, just at a time when it looked increasingly possible to decriminalise prostitution (at least for the under 18 year olds), governmental guidance ensured that this would not happen. In effect, this clause reinforced the centrality of a state-centred criminal justice response. By basing the type of intervention that a young person receives on an adjudication and assessment of their motivation (that is, are they voluntarily engaged in prostitution or are they forced), *Safeguarding* compels supporting organisations as well as statutory social services and criminal justice organisations to assess not simply a girl's prostituting activities but her wider relationships with men and her deeper psychological state of being. To put it another way, the provision of help, support and care exists as part of a continuum of possible interventions which include punitive criminal justice interventions. Creating such a continuum has the perverse effect of forcing supporting organisations to work with statutory organisations – even though the partnerships that might be forged can never be 'equal' partnerships, since the police and social services carry legal liabilities as well as legal powers that welfare-based, support organisations do not.

To summarise, the recognition of the plight of young people and children in prostitution created an imperative for policy reforms. Despite the laudable aims of those policy reforms, they are based on a totalising discourse of victimhood that extends the controls and regulations operated on young women as well as the supporting agencies – if only because when they encounter a young person of, for instance, 16 years old, they are compelled to break confidentiality, share information with statutory agencies and engage in a process of classification that *could potentially* result in the punishment of that young person. In short, young women are now enmeshed in tighter systems of control than before – in the name of their own protection.

From Supporting Sex Workers to Protecting Victims and Punishing Offenders

The momentum for reform of prostitution policy gained force in the early part of the first decade of the twenty-first century. Not only was *Safeguarding Children Involved in Prostitution* published in 2000, but by 2004 the Home Office had published its first consultation document on reforming prostitution policies and laws (entitled *Paying the Price*). The result of this consultation exercise, *A Coordinated Prostitution Strategy and a Summary of Responses to Paying the Price* was published in early 2006. At the time of writing this chapter in 2007, no specific legal reforms have taken place, although practice in many of the UK's larger cities and conurbations has come into line with the recommendations made. The main trend that has emerged both within the documents and in relation to practice has been a drift away from non-judgmental, harm-minimisation support towards a move to abolish prostitution altogether. The justification for such a policy change is official recognition of women's victimisation in prostitution – a recognition in part forced by the greater level of knowledge about the working conditions experienced by many of the UK's sex workers brought about by the sexual health and other support organisations in the 1990s. Deploying the same line of distinction between victims and 'persistent returners' evident in reforms with young people and prostitution, reforms to practice with adults in prostitution distinguish between the 'needy' and 'victimised' women in prostitution and the 'offenders' (both sex workers and those who abuse and exploit sex workers). These 'victims' of prostitution are constituted as women for whom the responsible local authority should not provide *non-judgmental* support, but support and services aimed specifically at getting the women to 'exit' or leave prostitution. At the same time, current proposals strengthen coercive criminal justice measures through: (i) creating a broader range of harsher disposals for offences of exploitation of sex workers or trafficking for the purposes of prostitution; and (ii) creating a broader range of harsher disposals for prostitution-related offences, such as soliciting or loitering. It is worthy of note that the proposals published in January 2006 do not require introduction via primary legislation. Instead, the proposals recommend to local authorities and police constabularies an approach that could be adopted within their locality which requires nothing more than a change in enforcement practice.

As mentioned above, these proposals are constituted by and within the distinction between victimised women not voluntarily engaged in prostitution and those who are. Such a conceptualisation creates an imperative for action, and the action that is recommended is a greater use of welfare based interventions – not as an alternative to criminal justice sanctions, but backed by the full range of criminal justice sanctions. In this way, the 'unwitting' victims of prostitution are compelled to seek help and the voluntarily engaged are given the choice to accept that help to leave or face harsher punishments. What is demonstrated in what follows is that the burden of regulation falls, yet again, on the more vulnerable sex workers – street-working women. It will also be demonstrated that two emerging trends noted in regards to young people have their echoes in current suggestions for reform in relation to adults. Firstly, like the young people, the entirety of street-working women's lives, the choices they make in their intimate relationships, their leisure activities, how they spend their money and so on become the object of regulation – not just their prostituting activities. Secondly, supporting organisations not normally associated with statutory services are being brought into closer and closer 'partnerships' with key criminal justice agencies (that is, police, probation, courts) in ways that limit their ability to offer the benevolent non-judgmental support that they have hitherto offered.

Paying the Price and *A Coordinated Strategy* regularly repeat that the 'problems' that need tackling are; (i) the exploitation of women and children, (ii) trafficking of individuals for commercial sexual exploitation, (iii) the ways in which debt and drug addiction trap individuals into prostitution and (iv) the links between drugs markets, serious and organised crime and prostitution. Throughout both documents there are constant references to 'pimps', 'traffickers', 'dealers', 'sexual abusers', 'coercers' and a host of other criminal men. Both documents heavily draw on the type of explanation for involvement in prostitution that was put forward in relation to young people where poverty, constrained social and economic difficulties that women experience and the ways in which women make choices to be involved in prostitution are rendered less important than the presence of coercive or exploitative individuals. To be clear, the problem of prostitution is now defined almost entirely in relation to gender and victimisation. Where men do appear in the policy documents, it is only as criminals. Nowhere is the issue of men *as sex workers* addressed. Instead, it is the presence of criminal men that is seen to be the driver of prostitution – men who exploit and abuse women, and men whose criminal activities contribute to the very destruction of local communities. As will be seen below, such a set of assumptions shapes the construction of the problem of prostitution as being a problem of *women*'s victimisation and the solution as being a paternalistic model of intervention in which women are saved.

As intimated above, the dominant official discourse now underpinning policy is a discourse of prostitution as victimisation in which an individual's experiences of victimisation are conflated with her status and agency. In policy documents, doubt is cast about any expression of choice on the part of the women:

> Debt and drug addiction play a major part in driving people into prostitution as a survival activity … Those involved in prostitution can be particularly difficult to reach, claiming that prostitution is their choice and that they don't want to leave – through a combination of fear, the process of normalization or in an effort to maintain their dignity (Home Office 2004, 55).

Such conceptions create the very conditions for increasing the levels of coercive and punitive regulation of women in prostitution. This occurs for two reasons: (i) the stereotype of the prostitute-victim is treated as though it is an adequate explanation; and (ii) by using an 'enforcement plus support' approach to regulation, the current reforms relocate the centrality of criminal justice responses to women who do not leave prostitution voluntarily. I will explain each of these in turn.

In *Safeguarding Children Involved in Prostitution*, *Paying the Price* and *A Coordinated Strategy*, individuals in prostitution are seen as victims because they do not voluntarily consent to sell sex. They are victims because something or someone else has forced or compelled them. Put another way, policy defines consent and voluntarism as the capacity to make a different choice than be involved in prostitution – or to choose not to work in prostitution. The key problem that policy now addresses is how to create the situation in which women make their own choice to leave prostitution. This is not unique to prostitution policy as the creation of responsible self-governing citizens lies at the heart of much neo-liberal governance strategies (Rose 1993). But, in regards to sex work specifically, such a simple and naïve understanding of the conditions in which women get involved in prostitution belie the economic and social realities so widely documented. It also contradicts the ethnographic research which argues that women and young people do make choices albeit not in conditions of their own choosing (Phoenix 2001; Sanders 2005). Recent ethnographic research also details the way in which many street workers who also identify as having problematic drug use claim that by doing sex work instead of crime, they are acting as socially responsible citizens (Durose 2007). The experiences of these women plainly do not fit the model of explanation framing current policy directions. So, whilst many street-working women suffer some form of victimisation and exploitation, they are not all victims waiting to be saved by the police or other agencies. Many are just poor women struggling to survive.

The 'enforcement plus support' approach reinforces the centrality of criminal justice sanctions in the regulation of prostitution. This is a result of the very demarcation between victims and offenders that is at the heart of current policy. On this point, *Paying the Price* is clear. The criminal law can and should be used to 'rigorously clamp down on unacceptable behaviour (i.e. voluntarily engaging in prostitution) and criminality'. This is an approach in which, unless there is the presence of a 'pimp' or other such controlling man, the responsibility for involvement in prostitution is placed solely within poor choices made by the individual and in which the question of necessity never appears. Here, the full force of criminal justice is used to compel women to leave *without* any attention being paid to the socio-economic circumstances that created the impetus for prostitution. In other words, greater and greater levels of intervention and control in women's lives are being justified on the grounds of 'helping' them whilst at the same time making the women responsible (as in blameworthy) for their own poverty and their attempts to survive it:

> The current offence of loitering or soliciting is a very low-level offence and, as such the court will usually only consider imposing a fine. This is said to have very little deterrent effect and does not address the underlying causes of the offending behaviour. To rectify this situation, the Government intends to publish proposals for legislative reform to provide a penalty specifically tailored to the needs of men and women in prostitution. The intention will be for the courts to be able to order an appropriate package of intervention to address the causes of the offending behaviour where that behaviour is persistent (Home Office 2006, 37).

In practice this means a variety of criminal justice interventions which include: voluntary self-referrals to outreach programmes; the use of civil Anti-Social Behaviour Orders (ASBOs) and Intervention Orders by the police and Local Authorities compelling women into drug treatment or other treatment programmes (breach of either of which constitutes the possibility of a prison sentence of up to five years); pre-charge diversion in which individuals are referred to drug intervention programmes; conditional discharges; mandatory drug testing and compulsory attendance at drug intervention programmes following charge as well as the full range of ordinary criminal justice sanctions following repeated conviction. The aim is clear:

> Under this staged approach those women (and men) who respond to informal referrals and seek help from support services to leave prostitution, and those who engage with the CJIT (Criminal Justice Integrated Team) workers to receive treatment and other support, *may* avoid further criminalisation. However, for those individuals who, for whatever reason, continue to be involved in street prostitution, the criminal justice system will respond with rehabilitative intervention to reduced re-offending and to protect local communities (Home Office 2006, 39).

Under this new 'coordinated' regulation system, it is not merely and only the individual's prostituting activities that become the focus of intervention and sanction. Instead it is the totality of their lives and relationships. Their patterns of drug use, the appropriateness of their housing, and their personal relationships with the men in their lives, their mental health, and their educational and work status and so on, all become the target of regulation. It is this very net-widening in terms of both the interventions and the object of intervention which creates the conditions in which women who engage in prostitution will have their lives more intensely governed and regulated than they have hitherto experienced. And, when their wider behaviour, actions, relationships and choices are judged and found wanting, they become, by definition, appropriate subjects of even harsher criminal justice punishments.

But, it is not just sex workers who become objects of intervention – the support organisations that sprang up in the 1990s are also subject to increasing levels of regulation by central government. Multi-agency organisations that offered non-judgmental support and advice are now located as the very organisations and agencies best placed to assess the women, work with them (and the police) and help them 'exit' prostitution. Take, for example, the experiences of one outreach project in the north of England. Whereas ten years ago the majority of their funds came from the regional health authority, now a significant proportion of their funds come directly from the Home Office. With that, a requirement of their funds is that they only work with women (not young people) who are actively working towards exiting prostitution. More than this, it is this organisation that is tasked by the courts with the responsibility for working with, and crucially reporting breaches and so on, to the criminal justice agencies, which then have it in their capacity to prosecute and seek further, harsher punishments. In other words, the radical potentiality of the organisation to support women in prostitution, to offer help and advice in a non-coercive and non-punitive fashion, is now limited by the relationship that the organisation has had to enter into with the statutory sector.

Conclusion

One of the abiding dynamics in prostitution policy reform has been the tendency of those who make policy to specify the 'distinct' social or individual characteristics of those involved in selling sex – characteristics that both explain their involvement in prostitution and mark them as different from the rest of the population. In seeking to address those defining characteristics policies are constructed and implemented in ways that do little more than further compound the separateness of the individuals in prostitution. What has been evident in the UK since the late 1980s has been a gradual challenge to the dominance of older notions of the problem of prostitution being the problem of nuisance caused by street prostitution to ordinary citizens. But this is not to say that this discourse has disappeared altogether. Since 1999, arrests for prostitution-related offences may well have fallen, but the use of Acceptable Behaviour Contracts and Anti-Social Behaviour Orders has increased dramatically. Many local authorities now claim, with pride, that they are able to police prostitution positively and escape the revolving door created through fining women by using ASBOs and CRASBOs. Regardless of local and regional differences in policing prostitution, other discourses have begun to emerge which have had a direct impact at the national level. Some of these discourses have worked to underpin the expansion of support for (particularly street-based) sex workers that occurred throughout the 1990s. Others inform lobby groups and political activism (such as the emergence of a discourse of prostitution as being a problem of human rights of sex workers). Others still have found favour with central government and underpin some of the marked changes in policy developed since the turn of the millennium. Particularly successful has been a discourse of totalising victimisation. It underpins reforms to policy regarding children and adults. In this chapter, I have traced some of the ways that such a discourse operates to create a tighter and closer system of regulation for street-working sex workers and support agencies alike. But the discourse of prostitution is not homogeneous or closed. It is contradictory especially in relation to the different ways that women in prostitution are constituted as being responsible (or not) for their situation, able to change (or not) their choices and blameworthy (or not). These contradictions have meant, in some cases, more progressive responses to the difficulties that women and children experience. In other cases, however, and as demonstrated in this chapter, it has meant a gradual but relentless tightening of control and regulation of some of the most politically, economically and socially marginalised individuals in prostitution – street-based sex workers.

References

Barnardos (1998), *Whose Daughter Next? Children Abused Through Prostitution* (Ilford: Barnardos).

Campbell, R. and M. O'Neill (eds) (2006), *Sex Work Now* (Cullompton: Willan).

Church, S., M. Henderson, M. Barnard and G. Hart (2001), 'Violence by Clients Towards Female Prostitutes in Different Work Settings: Questionnaire Survey', *British Medical Journal* 332, 524–5.

Department of Health/Home Office (2000), *Safeguarding Children Involved in* Prostitution (London: HMSO).

Durose, N. (2007), *Women's Illicit Drug Use*, PhD thesis, University of Bath.

ECP (1997), 'Campaigning for Legal Change' in G. Scambler and A. Scambler (eds), *Rethinking Prostitution* (London: Routledge).

EUROPAP (1994), *Final Report: European Intervention Projects AIDS Prevention for Prostitutes* (Ghent: Department of Public Health).

Faugier, J. and M. Sargeant (1997), 'Boyfriends, Pimps and Clients' in G. Scambler and A. Scambler (eds), *Rethinking Prostitution* (London: Routledge).

Hester, M. and N. Westmarland (2004), *Tackling Street Prostitution: Towards an Holistic Approach*, HORS 279 (London: Home Office).

Hill, M. and K. Tisdall (1997), *Children and Society* (London: Longman).

Home Office (2004), *Paying the Price: A Consultation Document* (London: HMSO).

Home Office (2006), *A Coordinated Prostitution Strategy and a Summary of Responses to Paying the Price* (London: HMSO).

Kinnell, H. (2006), 'Murder Made Easy' in R. Campbell and M. O'Neill (eds), *Sex Work Now* (Cullompton: Willan).

Lee, M. and R. O'Brien (1995), *The Game's Up: Redefining Child Prostitution* (London: The Children's Society).

Matthews, R. (2005), 'Policing Prostitution: Ten Years On', *British Journal of Criminology* 45, 877–95.

May, T., M. Edmunds and M. Hough (1999), *Street Business: The Links between Sex and Drug Markets*, Police Research Series Paper 118 (London: Home Office).

May, T. and G. Hunter (2006), 'Sex Work and Problem Drug Use in the UK: The Links, Problems and Possible Solutions' in R. Campbell and M. O'Neill (eds), *Sex Work Now* (Cullompton: Willan).

McKeganey, N. and M. Barnard (1996), *Sex Work on the Streets: Prostitutes and Their Clients* (Buckingham: Open University Press).

McLeod, E. (1982), *Women Working: Prostitution Now* (London: Croom Helm).

O'Neill, M. (2001), *Prostitution and Feminism* (Cambridge: Polity).

O'Neill, M. and R. Campbell (2001), *Working Together to Create Change: Walsall Prostitution Consultation Research* (Walsall South Health Action Zone).

Office for National Statistics, Annual Survey of Hours and Earnings (2006), available on line at <http://www.statistics.gov.uk/statbase/Product.asp?vlnk=13101>.

Phoenix, J. (2001), *Making Sense of Prostitution* (London: Palgrave).

Phoenix, J. (2002), 'Youth Prostitution Policy Reforms: New Discourse, Same Old Story' in P. Carlen (ed.), *Women and Punishment: A Struggle for Justice* (Cullompton: Willan).

Roberts, N. (1992), *Whores in History* (London: Harper Collins).

Rose, N. (1993), 'Governmentality, Authority and Expertise in Advanced Liberalism', *Economy and Society* 22:3, 283–99.

Sanders, T. (2005), *Sex Work: A Risky Business* (Cullompton: Willan).

Taylor, D. (2003), *Sex for Sale: New Challenges and New Dangers for Women Working on and off the Streets* (London: Mainliners).

UKNSWP (2004), *Response to 'Paying the Price' (Home Office Consultation)* (Manchester: UKNSWP).

Van Meeuwen, A., S. Swann, D. McNeish and S.S.M. Edwards (1998), *Whose Daughter Next? Children Abused Through Prostitution* (Ilford: Barnardos).

Ward, H. and S. Day (1997), 'Prostitute Women and Public Health', *British Medical Journal* 297, 1585.

Ward, S., S. Day and J. Weber (1999), 'Risky Business: Health and Safety in the Sex Industry Over a 9 Year Period', *Sexually Transmitted Infections* 75:5, 340–43.

Chapter 3

Wolfenden 50: Revisiting State Policy and the Politics of Sex Work in the UK

Sophie Day[1]

Introduction

Gay Pride, London 2007, followed a 'Wolfenden 50' conference at King's College, marking the fiftieth anniversary of the public report from the Committee on Homosexuality and Prostitution in the UK, which met from 1954 to 1957. The Report (Wolfenden 1957) recommended that homosexual behaviour between consenting adults should be decriminalised, as it was in 1967, constituting a cause for celebration. In contrast to the relatively liberal position taken on homosexuality and subsequently other 'private' activities such as suicide, abortion and divorce, prostitution was to be further criminalised. Insofar as prostitution constituted a 'public nuisance', the Wolfenden Committee recommended stiff penalties that were ushered into law with the Street Offences Act 1959.

The Report distilled certain lessons from the past by instituting an absolute contrast between the public and the private: the state had to intervene in the former and must refrain from meddling in the latter. As Davenport-Hines concludes, 'the most that can be claimed is that Wolfenden's Report was the finest flower of Victorian notions of privacy ...', which meant that 'the notion of privacy received its ultimate tribute: sexual outlaws were given tolerance within the law conditional on their acceptance of privacy' (Davenport-Hines 1991, 326–7). The Wolfenden Committee instituted a sharp distinction between vice and immorality that took place in 'public', to which severe sanctions were attached, and similar acts that occurred between consenting adults in 'private', which were tolerated in law, albeit subject to scrutiny by psychologists and state officials. This radical distinction between the private and the public had different consequences, however, for homosexual activity and prostitution because the Report reproduced, unquestioned, a male perspective. The man engaging in consensual homosexual activity was thereby equated with the man purchasing consensual sex, of whatever kind. The fact that his partner was

1 Thanks to members of the network, and especially to Vanessa Munro and Marina Della Giusta who hosted it, to Victoria Goddard, Frances Pine and Helen Ward for comments and references. I should like to thank also the many participants, colleagues and institutions with whom I have collaborated since I first conducted research on sex work in 1986. Projects have been supported by the Wellcome Trust, AVERT, the NHS Executive (North Thames) and the Jefferiss Research Trust.

another man engaging in reciprocal consensual and private activity in the one case and a woman (less often a man) earning her living in an occupation that is *ipso facto* 'public' in the other was never considered a legitimate concern. In this way, as Weeks has noted,

> … by the application of a single principle, the Report achieved an apparently contradictory series of effects: restrictive in one direction, liberal in the other. The unifying element was the belief that, by ceasing to be the guardian of private morality, the law would more effectively become the protector of public decency and order (Weeks 1992, 243).[2]

In the Report, the dominant sense of public and private prostitution related to visibility rather than payment, work practices or employment: public meant visible and private meant invisible.

The Report upheld the *status quo* in other respects and reaffirmed the abolitionism associated with the repeal of the Contagious Diseases legislation in the 1880s. The Wolfenden Committee reported an abolitionist approach in 119 countries by comparison with the 19 countries in which brothels were licensed by the state and registered in civil law (cited in Sion 1977). These figures spoke to long-lasting disputes about the regulation of prostitution: should the state 'profit' from sex work through taxation or fees? To what extent could the state refrain from intervention? Should prostitution be governed through civil or criminal codes?

The term 'abolitionism' comes from the early repeal movement in nineteenth-century Britain when campaigners sought to persuade the state to stop interfering in women's lives, to disavow a double standard about appropriate male and female behaviour and to avoid regulating and profiting from 'immorality'. These campaigners borrowed the term from the US anti-slavery campaigns: as McHugh notes, '… repealers so admired American abolitionism that they appropriated the term for themselves – an early work on the movement was entitled The New Abolitionists …' (McHugh 1980, 247).[3]

The Wolfenden Report reproduced the ambivalence of nineteenth-century abolitionism, specifically through two different connotations of the term. Some abolitionists fought to 'abolish' state intervention in prostitution; others to 'abolish' prostitution itself. The former considered the state despotic and discriminatory, even though some campaigners also disapproved of prostitution.[4] The latter, increasingly influential towards the end of the century, wanted to stop immoral behaviour among

---

2 This committee and the legislation have been discussed extensively prior to the fiftieth anniversary noted above: see, for example, Smart (1981), Hall et al. (1978), Bland et al. (1979), and Self (2003), as well as Weeks (1992).

3 See also Walkowitz 1980, 123. The inspiration from America may have been new but Bristow considers that legal activism over moral matters in the UK also developed from the seventeenth-century Societies for the Reformation of Manners (Bristow 1977).

4 A nineteenth-century activist argued in parliament that, 'the centralising, despotic, reforming state is not my idea of what a State ought to be, I like local influence and local good to be brought about by local people, and not either by the Home Secretary or the War Minister' (cited in McHugh 1980, 25).

women, to stop prostitution, even though they recognised too that the state was enforcing an inequitable double standard.

Britain has remained abolitionist in a formal sense but the terminology has lost its relevance. Commonly, abolitionists are considered now to campaign for the eradication of prostitution, and not for the removal of state regulations that discriminate against women and interfere needlessly in the lives of citizens. Moreover, it has become clear that all states regulate prostitution in one way or another and so the contrast between states that license businesses and/or prostitutes and those that do not seems less and less warranted. Various distinctions have been drawn between the British variant and other systems. Registration and licensing are distinguished from outright prohibition where prostitution is criminalised, as in much of the United States, and from those few states that address prostitution through the same laws that govern other businesses and activities (with such 'decriminalisation', there are no laws specific to prostitution in either criminal or civil codes). In practice, however, these different measures can look remarkably similar on the ground, combining toleration in some areas with repression in others through policies that change constantly as agents of law enforcement permit or fail to see certain types of sex work whilst penalising others. The differences depend too on the overall size of the sex industry, gender and immigration policies, welfare provision and policies towards minorities (Day and Ward 2004).

How to evaluate British abolitionism in relation to these other systems and how to mark this Wolfenden 50 anniversary in the annals of sex work emancipation? Presenting an earlier version of this chapter to the workshop convened in March 2006, I dwelt on the spaces of freedom offered by the peculiarities of the Wolfenden architecture, which allowed sex workers I knew in London to enjoy their jobs so long as they remained out of the public eye (see further below). Redrafting this paper less than two years later, I am struck by the ephemeral, even illusory, nature of this freedom as revealed through recent events. These events provide an occasion to reevaluate the advantages and disadvantages of what I shall term informal as compared to formal sex work politics. I summarise first the advantages that sex workers found through the Wolfenden system of abolitionism, drawing on fieldwork conducted in London during the 1980s and 1990s.[5] Sex workers I knew practised their occupation through informal economic and political activities. I then suggest a rupture associated with recent events in the UK, which include far-ranging policy reviews of sex work as well as punitive responses on the ground. Sanctions against sex work on the streets, involving UK women by and large, and work indoors on the part of 'migrants' have increased. Next, I review formal opposition to state rules

5 I conducted research with sex workers in London from 1986 to 2002. Anthropological fieldwork was concentrated in two periods: an initial study from 1986 to 1991, and a follow-up from 1998 to 2002. I conducted further research with Helen Ward through the Praed Street Project, that we established, which included interviewing and surveys, which were part of Dr Ward's clinical and epidemiological research, as well as a variety of interventions and collaborations in Europe. For an account of the fieldwork, focusing on the hundred women I knew well, and references to these other projects (which involved larger numbers), see Day (2007).

associated with the sex work movement that has developed since the 1970s and conclude with a discussion of possible developments in the informal and formal politics of sex work in the current impasse.

The Wolfenden Architecture in Mid-Twentieth-Century UK

The Street Offences Act 1959 is best considered together with another piece of legislation that preceded the Wolfenden Report, namely the Sexual Offences Act 1956. Together, these statutes approached prostitutes first as victims, in need of rescue like slaves (1956), and then as a nuisance to be confined within acceptable bounds of public decency (1959).

The 1956 legislation related to management and exploitation. It prohibited collaboration on the grounds that victims had to be protected from abuse and thus from their managers, agents and clients. Sex workers could not be employed nor could they employ others; they could not collaborate with colleagues or purchase services from associates. It was illegal to live on the earnings of prostitution and to exercise control over a prostitute.[6] In the later 1959 legislation, prostitution was presented as a form of 'private vice', which might be licit if it remained suitably hidden from view. As the Commissioners wrote, 'It is not … the function of the law to interfere in the private lives of citizens, or to seek to enforce any particular pattern of behaviour …' (Wolfenden 1957, 10). In permitting prostitution only 'in private', a double standard was upheld that allowed men to purchase services 'privately' in a domain that women, in fact, constituted as 'public' work. Men were not subjected to any sanction for buying services; this was considered a private choice. Sex workers, however, were forced to pretend that their work was in fact a matter of personal choice whilst remaining visible to potential customers. As Wolfenden apparently clarified in committee hearings, 'the client is indulging in a private vice but the prostitute is openly inciting to a particular course of behaviour and I do not see anything unjust in the law taking cognisance of that and penalising it accordingly' (cited in Self 2003, 108).

The Wolfenden architecture of the mid-twentieth century neither permitted nor prohibited sex work. It acknowledged that men (largely) needed to buy services and that women (mostly) might reasonably provide these so long as all transactions could be presented euphemistically in terms of private choice and personal desire. This stance meant that the state was not called upon to guarantee the usual infrastructure of commerce, whether in relation to webs of credit, debt and the money supply more generally, or to the specific nature of contracts, advertising, health and safety or taxation. To the contrary, the state could act as though the industry did not exist. Should sex work become worryingly visible, then the criminal justice system would come into play alongside various local government measures to displace and punish 'public' activity. Visible prostitution soon began to attract heavy penalties, explained by some scholars in relation to concerns about the breakdown of the family, growing

6 These laws (sections 30 and 31 of the 1956 Act) were rendered 'gender neutral' in the Sexual Offences Act 2003.

immigration and the Cold War. Certainly, sanctions against public prostitution were disproportionately felt by working-class and non-white women.[7]

Since the 1950s, the lines drawn between public and private have shifted in tandem with changing relations of gender, class and nation. For example, continuing disquiet about gender and class bias led to legislation against 'kerb-crawling' on the part of clients; and imprisonment as a direct sentence for loitering and soliciting was abolished (temporarily, as it transpired, when Anti-Social Behaviour Orders [ASBOs] were introduced in 1999).[8] In retrospect, however, it seems as though the Wolfenden architecture remained remarkably stable until the 1990s, when, Phoenix claims, 'the way that the sex industry is regulated and governed in England and Wales has been subject to what can only be described as a quiet revolution …' (2007, 7). This relative stability was associated with everyday attempts on the part of sex workers to occupy a small space outside the formal economy but not yet illegal, conducting an informal political life beyond the reach of the state in association with their informal economic activities, that likewise remained unregulated, albeit demanding fast footwork every time some new rule was instituted.

The legislation of the 1950s encouraged women to work discreetly. Prostitution had been individualised and disconnected from the infrastructure that made most forms of activity possible, but it did allow participants to operate a parallel world in which they recognised what they did as a form of work. As far as sex workers I knew were concerned, the peculiar contortions of the law created areas in which they could operate freely so long as they remained inconspicuous and, ideally, invisible. They were forced to pretend that their occupation was a matter of personal lifestyle, as their public activities had to look private in order to be legal. Of course, they still had to remain visible to potential customers. The peculiarities of this legislation have been fundamental to the conduct of sex work in London, for what is private from one perspective is public from another and what is work from one perspective is vice from another. As far as sex workers are concerned, clear limits to state intervention should allow them to work freely: they should be able to represent sex 'work' as 'private' vice to state officials. Officials constantly threaten to interfere by reading so-called private vice in the terms of traditional concerns about public order, public health or public decency. Moreover, they scrutinise private vice to make sure that it is conducted in a solitary and individualised fashion that precludes everyday business activities and employment relations. Yet, as I have argued elsewhere (Day 2007), the Wolfenden prescriptions also created, paradoxically, an informal 'free' niche market in matters of 'private vice'. In the shadows, where the abolitionist state did not penetrate, sex workers were, and still are in some circumstances, left to themselves: with no rules and regulations to follow and no inspections. Abolitionism did not simply limit the market, it created one.[9]

---

7 See, further, references in footnote 1 above.

8 Two government committees had reported by 1986: the Vagrancy and Street Offences Committee (1974–1976), and the Criminal Law Revision Committee (1982 and 1985).

9 See Day (2007) for the details of this argument and an account of London sex work as an informal economic activity.

In brief, women I knew enjoyed working freelance without any of the inspections, routines, audits and diktats associated with other jobs. With luck, they could avoid officials, since they were engaged in purely private affairs. They could ignore the interfering, despotic state and act as though it did not exist. It was difficult to achieve this position because, of course, sex workers had to attract their clientele whilst avoiding 'public' activity, that is, visible activity – perhaps on the streets, through explicit advertising, within the normal occupational structures of contracts of employment rendering them either employers or employees, and so forth.

Women I knew in London during the 1980s and 1990s were concerned above all to protect their 'privacy': they boasted other jobs and other identities to families and friends as well as to state officials; they concealed their occupation and kept the secrets of associates. Many of these women were active in identity politics, especially in relation to gender and sexuality; many joined NGOs, participated in public demonstrations, and actively fostered the production of positive images of sex work and sex workers. This relatively formal or official politics, however, was rarely tied to a sex worker identity. Informally, sex workers inducted novices, looked after each others' children, offered credit, lodgings, clientele and other benefits to each other. Individuals took the greatest care to respect each others' privacy and to hold each others' secrets in this informal politics of cooperation and self organisation.

In between the formal and the illegal, sex workers enjoyed working on their own behalf or attempting to do so, operating autonomously without a manager or tiresome work routines and state rules, free to enjoy 'the game' of 'hustling'. It was never an easy game and, during the 1980s and 1990s, sex workers had to reinvent their practices repeatedly as state rules or local schemes closed down areas of work or targeted particular players, such as clients, with new sanctions. Thus, central London streets were heavily policed from the 1990s and largely closed: women who moved to indoor work or suburban areas soon found themselves under surveillance. Urban regeneration schemes deterred clients through traffic control and fuelled local opposition to the sex industry on the part of both residents' associations and vigilantes.

More recently, a raft of new measures has been instituted in the UK and further changes are likely to be introduced with the Criminal Justice and Immigration Bill currently in Parliament. Such developments, which have occurred since I presented an earlier version of this chapter constitute, I argue below, a break with the Wolfenden architecture. Indeed, since 2006, the small space of licit sex work that I have hitherto identified has been eroded through a series of developments. The limits to freelance work and informal politics in an increasingly precarious informal economy have become more obvious.

Prohibition in the UK

Some recent initiatives in the UK offer fitting redress against the iniquities of the mid-twentieth-century legislation. Thus, laws were rendered 'gender neutral' in the Sexual Offences Act 2003 (which came into effect in 2004) and the Criminal Justice and Immigration Bill 2007, if passed in its current form, will lead to the repeal of the infamous term, 'common prostitute'.[10] The revolution in prostitution control, however, is repressive and discriminatory overall. Anti-Social Behaviour Orders were introduced in 1999 to promote public order by restricting those who had caused alarm, distress or harassment. They have been used against sex workers outdoors, reintroducing prison sentences for loitering and soliciting and carrying much heavier sanctions than the three months' imprisonment previously available under the Street Offences Act 1959. There has been a concerted crackdown on 'illegal migration' (associated with a panic about 'trafficking') and on advertising, as well as attempts to criminalise both buying and selling sex *per se*. British policy-makers have collaborated closely with experts in Europe, notably Sweden, where the industry has been extensively criminalised, and the United States, but they have shown little interest in moves to 'normalise' sex work through, for example, decriminalisation. The Prostitution Reform Act 2003 in New Zealand repealed all previous legislation and legalised contracts for commercial sexual exchanges, preserving criminal justice sanctions only for the purchase of sex from those under the age of 18. This legislation is upheld by sex worker activists as a model to follow but it has not, it seems, ignited the interest of UK politicians.

A government consultation occurred in 2004 with the Home Office publication, *Paying the Price* (Home Office 2004). This document describes the negative impact of prostitution on individuals and on the wider community in some detail: prostitution apparently leads to a life of crime, drug addiction and social exclusion. Therefore, the consultation exercise was focused on the prevention of prostitution, exiting strategies for those already involved, and sanctions against other people involved. 'Pimps, traffickers and exploiters' (often known as agents and managers) as well as clients are considered to be more exploitative or abusive than in other sectors of the economy.

While the consultation saw prostitution as a problem, which led to more problems in the form of crime and disorder, and while it considered that prostitutes had to be encouraged to 'exit' the trade, the document nonetheless also outlined measures that might allow women to work more safely. In particular, two proposals were discussed: first, managed or 'toleration' zones for street work, that is, demarcated and non-residential areas where sex workers could operate legally and in relative safety; and second, cooperative work indoors that would involve a change to the law on brothels by allowing two or three women to work together.

The strategy eventually published (Home Office 2006), distilling the best of a decade of Home Office papers and consultations, ruled out toleration zones. It adopted a punitive stance akin to US prohibitionism, allowing police greater powers against street work, including loitering and soliciting and kerb-crawling on the part of clients. Legal and medical interventions meant that penalties rose dramatically and now include compulsory medical treatment orders for sex workers and rehabilitation programmes for clients. Street work has been basically prohibited. Indoor work is

---

10 The offence of being a common prostitute applies only to women working outdoors who are more likely to be working-class and non-white and it is the only offence in which previous convictions can be made known in court before sentencing.

curtailed through policies of disruption and increasing reliance on regulation, often indirectly by other government offices via migration and terrorism measures.

In December 2006, the bodies of five young women were found in Ipswich: all sex workers, all murdered. Huge sympathy and support on the part of residents, local government, the media and others was eclipsed rapidly by a backlash. In April 2007, Ipswich devised a local street prostitution strategy, mirroring that of the Home Office. The Executive Summary of this Ipswich report states: 'there is an overall strategic aim to remove street prostitution from Ipswich …' We are told, 'the key objectives must be to ensure that individuals do not become involved in street prostitution in the first instance. If they do then we need to make sure that opportunities are created for them to leave …' (Ipswich 2007). This policy necessitates zero tolerance of clients. Anti-social behaviour legislation, CCTV and more police patrols will provide the main means to this end. As promised, the government, in May 2007, announced a new crackdown on clients: the current demons of the piece. A six-week advertising campaign in seven cities was launched to deter kerb-crawling.

As noted, the government's *Coordinated Prostitution Strategy* had announced suppression of street work with a 'sweetener', acknowledging safety issues in a promise to change the definition of a brothel so that two prostitutes could work together (Home Office 2006, 61). The *Guardian* reported, 'Ms MacTaggart justified the decision to relax the law on brothels as a necessary harm-reduction measure and insisted that two or three women working together in a flat could operate in a way that was not disruptive to neighbours' (*Guardian* 2006a). A Regulatory Impact Assessment was then circulated and it was at this point that the recommendation to allow two or three individuals to work together indoors disappeared.

New measures to rehabilitate fallen women, through compulsory drug and alcohol treatment, have joined the notorious and ever-more complex Anti-Social Behaviour Orders.[11] Other initiatives focus on work indoors more than on the streets, as the government tries to stem migration into the UK sex industry under the rubric of 'anti-trafficking' discourses. The categories of public and private that constituted a fulcrum around which the abolitionist consensus was sustained have been redefined along with related terms such as male and female, upper and lower status, foreign and local, criminal and deviant. In effect, 'private vice' has been redefined in terms of 'violence against women'. The state acknowledges a role in protecting its citizens and, drawing on the protectionist language of abolitionism, asks how to protect women from violence. On the anniversary of the Ipswich murders, the answer seems to be prohibition. Sex work is barred because it is dangerous for women. To cite just one of the numerous examples in the media over this period, the Press Association reports that the Home Office considers street prostitution 'inherently dangerous'

---

11 Clause 72 of the Criminal Justice and Immigration Bill (2007) requires anyone arrested for loitering or soliciting to attend a series of three meetings with a supervisor approved by the court 'to promote rehabilitation, by assisting the offender to address the causes of their involvement in prostitution and to find ways of ending that involvement'. Failure to attend results in a summons back to court and a possible 72-hours imprisonment. Magistrates would have powers to make subsequent orders so that women could be cycled repetitively through broken supervision meetings, court orders and imprisonment.

and so 'the best way to protect men and women is to prevent them from becoming involved in the first place' (*Guardian* 2007). Indoors, victims take a particular form in the (singular) person of the 'trafficked migrant' or undocumented worker who must be repatriated in the name of protection. Outdoors, victims also take a particular form as the 'local drug addict' who must be rehabilitated.

These repressive measures may have been motivated by attempts to appeal to the electorate through 'cleaning up' the streets, neighbourhoods and cities of the UK, through 'being tough' on immigration or 'protecting' the family and safeguarding its young. Work conditions are certainly not mentioned in this new prohibitionist policy. There is no reference to occupational health or safety: nothing about how to prevent murder, rape or robbery in the highly individualised occupation of sex *work* in the UK; no mention of other workplace protection such as the security that normally accompanies pay in the form of contracts, sick leave, insurance and pensions. There is no acknowledgement of rights at work that generally involve public collaboration with colleagues relating to the duties imposed by employers or requested of employees, and exchanged in business dealings with customers and agents. It is claimed that no-one would sell sex if they had other options. Therefore, sex workers are to be redeemed, rehabilitated or reintegrated – to use the term popularised in recent policy statements (Day 2007) – by drug and alcohol centres, social workers and probation staff, so that they can learn to work 'properly', renounce their past sins and learn to confine their so-called sexuality within the private sphere. Clients must now learn about moral behaviour within this private sphere as well. Since sex work has no public protection – through trade unions, health and safety legislation, state inspection and so forth – in the way of (other) occupations, these new rules are to be overseen by the police. The resulting patterns of control have been contested in terms of the confusion they cause, and risk creating further problems of public order and health, as well as infringing civil liberties.

The Sex Work Movement

The term sex work was coined in the 1970s (Leigh 1997) and activists formed a loose collective internationally in relation to this claim. With the growth of social movements for civil and other rights, activists have campaigned for public recognition of the occupation, for the dignity of sex work and for a visible place at the heart of social life. I have suggested (Day 2007) that this more public, formal or official sex worker activism shares much with the everyday and largely hidden world of sex work. It is clearly distinct, however, in the explicit recognition of, and argument with, state regimes. While many women I knew acted as though they operated outside the realm of the nation state and its local manifestations, and assumed that any dealings with officials would only make life more difficult, activists aim for state and social reform. Campaigns generally assert that 'slavery' and abuse result from systems of prostitution control and stigmatisation, not from the work itself or indeed sexual relations more generally – it is argued cogently that commercial sex hardly accounts for the oppression of women. For these reasons, sex workers and associated activists became involved in a range of reforms including those introduced since the 1990s in Germany, the Netherlands and New Zealand and, previously, parts of Australia. Individuals and organisations have been involved in the drafting of legislation and appeals to international and national tribunals dealing with a range of occupational, civil and human rights. They have negotiated with unions, insurance companies and employers' bodies. New forms of activism such as those addressing rights to free movement have developed.[12]

Yet, opposition to the state has also led to difficulties. Apparently positive reforms that recognise sex work in some countries have led to the loss of autonomy, as state rules continue to favour capital over labour. Activists argued that sex work should be seen simply as a business, subject to normal regulations of financing, profit and taxation. Subsequently, they emphasised the need to protect small business interests against monopoly capital since political efforts towards decriminalisation or 'normalisation' also led to economic centralisation along with fiscal policies that penalised freelance workers. During the 1990s, activists found that neoliberal principles, which advocate toleration of sex work and often the repeal of prostitution laws because of the money generated by the industry, operate in the interests of employers and not workers. New regulations, like the old, seemed to be designed to benefit business interests and clients more than workers. Thus, cooperation with potential allies among brothel owners or business managers in various campaigns foundered as these groups opposed unionisation – effectively and with great vehemence in the Netherlands and San Francisco (Visser 2004; Chapkis 1997). Similarly, the recognition of sex work in European countries has divided sex workers into two cadres, the local and the 'foreign'. Activists have found that they legitimised unwittingly EU immigration policies that disadvantaged the undocumented even more than previous regimes, since these migrants are excluded from the limited recognition offered by the state. So-called normalisation in the Netherlands led to lower earnings and divisions within the sex worker movement.

It has proved difficult, therefore, to assess the benefits of reforms removing criminal sanctions and recognising the occupation of sex workers. Certain avenues have opened up in relation to union activity, health and safety, pension or holiday rights. Others have closed as governments introduced systems of surveillance, including new regimes for discriminating between those to be included within the new systems and those who are prohibited from working.

An Impasse

When I discussed sex work politics in the 2006 workshop, I emphasised the considerable success of what I have called informal politics. Sex workers have succeeded in creating a parallel universe partially independent of the state and the regimes governing most jobs. They organise their own political and economic lives in the shadows and gain

12 Campaigns against restrictions on non-nationals have advocated short-term working visas for non-nationals or, in the case of the self-employed, more realistic requirements for their business plans. Employers in legal brothels could sponsor workers from other countries so as to minimise the enormous costs currently faced by illegal migrants and then workers would only have to repay their employers the cost of travel.

significant autonomy within this world, which often shelters the most vulnerable – such as those who do not hold the relevant legal papers or who are criminalised in some other way. While disapproval of sex work has limited the alliances between workers and other networks of self-employed people, union members or associations of informal home workers, the stigma has goaded sex workers into creating and fostering long-term and effective associations providing welfare, advocacy, work and training, which spill outside the sex industry as women move from one job to another. I found that women could bypass many state officials and act as though they were irrelevant to their lives. Moreover, sex workers I knew avoided social stigma by hiding their occupational identity and developing aliases to use with friends, families and in other jobs. Nonetheless, this process of concealment is costly. It creates an extreme separation between sex work and other jobs, isolating sex workers from other people and enabling in turn the interpolation of myth, stigma and moral panic.

The more public activist politics has also been successful. Actions in association with other feminists have been effective against, for example, the apparently natural and gendered distinctions between private and public affairs. Cultural initiatives have also attracted attention: Indian Durbars have drawn support from around the world; German model brothels set up by sex workers have shown what reasonable work conditions might look like; commemorative events and monuments have attracted visitors to statues, museums and annual events to remember the dead and campaign against violence to sex workers; the symbolic 'red umbrellas' appear in protests and carnivals of many kinds.

The extreme sanctions against sex work and widespread disapproval of the occupation have made formal politics especially difficult, with each new development stalled by apparently extraneous issues, such as support for capital or immigration control. In the current impasse, sex worker activists have responded to new government initiatives with incredulity, dismay and counter-initiatives. They have queried government data, built alliances with non-sex workers and organised numerous campaigns. They have created alliances within the trade union movement, among human rights campaigners, libertarians and others. Over 850 responses were made to *Paying the Price*, and some of those from sex worker organisations, unions, academics and other associates have since been published independently on websites and in journals, as they were ignored in the subsequent strategy.[13] Campaigns include the Safety First Coalition, co-ordinated by the English Collective of Prostitutes, to push for the decriminalisation of sex work in the wake of the Ipswich murders and counter to the new prohibitionism. The founding members include Phillida Bunkle, a former New Zealand MP who helped introduce decriminalisation in New Zealand; Pauline Campbell, mother of Sarah Campbell, who died in the 'care' of HMP Styal as well as Ipswich residents.[14] The situation in the UK today causes only anger and cynicism in the sex work movement.

---

13 See Dr Goodyear's useful website, <http://myweb.dal.ca/mgoodyea/uksex.htm>, where a number of these responses are posted or referenced including articles on the original consultation, the eventual strategy and related research findings. Goodyear has also posted an important article on the site, 'Remembering Ipswich'.

14 See <http://www.prostitutescollective.net/>.

Should sex workers 'avoid' or 'negotiate with' state officials? Are self-organisation and self-representation more attainable in the informal or the formal realm? What sort of political organisation might keep an 'interfering' and 'despotic' state at arm's length and yet win concessions? My comments indicate the failures as well as the successes of sex work politics and the quandaries we face: what next? It is unclear whether strategies of avoidance and self-organisation in the shadows will be effective against the new government repression. No doubt, sex workers will continue to evade new regulations and hide from agents of law enforcement but, perhaps, within smaller and smaller interstices of the law. If the occupation remains 'private' or hidden, how can sex workers unionise and campaign for their occupational or, indeed, civil and human rights? The absolute break between sex work and other jobs and activities sustained by most of the women I knew constrains political life. Whatever the political passions of these women, their informal activities are hidden by the secrets of this private-yet-public world. The moral panics surrounding government interventions in relation to the 'crack whore' and the 'trafficked victim' have also intensified stigma against all sex workers (and indeed other players in the industry) and it is hard to see how this renewed stigma can be countered without the visibility and transparency of a more formal politics to which non-sex workers can subscribe.

Whether or not activists identify publicly as sex workers, they share a common platform of direct confrontation with the state and a more general process of culture building to destigmatise the status of 'whore'. On the other hand, these contrasting strategies of confrontation in sex work activism may have succeeded merely in reinscribing power and legitimising the position of the state. It has proved difficult to reform sex work without allotting the state a larger regulatory role.

Discussion

Relevant debates about political organising can be summarised for the present purposes into two positions reflecting what I have called informal politics on the one hand, often represented as a negative tactic or strategy of state avoidance, and formal politics on the other, represented as a contrasting tactic of engagement with the politically powerful based on a positive vision of possible change. Past experience suggests that strategies of concealment are a necessary reflex or protection against the particular stigma of the sex industry. Past experience also indicates that sex workers have developed particular skills in a politics that is at least partially surreptitious, invisible and disorganised (Bull 2000); they have generally found new places to hide. Recently introduced UK regulations, however, damage sex workers and it is possible that formal opposition may yet limit their scope, both through protest against specific initiatives and through a more broadly-based social movement.

In this context, it is worth emphasising that informal and formal politics (or negative and positive tactics) co-exist in the sex industry. Close attention to the precise forms of co-existence and points of articulation may help the development of political action. Who can front for whom? How are workers' organisations sustained beyond the reach of state rules? How can the specific advantages of both informal and formal politics be combined? It may prove possible to bargain with the state and yet still operate in 'secret'.

Affiliation to GMB (Britain's General Union) provides a recent example of successful mediation between, and articulation of, these political forms. Models of trade union and related activity suggest a bargain with the state in which union democracy – rules of representation and participation for example – are open to scrutiny, so that the organisation seems transparent to the state. Contrast these with models of illegal or informal organisations, such as the mafia, where only key nodes or persons are visible while everyone else remains out of sight. Negotiators of this kind have been important in sex work activism where they have mediated between sex workers, business interests and the state. Thus, the International Union of Sex Workers (IUSW), affiliated to GMB in 2002, and GMB representatives, have been advocates on behalf of sex workers in campaigns for employment, health and safety and contractual rights in more formal sectors of the industry, such as the chat lines and clubs (which have multiplied since the 1970s).[15] Whilst affiliated to GMB, IUSW operates more autonomously than other branches because of the requirement of privacy: for fear of stigma and criminal sanctions. Political action in sex work necessitates this process of 'hiding' as well as 'visible' protest.

In a European project on sex work,[16] we found that health workers and lawyers could provide similar mediation: identities and roles changed so that the boundaries between self-organisation and other forms of representation were blurred. A woman who is a sex worker in one situation is recognised officially as a NGO/GO interpreter or health worker in another, perhaps using a different name. Transparent to the state and associated with a particular national territory, these advocates, in their formal NGO/GO positions, hide all the visible traces of the network of sex workers, spanning the entire continent. Research on other social movements – relating to asylum seekers, for example – has shown similarly how such negotiating points can remain fixed whilst those they represent come and go – often across national borders. Such patterns of movement create relatively long-lasting and far-flung political constituencies beyond the particular cycles of migration associated with a given individual or community (Appadurai 1996). These are simultaneously economic and cultural circuits: opposition to the repatriation of undocumented workers has been accompanied by transfers of money through remittances, and of the information that is so critical to political action.

Information technologies allow constituencies to remain (ideally) hidden through a 'virtual' society and they have been important to grassroots organising. Despite many claims opposing the rigidity of labour organisations to the mobility of capital and its networked elites, it is clear from sex work politics that new forms of organisation and opposition are not only possible but effective. Sex workers can be as cosmopolitan as those conventionally considered members of the elite, as skilled at managing the plural identities appropriate to one nation state or another, and accomplished at hiding from regulatory bodies. They have stubbornly refused to remain anchored within the local or national arena for political purposes whilst moving across the world 'merely' to find work.

---

15 See for example, <http://www.indymedia.org/en/2006/01/832371.shtml, 2006>.

16 See <www.europap.net>.

Consider then how these parallel worlds might be consolidated. Credit unions, banks and allied systems of capital formation including social security *vis-à-vis* the state have been established across the world through organisations of informal or illegal workers such as SEWA, the Self Employed Women's Association.[17] Durbar is a sex workers' organisation based in West Bengal (Kolkata) with 65,000 members that has similarly entwined economic and political aims and plans its own hospital so as to provide welfare to members denied state provision.[18] Organisations of homeworkers in the 'informal economy' have affiliated to trade unions at the same time as organising independently to obtain credit, social security and support for production and marketing.[19] In many of these associations, the protection and expertise offered by 'official' union representatives has been reciprocated by so-called migrants who have revived careworn political and bureaucratic structures (and, in quantitative terms, a rank and file membership).[20]

Analysis of informal and often illegal organising presents a challenge to those who have read an end to politics in the great projects of informalisation and privatisation over recent years. Although sex workers have been unable to win concessions from the UK regime, they have maintained significant autonomy in parallel worlds outside the ruling system. Forced into this 'negative' stance, they have nonetheless provided the services conventionally distributed through states and, perhaps unintentionally, enabled increasing representation and participation among people of different nationalities moving from one job or country to another. These parallel worlds include sex worker activists. Their more visible and transparent politics do not seem to have achieved more than limited state protection through health and safety measures and minimal guarantees enabling the workforce to reproduce itself. Although formal opposition has, therefore, failed likewise to foster social inclusion, justice or a living wage, it has begun to resonate widely with general social opposition to moralism and repression and a broad critique of government policy. In the light of events since 2006, I consider it unwise to credit state policies with any coherence or to imagine that the many critiques of these policies and practices will elicit any rational response. Specific demands, even if they elicit concessions, may lead to further regulation. Yet, it does not seem that simply avoiding state officials represents a viable alternative in the context of increasing discrimination. New forms of political organising that combine formal and informal politics may prove critical to the project of social change.

---

17 See <http://www.sewa.org>. For an earlier account, see Jhabvala (1994).

18 See <http://www.durbar.org/>.

19 See, for the UK, <http://www.ngh.org.uk>.

20 Contemporary unionisation builds on past campaigns: the *Guardian* reported activities on behalf of undocumented workers: 'The TGWU's international branch was formed in the 1970s by Portuguese refugees who came to Britain during Portugal's military dictatorship and worked in the hotel and restaurant trade' (*Guardian* 2006b). Since then, members from many countries have collectively built the branch. Note, however, the difficulties that union organisers have faced in negotiating with other 'official' unions closely associated with the state and companies; see for example Tirado (1994) on garment workers in Mexico.

References

Appadurai, A. (1996), *Modernity at Large: Cultural Dimensions of Globalization* (Minneapolis, MN: University of Minnesota Press).

Bland, L., T. McCabe and F. Mort (1979), 'Sexuality and Reproduction: Three "Official" Instances' in M. Barrett, P. Corrigan, A. Kuhn and J. Wolff (eds), *Ideology and Cultural Production* (London: Croom Helm), 78–111.

Bristow, E.J. (1977), *Vice and Vigilance: Purity Movements in Britain since 1700* (Dublin: Gill and Macmillan).

Bull, M. (2000), *Seeing Things Hidden: Apocalypse, Vision and Totality* (London: Verso).

Chapkis, W. (1997), *Live Sex Acts: Women Performing Erotic Labor* (New York: Routledge).

Davenport-Hines, R. (1991), *Sex, Death and Punishment: Attitudes to Sex and Sexuality in Britain since the Renaissance* (Glasgow: Fontana).

Day, S. (2007), *On the Game: Women and Sex Work* (London: Pluto).

Day, S. and H. Ward (eds) (2004), *Sex Work, Mobility and Health in Europe* (London: Routledge and Kegan Paul).

Fortunati, L. (1995), *The Arcane of Reproduction: Housework, Prostitution, Labor and Capital* (trans. H. Creek, (ed.) J. Fleming) (New York: Autonomedia).

The *Guardian* (2006a), 'Small Worker-run Brothels Proposed to Deter Exploitation of Prostitutes', 18 January 2006.

The *Guardian* (2006b), 'Our Eyes Have Been Opened by the Abuse', 29 April 2006.

The *Guardian* (2007), 'New Crackdown Targets Kerb-crawlers' (Press Association, 12 May 2007).

Hall, S., C. Critcher, T. Jefferson, J. Clarke and B. Roberts (1978), *Policing the Crisis: Mugging, the State and Law and Order* (London: Macmillan).

Home Office (2004), *Paying the Price: A Consultation Paper on Prostitution* (London: HMSO).

Home Office (2006), *A Coordinated Prostitution Strategy and a Summary of Responses to Paying the Price* (London: HMSO).

Ipswich (2007), 'Ipswich Street Prostitution Strategy' (Ipswich: Crime and Disorder Reduction Partnership) available at <http://www.ipswich.gov.uk/NR/rdonlyres/2780A615-452E-4356-995E-E083B06FF648/0/DraftIpswichStreetProstitutionStrategy.pdf>.

Jhabvala, R. (1994), 'Self-Employed Women's Association: Organising Women by Struggle and Development' in S. Rowbotham and S. Mitter (eds), *Dignity and Daily Bread: New Forms of Economic Organising Among Poor Women in the Third World and the First* (London and New York: Routledge), 114–38.

Leigh, C. (1997), 'Inventing Sex Work' in J. Nagle (ed.), *Whores and Other Feminists* (New York and London: Routledge), 223–31.

McHugh, P. (1980), *Prostitution and Victorian Social Reform* (London: Croom Helm).

Phoenix, J. (2007), 'Regulating Prostitution: Different Problems, Different Solutions, Same Old Story', *Community Safety Journal* 6:1, 7–10.

Self, H. (2003), *Prostitution, Women and Misuse of the Law: The Fallen Daughters of Eve* (London: Frank Cass).

Sion, A.A. (1977), *Prostitution and the Law* (London: Faber and Faber).

Smart, C. (1981), 'Law and the Control of Women's Sexuality: The Case of the 1950s' in B. Hutter and G. Williams (eds), *Controlling Women: The Normal and the Deviant* (London: Croom Helm), 40–60.

Tirado, S. (1994), 'Weaving Dreams, Constructing Realities: The Nineteenth of September National Union of Garment Workers in Mexico' in S. Rowbotham and S. Mitter (eds), *Dignity and Daily Bread: New Forms of Economic Organising among Poor Women in the Third World and the First* (London and New York: Routledge), 100–113.

Visser, J. (with A. Randers-Pehrson, S. Day and H. Ward) (2004), 'Policies Towards the Sex Industry in Europe: New Models of Control' in S. Day and H. Ward (eds), *Sex Work, Mobility and Health in Europe* (London: Kegan Paul), 241–57.

Walkowitz, J. (1980), *Prostitution and Victorian Society: Women, Class and the State* (Cambridge: Cambridge University Press).

Weeks, J. (1981 [1992]), *Sex, Politics and Society: The Regulation of Sexuality Since 1800* 2nd edn (London: Longman).

Wolfenden Report (1957), *Report of the Committee on Homosexual Offences and Prostitution*, Committee on Homosexual Offences and Prostitution (London: HMSO).

Chapter 4

The Construction of Prostitutes and Clients in French Policy Debates

Gill Allwood

This chapter examines French policy debates on prostitution between 1997 and 2007, focusing in particular on the way in which prostitutes, clients and the relations between them have been constructed by the various actors involved. It examines the consequences of these constructions for both policy outputs and implementation. Finally, it discusses the way in which relations between prostitutes and clients have been affected by recent changes in prostitution policy and surrounding representations of the issue.

France has been abolitionist since 1960 when it ratified the 1949 UN Convention on the Suppression of the Traffic in Persons and of the Exploitation of the Prostitution of Others. State controlled brothels were closed in 1946, but police files on prostitutes were maintained until 1960. The foundations of state abolitionism were laid in a series of policy measures in the early 1960s, but for most of the following 30 years, implementation varied locally, and prostitution rarely appeared on the political agenda. The exceptions were a brief mobilisation of prostitutes' rights groups against police harassment in 1975 and debates surrounding a suggestion in 1990 by the former Minister for Health (1986–1988), Michèle Barzach (RPR), that state brothels be reopened in order to reduce the risks to public health, and in particular, the risk of the spread of HIV/AIDS (Mazur 2004). Prostitution policy consisted of harsh penalties for those who profited from the earnings of prostitution alongside social protection measures for those who agreed to exit. Prostitution itself was a civil liberty, although soliciting was a minor offence, and clients were not mentioned.

In the late 1990s, the question of what to do about prostitution re-emerged in French public and political debate because of its increased visibility both in areas of French cities which had traditionally been associated with the sex industry, and elsewhere. The debate centred on street prostitution, which was the most visible and which was defined as the most threatening to public order and to the well-being of the women and girls involved. France was also involved in international negotiations on anti-trafficking measures, and negotiators were aware of the pressure from some quarters, in particular the Netherlands (Outshoorn 2000) and the International Labour Office (Lim 1998), to decriminalise and regulate sex work as a proposed means of combating sex trafficking. The French perceived an international push towards regulation, and resisted this, making prostitution policy a marker of French national identity, and constructing the French approach as the epitome of abolitionism.

At the same time, state feminists within the left-wing Jospin government (1997–2002) were pursuing an anti-male-violence campaign, which involved coordinated policy initiatives and government-sponsored research projects, conferences and campaigns. Prostitution was included within this campaign and was defined by the Minister for Women's Rights, Nicole Péry, as a form of violence towards women. At the UN Beijing +5 Conference in New York in 2000, Péry re-affirmed her country's commitment to the 1949 Convention which states that 'prostitution and the accompanying evil of the traffic in persons' are 'incompatible with the dignity and worth of the human person' and condemns any person who exploits the prostitution of another with or without their consent (Péry 2001). Foreign Minister, Hubert Védrine, also reaffirmed the French commitment to abolitionism in various international negotiations on trafficking and child prostitution and pornography; and in 1999, the newly created Delegation for Women's Rights in the Senate chose prostitution as its first subject of enquiry and produced a lengthy and influential report authored by Senator Dinah Derycke, which praised state abolitionism, but criticised the way in which it was implemented (Derycke 2001). The term 'abolitionism' was used in these debates and pronouncements to refer both to the abolition of all laws and measures that make any distinction between prostitutes and other individuals and to the abolition of prostitution itself.

The close fit between government discourse on prostitution and the socially and politically dominant abolitionist frame made it acceptable to a broad coalition of abolitionist groups and individuals, including powerful secular and Catholic NGOs, politicians of the left and right and, also, as revealed by a series of hostile debates, most French feminists. Abolitionist discourse became so dominant during the Jospin government that it came to be presented as inevitable and neutral and indeed its proponents explicitly stated that their position was non-ideological (Nor 2001) or situated outside the abolition–regulation dichotomy (Derycke 2001). Abolitionist organisations had effective access to policy-makers and the resources to fund conferences and publications. A high-profile conference at UNESCO in Paris in 2000, organised by the abolitionist NGO, Fondation Scelles, was supported by prominent public figures including leading lights on the Republican left, founder of the Mouvement des Citoyens party and presidential candidate, Jean-Pierre Chevènement, and philosopher and academic, Sylviane Agacinski. The 35 signatories of a declaration in *Le Nouvel Observateur* that the body is not a commodity included prominent political figures François Hollande, Robert Hue and Dominique Voynet. Pronounced media interest manifested itself in high profile debates polarising opinion around sex work or violence; free or forced; sex workers or victims. Questions of agency, coercion and structural oppression were at the centre of feminist debates, which also tended to polarise around those who supported sex workers' rights and those who advocated the eradication of prostitution.

The 2002 presidential and parliamentary elections were to have a significant impact on prostitution policy debates, however. These elections were dominated by the issue of 'security', encompassing law and order, as well as anti-terrorism and anti-immigration. The defeat of the outgoing Prime Minister and Socialist Party candidate Lionel Jospin in the first round of the presidential election by extreme right Jean-Marie Le Pen sent shock waves throughout the country. The right wing

Jacques Chirac then benefited from the vote 'to save the Republic', and his victory was followed by that of a right wing parliamentary majority under Jean-Pierre Raffarin. The new Minister for the Interior, Nicolas Sarkozy, immediately announced his intention to table a Domestic Security Bill, and it was this that was to redefine prostitution and transform prostitution policy.

The Domestic Security Bill reclassified soliciting as a serious offence, incurring a prison sentence (six months in the original, two months as the result of a successful amendment during the parliamentary debates) as well as a more substantial fine. It reintroduced 'passive soliciting', removed from the New Penal Code in 1994 (by a right-wing majority). Sarkozy, arguing that it was inconvenient for the police to have to obtain evidence of active soliciting, proposed the insertion of a new article in the Penal Code (Article 225-10-1) creating a serious offence of soliciting by any means including 'dress or posture'. The reference to 'dress' caused an outcry and was removed by a government amendment during the Senate debate. The version that was passed by the Senate refers to 'a posture, even passive' (Senate 2002a). The Domestic Security Law also states that foreigners who contravene the Penal Code or behave in a way which disrupts public order can have their visitors' permits removed. Foreign nationals accused of soliciting, whether actively or passively, can therefore now be deported, whether they are legally present in the country or not. They may be given temporary leave to remain in the country and to work in exchange for denouncing their pimp or trafficker. This applies until the case has been heard, and in the event of a conviction, becomes permanent (Article 76).

The Domestic Security Law contains measures aimed not only at street prostitutes, but also beggars, travellers and young people. Its supporters, in particular Sarkozy himself, argued that these were necessary in order to remove the sources of 'anxiety and legitimate exasperation' that affect large sections of the population. Its critics, including parties of the left, trade unions and associations concerned with human rights, poverty and social justice, claimed that it was an attack on the poor, criminalising begging, soliciting and loitering, rather than fighting against social exclusion (Tubiana, Marcus et al. 2002). They accused Sarkozy of exploiting the climate of insecurity and argued that 'no-one chooses to be a beggar or a prostitute, to live in neighbourhoods with no facilities and no public services' (Senate 2002a). In the Senate, critics accused Sarkozy of being interested only in cleaning up the streets, rather than fighting the criminal networks that are responsible for exploiting women and girls in prostitution. They denounced the redefinition of prostitution as a law and order issue and argued that these measures would push prostitutes underground, damaging prevention and public health and hindering the work of the community health and HIV/AIDS prevention associations that provide outreach services (Luc 2002; Mahéas 2002). Claude Boucher from the Bus des Femmes, a support service in Paris run by prostitutes and former prostitutes, insisted that many women she meets work as prostitutes in order to preserve their dignity, since neither social security benefits nor the minimum wage are enough to live on. Treating them as criminals would make their lives more dangerous, she argued: 'This is a law against those who are excluded, against the most vulnerable' (Délégation de l'Assemblée nationale aux droits des femmes et à l'égalité des chances entre les hommes et les femmes 2002).

In April 2006, PCF Senator, Nicole Borvo, tabled a Private Member's Bill (2006) which aimed to undo what she perceived as the harmful effects of Sarkozy's law. Very much in the spirit of Dinah Derycke's report for the Senate's Delegation for Women's Rights five years earlier, Borvo's Bill is based on the view that prostitution takes place within a framework of domination and is a form of violence. It calls for an end to the exploitation and commodification of the human body and rejects the distinction between free and forced prostitution. It criticises the Domestic Security Law for constructing prostitution as a law and order issue and claims that it has been ineffective in addressing the organised crime responsible for trafficking, which, in contrast to prostitution, should be the target of criminal justice measures. It argues that the criminalisation of passive soliciting has not reduced prostitution, but has changed the status of prostitutes from victims to criminals. Again reminiscent of the recommendations of the Derycke report, Borvo's Bill calls for coherent government policy on prostitution, which stresses prevention and support for prostitutes, combined with harsh measures aimed at those who profit from it. Like most Private Members' Bills, it has not made it onto the parliamentary agenda, but does suggest an alternative frame which could re-emerge in the future.

Constructing Prostitutes in Policy Debates

Under the Jospin government, the dominant representation of prostitutes in national policy debates was as victims who needed to be saved and reintegrated into society. This view was held by state feminists, government ministers, members of parliament, and the heterogeneous and powerful abolitionist lobby. It dominated the Derycke report on public policy and prostitution (Derycke 2001), the report on prostitution which was part of the work of the National Commission on Violence Towards Women (Marcovich 2002), and related debates which took place within the government's extensive enquiries into modern forms of slavery (Vidalies 2002b). Consultation on prostitution and related policy provided an opportunity for civil society organisations to enter policy debates, for example, by giving evidence to parliamentary committees, such as the Law Commission and the Women's Rights Delegations in each chamber, and, although some of those who gave evidence constructed prostitutes as workers denied access to decent living and working conditions, they formed the minority.

At the same time, at the municipal level, prostitutes (but not clients) were constructed as a source of public nuisance who needed to be confined to certain locations. In the summer of 2002, Françoise de Panafieu, UMP deputy for the 17th arrondissement in Paris, led a high-profile campaign against the effects of street prostitution in her neighbourhood. Responding to pressure by local residents' groups, mayors on both the right and the left were introducing by-laws that, implicitly at first, then more explicitly, banned prostitution in certain areas. Nicolas Sarkozy built on this public nuisance discourse when he became Minister of the Interior in 2002. He combined it with elements of the discourse around insecurity which had dominated the presidential and parliamentary elections and which he used to justify his Domestic Security Bill. He represented prostitutes as a danger to citizens' sense of security, but also as victims who needed to be saved, and as potentially useful witnesses in trafficking cases. The coherence of these apparently contradictory representations depended on his almost exclusive concern with foreign women in prostitution, a category he homogenised and opposed to the unproblematic 'traditional' (French) prostitutes who work in clearly delineated parts of town and whom he rather warmly represents as part of the national cultural heritage.

In his presentation of the bill, he argued that the problem that needed addressing was not 'classic prostitution', but the presence of the 'poor foreign girls', victims of violent traffickers and pimps, who cause problems for the local residents. The solution he proposed was to rescue them from their traffickers and return them to their homes; and he argued that the only way this could be done was by making soliciting an arrestable offence, so that the victims of trafficking could be arrested and returned to their families: 'Far be it from me to suggest punishing these poor girls: the offence that we are creating must come to their aid ... I hope that these women will have a better future than facing degrading encounters night after night' (Sarkozy 2002a). He states that 'taking them home' is a humanitarian duty (Sarkozy 2002b).

The inability to speak French becomes an important marker of Otherness in the construction of the foreign prostitute/victim of trafficking. Sarkozy portrays this as a major obstacle (and in his more recent [2006] immigration laws, a minimum requirement for the non-deportation of children born in France to foreign parents). The inability to speak French exacerbates prostitutes' status as victims and justifies their rescue: 'They become prisoners of a criminal gang because they are in a country – ours – whose language they do not speak, where they do not know anyone and where they are controlled by their pimps. If soliciting is recognized as a serious offence, the police will be able to take these girls home' (Sarkozy 2002b), returning them, as his critics have pointed out, to the very conditions which prompted their departure in the first place (Borillo, Fassin et al. 2002).

Both the abolitionist construction of the problem of prostitution that dominated the discourse of the Jospin government and Sarkozy's reframing of the issue as one of security and immigration deny agency to the women concerned. This is not to say that there are no abolitionists who recognise the subjecthood of women in prostitution and their individual actions within the structural constraints of patriarchy and capitalism, for example, Claudie Lesselier (Lesselier 2005), but Senator Dinah Derycke's claim that 'all prostitutes hope to leave prostitution one day or another, no matter what they might say' (Derycke 2001, 26) suggests that, even when they do intervene in public debates, their words are not accorded any validity. Even when they are not physically excluded from conferences and meetings, as they were from the UNESCO conference in Paris in May 2000 (Fondation Scelles 2000), their discourse can be undermined by the view that they cannot understand their exploitation or that they are the mouthpieces of their pimps. Abolitionist groups such as Le Mouvement du Nid and Fondation Scelles represent prostitutes as absolute victims, plunged into despair, solitude and desperation (Lemettre 2002). Phillippe Scelles, of the Fondation Scelles, for example, declared: 'prostitution is not an expression of women's freedom, but of their profound misery, the tragedy of destiny, a descent into hell' (Fondation Scelles 2000, 5–6).

A disparate minority accords them some measure of subjecthood, although those who campaign for sex workers' rights, such as the associations Cabiria and the Bus des Femmes, struggle in the face of an overwhelming domination of policy debates by abolitionists. The research project funded by the Paris City Council and conducted by Janine Mossuz-Lavau and Elisabeth Handman has made a significant contribution to giving voice to sex workers within public and policy debates and aims to fill the silence broken only by the occasional autobiography by a former prostitute or a prostitutes' rights activist (Handman and Mossuz-Lavau 2005).

The internet is also offering some opportunity for sex workers to express their opinions – on the feminist website Les Pénélopes, on the site of the community health group Cabiria, and on the newer site of the recently formed group Les Putes (Whores), for example. Cabiria publishes regular research reports and has links with organisations in other European countries, including research links as part of the EU funded DAPHNE programme. In terms of access to the national media and to policy-makers, however, those who represent prostitutes as subjects and agents are not those who are working with them on the ground. Instead, they are a small number of intellectuals who take a liberal individual rights approach to prostitution, making it a question of choice and, in some cases, self-expression (E. Badinter 2002; Borillo 2002; Iacub, Millet et al. 2002; E. Badinter 2003).

The Client

Until recently, French policy-makers ignored the clients of prostitutes above the age of consent, which is 15. The Derycke report drew attention to the way in which the client 'benefits from a sort of consensual indulgence on the part of society' (Derycke 2001, 24) and argued that he could no longer be ignored. It found that clients are ordinary men from all parts of society, and it argued that they should be made to take responsibility for their actions, whether this was through criminalisation or education (Derycke 2001, 44). The introduction in Sweden of a law criminalising the client of prostitution drew attention to the way in which French policy had been silent in this respect. Could the problem of prostitution be resolved by focusing on demand rather than, or as well as, supply?

The first parliamentary debate on clients of prostitution came about indirectly, when, in November 2001, a government amendment was added to a bill on parental authority, proposing the criminalisation of clients of prostitutes under the age of 18. The main concern was 15–18 year-olds who are above the age of consent and therefore were not covered by the law on underage sex. The amendment proposed the creation of a new offence in the criminal law, which would apply not only when the act was committed in France, but when it was committed in another country by a person with French nationality or normally resident in France. The final version, passed into law on 4 March 2002, imposes a sentence of three years in prison and a fine of 45,000 Euros for soliciting, accepting or obtaining, in exchange for payment or the promise of payment, sexual relations from a minor who participates in prostitution, even occasionally. Article 225-12-2 increases the penalties to five years in prison and 75,000 Euros fine when there are aggravating factors (Rozier 2002, 22–3).

The trigger for the amendment, which bore little relation to the bill to which it was attached, seemed to be the presence of underage prostitutes on the streets of Paris. The salient characteristics of the minors who were to be protected by the law which were highlighted by the then Minister for Justice were that they were foreign, brought into France by traffickers, and unable to speak French (Lebranchu 2001). The increase since the late 1990s in the number of underage prostitutes on the streets of Paris (estimated by UNICEF at the time at 8,000) had already led the association, the Bus des Femmes, to stop distributing condoms to under-18s as a symbolic protest against the inertia of the state (Borvo 2001). Lebranchu argued that, 'even if the pimp is the most at fault, we must, in the words of the Paris public prosecutor, "destroy the market"' (Lebranchu 2001). This focus on removing demand in order to reduce the number of underage prostitutes on the streets is in contrast to the responses proposed to adult prostitution, arguably because there is a consensus that child prostitution is wrong and must be stopped. It was left-wing women who spoke in favour of the amendment: Nicole Borvo, Dinah Derycke, Marylise Lebranchu and Ségolène Royal. Ségolène Royal, Minister for the Family, Children and the Disabled, claimed, 'the associations that help them escape this slavery are clear: child prostitution exists because clients exist ... We are therefore committed to finding a way of dissuading clients and pimps, because, without clients, there will be no pimps' (Royal 2002). Lebranchu argued that the harsh penalisation of clients would dissuade pimps from putting under-18s on the street, just as ten-year sentences for sexual assault of under-15s in exchange for payment has dissuaded them from putting children of this age on the street (Lebranchu 2001).

There was no consensus amongst members of parliament on the criminalisation of the clients of underage prostitutes as opposed to the prohibition of underage prostitution. Prohibition was advocated by Robert Badinter, former Minister for Justice and PS Senator, in order to take into account 'the not just pitiable, but tragic, condition of children, mostly foreign, in prostitution' (R. Badinter 2002). Michel Dreyfus-Schmidt suggested that prohibition of underage prostitution would enable the police to arrest underage prostitutes, who might then gain access to opportunities for rehabilitation (Dreyfus-Schmidt 2001).

The Domestic Security Law extended the penalties introduced in 2002 for clients of underage prostitutes to clients of prostitutes with a 'particular vulnerability', apparent or known to the client, as the result of illness, physical or mental disability, or pregnancy (Senate 2002b). The PS called, unsuccessfully, for the removal of this article, which, they argued, discriminated against disabled or pregnant women in prostitution (Mahéas 2002). Johanne Vernier, lawyer and member of le Gisti, argued that if the 'particular vulnerability' does not affect the individual's decision-making capacity, then she should be free to prostitute herself, since prostitution is not illegal. If her decision-making capacity is affected, then she is already protected by laws on rape and sexual assault (Vernier 2005b).

The criminalisation of all clients of prostitution was also discussed within the debates on passive soliciting in the Senate in November 2002. Nicole Borvo, for example, stated that 'if there are lots of prostitutes and if prostitution can be lucrative for some, it is because there are lots of clients!' (Borvo 2002). 'The clients must be made to take responsibility for their actions. The debate on criminalization is open.' However, in the face of concerns that penalising the clients would push prostitutes underground and exacerbate their problems, Borvo recommended instead public information campaigns to raise awareness of prostitution and trafficking (Borvo 2002).

Bernard Lemettre, president of the Mouvement du Nid, was also hesitant about penalisation, calling instead for a better understanding of clients and how society constructs them. He portrays the client as a lonely individual who does not really understand what he has done wrong. After hearing his evidence to the committee, member of the Women's Rights Delegation, Danièle Bousquet, commented: 'I share your view that criminalisation is not the only possible response because the client, in the current context, does not understand how it is that he has done something abominable' (Lemettre 2002).

Claudine Legardinier, a journalist associated with the Nid and present in the same hearing, was much less indulgent, arguing that society is increasingly requiring men to take responsibility for their actions, but not with regards to prostitution: 'as soon as clients have got their money out, they have the right to do anything – and especially the right not to ask themselves any questions about the journey that has brought the young woman to where she is today. They buy – excuse the expression – the right not to give a damn' (Legardinier 2002). Legardinier calls for a range of measures, including education and a re-examination of masculinity, intended to reduce demand and to make men recognise their role and their responsibilities.

Laura Duchêne (PCF and member of the network Pour un Monde Sans Exploitation Sexuelle) states that feminists were initially in favour of the criminalisation of clients, but evidence from associations on the ground led them to believe that France is not ready for this. She argues that it would obscure other problems and would be counter-productive, increasing the marginalisation of prostitutes, hindering their access to care and exposing them to more violence (Duchêne 2002, 13). She argues that what is currently needed in France is better sex education in schools, a debate within the political parties, and public information campaigns (Duchêne 2002, 13). Le Nid and Fondation Scelles have both launched education and information campaigns. In August 2005, Fondation Scelles launched an awareness raising campaign around clients of prostitution, attempting to convey the message that criminal networks function because of demand (Fondation Scelles 2005).

Policy debates on the client are recent and concern only clients of street prostitution. This coincides with a reported move by middle-class men away from street prostitution to more discreet forms where the client is better protected from any problems with the law and is more anonymous (Simon 2002; Welzer-Lang 2003, 6). The first major academic study of clients, conducted by sociologist Said Bouamama, found that street prostitution is still the most popular form, particularly for clients with less money (Bouamama 2004, 30), but that other forms are developing quickly: 39.7 per cent of participants in the study were clients of more than one type of prostitution (Bouamama 2004, 138). PS Deputy, Alain Vidalies, labelled society's reaction to the public nuisance caused by street prostitution hypocritical, given the way that other forms of commercial sex are ignored (Vidalies 2002a). A Private Member's Bill tabled by Nicole Borvo in 2006 criticises the current impunity for those who profit from 'hidden' forms of prostitution in bars and saunas.

Prostitute–Client Relations

In principle, at least, the law before 2002 criminalised only the exploitation of prostitution and set out harsh penalties for those who profited from it, whether they were landlords, hotel owners or pimps. Prostitutes were constructed as victims of prostitution, and, although active soliciting was considered a minor offence, prostitution itself was not illegal. Critics of the Domestic Security Law argued that criminalising prostitutes would shift the power relations between prostitutes, clients and pimps, and that this would make the lives of prostitutes more difficult. They objected to the change in emphasis from targeting pimps to targeting prostitutes, and argued that it was the introduction of passive soliciting that most affected the relation between prostitutes and clients. In the parliamentary debates on the Domestic Security Bill, Jacques Mahéas (PS) argued that criminalising passive soliciting would push prostitution underground making it more dangerous for prostitutes, and disadvantaging them in relation to clients, pimps and the police (Mahéas 2002). Studies of the impact of the law suggest that he was right.

Evidence of the impact of the Domestic Security Law can be gathered from the police, support associations and journalistic reports, which began to appear within months of the introduction of the law. The evidence suggests that the law has not affected demand, but has had a significant impact on supply and on the relations between prostitutes, clients and pimps. Clients have nothing to fear from the new measures, and there are many reports of them becoming more violent and demanding unprotected sex more frequently. *L'Humanité* (29 June 2005) quotes a 'traditional prostitute' in her sixties, who claims that 'violence has increased ... We are often asked for unprotected sex. And when a prostitute, because of police harassment, has not been able to work for three days, sometimes she resigns herself to agreeing. This law, in fact, has simply reinforced the power of the police and of clients over women' (Mouloud 2005).

Deteriorating relations between prostitutes and the police mean that prostitutes are no longer protected from violent clients, and the clients know this. *Libération* quotes a prostitute who says: 'before, when we saw a police car, we felt reassured. The clients knew that we had good relations with them. Now, as soon as we see the officers, we hide. The clients have understood that we are no longer protected, and they do what they want' (Grosjean 2003).

Prostitutes have moved from more public to more isolated areas and work much later in the night in an attempt to avoid arrest. This not only increases the risk of violence, but makes it more difficult for the support associations to maintain contact with them (Handman and Mossuz-Lavau 2005, 34). Police harassment is widely reported by prostitutes and support associations (Grosjean 2003). Some prostitutes have organised in an attempt to deal with it, building up funds to pay fines and staging protests. Act Up reports that African prostitutes from the Bois de Vincennes created a collective in March 2005 in an attempt to defend themselves against police harassment. A member of the collective states that the women are sometimes held for 72 hours, are repeatedly fined, and report being badly treated by the police (Act Up 2005). Traffickers have put more women on the streets to compensate for the possibility of deportations (Grosjean 2003). They keep tighter control over the women and use more violence towards them. Claude Boucher of the Bus des Femmes claims that traffickers show no fear of the authorities. Their victims, on the other hand, are scared of the police, the courts, clients and passers-by (Grosjean 2003).

The measures introduced by the Domestic Security Law were intended to target foreigners. Head of the BRP (Brigade de Répression du Proxénétisme – vice squad), Daniel Rigourd, told the Women's Rights Delegation in November 2002: 'let's not beat about the bush, it is foreign prostitution that is targeted, prostitution controlled by mafia-type organisations' (Rigourd 2002). The distinction between 'traditional' and 'foreign' prostitutes was reinforced by the Ministry for the Interior, the police and the media. It divided prostitutes and tempered organised opposition to the Bill, which was more likely to depend on 'French' prostitutes than those who risked deportation. A report in *Le Monde* on a demonstration by sex workers against Sarkozy's proposals stated, 'the young undocumented foreign women held by criminal networks are not part of this demonstration. There is even evidence of a certain amount of animosity towards them on the part of the so-called "traditional prostitutes"': '"they are dirty workers; they leave condoms on the ground. It is because of them that we have to put up with Sarkozy's bill" stated a young woman who works in rue Saint-Denis' (Fabre and Krémer 2002). Claude Boucher, of the Bus des Femmes, also claims, 'traditional prostitutes and these slaves are completely different. Traditional prostitutes did not come into prostitution because it was their dream job, but that doesn't make them victims. If they have made this difficult choice, it is in order to escape the indignity of poverty' (Boucher 2002).

Although in the months immediately following the introduction of the Domestic Security Law, the police arrested mostly foreign prostitutes, by 2004, they were arresting 'traditionals' too (Handman and Mossuz-Lavau 2005, 36). *L'Humanité* (21 February 2006) reported the occupation of an employment agency by 'traditionals' from the Bois de Vincennes, protesting against police harassment which prevents them from working. They stated that the police give them on-the-spot fines because the public prosecutors will not pursue the cases. Judges, too, appear to be reluctant to impose large fines and prison sentences for what they see as a social problem (Mouloud 2005). Some judges refuse to apply the law on passive soliciting and release the accused immediately. Others only impose fines, but these fines are heavy enough (350–1000 Euros) to send the women straight back onto the streets to raise the money. Sometimes the camper vans in which the women work are confiscated, and sometimes they receive prison sentences, which may or may not be suspended. Some judges ignore previous convictions and give suspended sentences every time (Handman and Mossuz-Lavau 2005, 36).

The Lyon-based NGO, Cabiria, stated that some prostitutes had already been making racist comments about migrant women, but tensions within the community have exacerbated, transforming turf wars into hatred for foreigners (Monnet 2003). Part of the reason for hostility towards migrant women in prostitution on the part of French 'traditional' prostitutes is their belief that many of them are working for pimps. Migrant women are blamed for the degradation of working conditions, the fall in prices and the increasingly difficult relations with the police (Pagès 2006). Associations report that traditional prostitutes are suffering from the competition of trafficked women, from the fall in prices brought about by their presence and by the shift in bargaining power between prostitutes and clients. Some have lost their homes and go to the associations to beg for help. Government promises of alternative employment for those who choose to exit have amounted to nothing more than a few hours of cleaning a week (Grosjean 2003). Head of the vice squad, Daniel Rigourd claims there are few French prostitutes still on the streets in Paris. In Rue Saint-Denis, there are 350 prostitutes, 'real French-French women', aged 40–70 (Rigourd 2002). Most French prostitutes have moved off the street, where competition is fierce, into apartments (Rigourd 2002). There are also escort agencies and bars.

Some temporary residence permits have been issued, but a small number in relation to the number of arrests. According to OCRTEH, 104 temporary residence permits were issued between March 2003 and September 2004 to prostitutes who have denounced their pimps. Those who have no papers and do not denounce their pimp are deported through administrative, not judicial, channels (Handman and Mossuz-Lavau 2005, 37). *L'Humanité* reports, 'the law, which was intended to help dismantle criminal networks and free foreign prostitutes from their grasp, has turned out to be a new deportation machine. Since the end of 2003, more than 300 women from Eastern Europe have been deported' (Mouloud 2005). In Paris, between 1 April 2003 and 1 May 2004, 3,192 prostitutes were detained in custody and only 158 gave evidence. Vernier argues,

> ... either the majority of people in prostitution are not victims of traffickers or pimps, or the conditions in which they are asked to denounce them are unfavourable. Prostitutes on the street have therefore become the prime target of criminal law in order to fight against pimping and trafficking. But punishing all prostitutes in order to reach this goal assumes that they are all victims. On the one hand, penalizing prostitutes who do not have a pimp or trafficker is a kind of 'collateral damage' in the war on pimping and trafficking. On the other hand, prostitutes who are victims of pimps and traffickers are penalized in their own interest (Vernier 2005a, 137).

The government claims that the Domestic Security Law has reduced the public nuisance caused by some forms of prostitution and has had an impact on trafficking. Charges for soliciting have certainly increased, and Sarkozy claims that, in 2004, 47 international prostitution rings were dismantled, compared with 39 in 2003 (Sarkozy 2005). The opposition claims that, although visible prostitution can be shown to have declined since the introduction of the Domestic Security Law,

> ... all the associations on the ground agree that prostitution has not decreased. As we feared, the law and order approach simply moved it to less exposed areas, making it more dangerous and less visible, leaving prostitutes exposed to violence on the part of clients and increased health risks. At the same time, the humanitarian part, including support for victims, does not seem to be living up to its promises in terms of places in accommodation, and access to training (Mahéas 2005).

A joint report published in February 2007 by the human rights organisation, the Ligue des Droits de l'homme, and two trade unions for members of the legal profession, the Syndicat de la Magistrature and the Syndicat des Avocats de France, concludes that the law does not fight against pimping, but against prostitutes and has not affected organised crime. The authors state that there are few convictions, but the number of arrests is increasing, because it is an easy way for the police to meet their targets. Prostitutes are 'handcuffed, insulted and searched before being held in custody. Transsexuals are the most likely to be strip searched, humiliated and treated like freaks. It is not unusual for custody to last much longer than the investigation requires' (Ligue des droits de l'homme, Syndicat de la Magistrature et al. 2007).

By criminalising passive soliciting, the Domestic Security Law has tipped the balance of power in favour of clients. They could, in theory, be charged with soliciting, but in practice, they are usually left alone. The risk of being arrested for soliciting – with large fines, a possible prison sentence and likely overnight custody – means prostitutes have less time to negotiate safe practices and to assess dangerous clients. They have also been pushed into more isolated neighbourhoods. Foreign prostitutes risk deportation, even if they are legally present. These factors have pushed prices down and risky practices up. There is less police protection from violence, and it is more difficult to access the support associations.

Conclusion

The various strategies that have been deployed or suggested in response to prostitution in France have different effects on supply, demand and the relation between the two. The harsh penalisation of those who profit from prostitution has been one of the cornerstones of French abolitionism since the ratification of the 1949 UN Convention in 1960. While the aim of prostitution policy is still, in theory, to track down and convict pimps and traffickers, critics argue that the limited resources committed to counter-trafficking undermine the seriousness of this intent. Arresting prostitutes in the hope that they will give crucial evidence against their exploiters is cheap, but not the most effective way of unravelling large transnational networks. It operates more effectively as an anti-immigration policy, pandering to popular anti-immigrant sentiment and reinforcing the law and order agenda.

The other cornerstone of French abolitionism, which the current government has not actually rejected, is the provision of social protection and reintegration for those victims of prostitution who choose to leave. Due to the failure to set up state agencies, despite the provisions of a series of laws in the 1960s, these services have been provided by NGOs, with some measure of state funding. They have become more precarious, however, due to cuts in funding, to the dramatic increase in demand for services since the first arrival of trafficked women in 1997, and as a result of changing working practices since March 2003.

French prostitution policy is perhaps more than ever marked by contradictions and inconsistencies. If the problem is the presence of unwanted migrants, then the current policy has developed into an effective solution. Similarly, if the problem is the visibility of street prostitution in middle-class neighbourhoods, then there has been some success in reducing it. But for many critics of Sarkozy's approach, the 'problem' of prostitution has been wrongly constructed, and inherent in this construction is the representation of women in prostitution either as helpless victims, criminals or immigrants who need to be 'taken home'.

References

Act Up (2005), *Le noir est une couleur: rencontre avec Marianne, membere du collectif de Vincennes*, retrieved 12 September 2005 from <http://www.actupparis.org/article2065.html>.

Badinter, E. (2002), 'Si c'est leur choix', *Le Nouvel Observateur* (Paris), 1972.

Badinter, E. (2003), 'Le féminisme d'Elisabeth Badinter', *L'Humanité* (Paris), 23.

Badinter, R. (2002), Senate Debate 14 February 2002, retrieved 16 May 2006 from <http://www.senat.fr>.

Borillo, D. (2002), 'La Liberté de se Prostituer: En l'absence d'exploitation, vendre son corps est un métier comme un autre', *Libération.*

Borillo, D., E. Fassin et al. (2002), 'Non à la guerre aux prostituées', *Le Monde.*

Borvo, N. (2001), Senate Debate 21 November 2001, retrieved from <http://www.senat.fr/seances/s200111/s20011121/sc20011121042.html >.

Borvo, N. (2002), Senate Debate 14 November 2002, retrieved from <http://www.senat.fr>.

Bouamama, S. (2004), *L'homme en question: le processus du devenir-client de la prostitution* (Le mouvement du nid and IFAR).

Boucher, C. (2002), 'Défendre les travailleuses du sexe', *Le Nouvel Observateur* (Paris), 1972.

Délégation de l'Assemblée nationale aux droits des femmes et à l'égalité des chances entre les hommes et les femmes (2002), 'Compte rendu no. 2, 15 Octobre, Présidence de Marie-Jo Zimmermann', retrieved from <http://www.assemblee_nationale.fr/12/cr-delf/02-03/c0203002.asp>.

Derycke, D. (2001), *Rapport d'activité 2000: les politiques publiques et la prostitution*, Délégation du Sénat dux droits des femmes et à l'égalité des chances entre les hommes et les femmes, <www.senat.fr>.

Dreyfus-Schmidt (2001), Senate Debate 21 November 2001, retrieved from <http://www.senat.fr/seances/s200111/s20011121/sc20011121042.html>.

Duchêne, L. (2002), 'Le PC dans un processus d'abolition de la prostitution,' *Prostitution et Société*, 12–13.

Fabre, C. and P. Krémer (2002), 'Plusieurs centaines de "personnes prostituées" se sont rassemblées à Paris contre le projet Sarkozy', *Le Monde* (Paris).

Fondation Scelles (2000), *Actes du colloque du 16 mai 2000, tenu à l'UNESCO, Paris*. Le peuple de l'abîme. La prostitution aujourd'hui, UNESCO Paris.

Fondation Scelles (2005), 'La Fondation Scelles présente la première déclaration de sensibilisation des clients de personnes prostituées: Et si on parlait prostitution', retrieved 1 September 2005 from <http://www.fondationscelles.org>.

Grosjean, B. (2003), 'Des filles de joie bien à la peine', *Libération* (Paris).

Handman, M.-E. and J. Mossuz-Lavau (eds) (2005), *La Prostitution à Paris* (Paris: Editions de la Martinière).

Iacub, M., C. Millet et al. (2002), 'Ni coupables ni victimes: libres de se prostituer', *Le Monde* (Paris).

Lebranchu, M. (2001), Senate Debate 21 November 2001, retrieved from <http://www/senat.fr/seances/s200111/s20011121/sc20011121042.html>.

Legardinier, C. (2002), 'Audition de Claudine Legardinier', journaliste par la Délégation de l'Assemblée nationale aux droits des femmes et à l'égalité des chances entre les hommes et les femmes. Paris, Assemblée nationale.

Lemettre, B. (2002), 'Audition de Bernard Lemettre', président du Mouvement du Nid par la Délégation de l'Assemblée nationale aux droits des femmes et à l'égalité des chances entre les hommes et les femmes. Paris, Assemblée nationale.

Lesselier, C. (2005), 'Prostitution et Violence contre les femmes', *Forum national de la Fasti: Prostitution: L'exploitation des femmes étrangères* (Paris).

Ligue des droits de l'homme, Syndicat de la Magistrature et al. (2007), 'Des nouvelles zones de non-droit: Des prostituées face à l'arbitraire policier', retrieved 1 March 2007 from <http://www.syndicat-magistrature.org>.

Lim, L.L. (ed.) (1998), *The Sex Sector: The Economic and Social Bases of Prostitution in Southeast Asia* (Geneva: International Labour Office).

Luc, H. (2002), Senate Debate 14 November 2002, retrieved 9 May 2006 from <http://www.senat.fr>.

Mahéas, J. (2002), Senate Debate 14 November 2002, retrieved from <http://www.senat.fr>.

Mahéas, J. (2005), 'Bilan de la loi pour la sécurité intérieure en ce qui concerne la prostitution', Question écrite no. 17416. Publiée dans le JO Sénat du 5 mai 2005, page 1245, retrieved 24 February 2006 from <http://www.senat.fr>.

Marcovich, M. (2002), *Le système de la prostitution. Une violence à l'encontre des femmes* (Paris: Commission nationale contre les violences envers les femmes).

Mazur, A. (2004), 'Prostitute Movements Face Elite Apathy and Gender-Biased Universalism in France' in J. Outshoorn (ed.), *The Politics of Prostitution: Women's Movements, Democratic States, and the Globalization of Sex Commerce* (Cambridge: Cambridge University Press), 123–43.

Monnet, C. (2003), 'Répression et prostitution', *Passant* 44 (avril–mai).

Mouloud, L. (2005), 'Prostitutio – Le racolage à l'index', *l'Humanité.*

Nor, M. (2001), *La Prostitution* (Paris: Le Cavalier Bleu).

Outshoorn, J. (2000), 'Legalizing Prostitution as Sexual Service: The Case of the Netherlands', *ECPR Joint Sessions Workshop 12*, Copenhagen.

Pagès, Y. (2006), 'Prostitution' in S. Beaud, J. Confavreux and J. Lindgaard (eds), *La France Invisible* (Paris: La Découverte), 305–15.

Péry, N. (2001), 'Actualités', retrieved 21 October 2001 from <http://www.social.gouv.fr/femmes/actu/doss>.

Rigourd, D. (2002), 'Audition de M. Daniel Rigourd par la délégation aux droits des femmes et à l'égalité des chances entre les hommes et les femmes', Compte rendu no. 6. Mercredi 13 novembre 2002. Retrieved 9 May 2006 from <http://recherche.assemblee-nationale.fr>.

Royal, S. (2002), Senate Debate 7 February 2002, retrieved 16 May 2006 from <http://www.senat.fr>.

Rozier, J. (2002), 'Rapport d'information fait au nom de la délégation du Sénat aux droits des femmes et à l'égalité des chances entre les hommes et les femmes sur le projet de loi no. 30 (2002–2003) pour la sécurité intérieure' (Paris: Le Sénat).

Sarkozy, N. (2002a), Senate Debate 13 November 2002, retrieved 13 November 2002 from <http://www.senat.fr>.

Sarkozy, N. (2002b), Senate Debate 14 November 2002, retrieved 9 May 2006 from <http://www.senat.fr>.

Sarkozy, N. (2005), 'Bilan de la loi pour la sécurité intérieure en ce qui concerne la prostitution', question écrite no. 17416. Publiée dans le JO Sénat du 5 mai 2005, page 2723, retrieved 24 February 2006 from <http://www.senat.fr>.

Senate (2002a), 'Compte rendu analytique officiel de la séance du 14 novembre'.

Senate (2002b), 'Compte rendu intégral des débats du Sénat: Séance du 14 novembre 2002', retrieved from <http://www.senat.fr>.

Simon, C. (2002), 'Clients de la prostitution', *Le Monde* (Paris).

Tubiana, M., B. Marcus et al. (2002), 'Lettre ouverte à Monsieur Sarkozy', *Le Nouvel Observateur*.

Vernier, J. (2005a), 'La Loi pour la sécurité intérieure: punir les victimes du proxénétisme pour mieux les protéger?' in M.-E. Handman and J. Mossuz-Lavau, *La Prostitution à Paris* (Paris: Editions de la Martinière), 121–52.

Vernier, J. (2005b), 'La pénalisation des prostitués selon la LSI', *Plein Droit*, 65–6.

Vidalies, A. (2002a), 'L'Expression "travailleur du sexe" ne doit pas être taboue', *Le Monde* (Paris).

Vidalies, A. (2002b), 'Rapport d'information par la mission d'information commune sur les diverses formes de l'esclavage moderne', Assemblée nationale, No. 3459.

Welzer-Lang, D. (2003), 'Quand le sexe travaille ou Une loi peut en cacher une autre', retrieved 3 February 2003 from <http://www.multisexualites-et-sida.org/yapasque/client.html>.

Chapter 5

Exploring Exploitation: Trafficking in Sex, Work and Sex Work

Vanessa E. Munro[1]

Asserting that the concept of exploitation is both 'ambiguous and ill-defined', John Lawrence Hill has lamented the fact that, in its current state, this concept has been so widely applied, taking on what he argues to be 'an open-textured and almost all-encompassing meaning' (Hill 1994, 632). Echoing a similar sentiment, Alan Wertheimer has noted that 'although we frequently claim that some act, practice or transaction is exploitative, the concept of exploitation is typically invoked without much analysis or argument' (Wertheimer 1996, 5; Wertheimer 1997). As both these theorists rightly point out, this is problematic, not so much because such claims are false (although they may be), but because they inappropriately presume that the meaning and significance of exploitation is obvious. On the contrary, as this chapter will seek to illustrate, disputes over what constitutes exploitation are rife in social, political and moral theory, as are debates over its normative import once established.

Although this chapter does not purport to offer a solution to these debates over the meaning of exploitation, either in general or in the specific contexts of sex and labour trafficking, it does hope to move beyond treating this concept merely as a 'rhetorical placeholder for expressing disapproval' (Wertheimer 1996, 5). More specifically, it seeks to highlight the difficult questions that must be addressed if we are to give meaning to an exploitation claim in these contexts and if we are, in turn, to respond appropriately to its assertion. In broad terms, then, the discussion that follows can be broken down into three main parts. In the first part, the general debates that have marked the terrain in which the concept of exploitation has been theorised and interrogated will be considered. In the second part, discussion will turn directly to the issue of people trafficking, highlighting the role that claims of exploitation have played in framing contemporary national and international legal responses thereto. As part of this discussion, the extent to which exploitation has been defined and responded to in different ways in the contexts of sex and labour

1 With the usual caveats, I would like to thank Marina Della Giusta, Sharron FitzGerald, Jo Phoenix and David Archard for their comments on an earlier draft. I would also like to acknowledge the extent to which this chapter has benefited from discussion with collaborators in the Supply/Demand Dynamic Expert Seminars, hosted at King's College London during 2005/2006. I am grateful to the British Academy and the ESRC for funding the organisation of these meetings.

trafficking will also be examined. With this in mind, in the third part of the chapter, tentative suggestions will be made about the implications of these divergent uses of exploitation for the development of a coherent and effective legal response. In a context in which people trafficking engages a range of competing agendas on – amongst other things – organised crime, immigration, labour relations and prostitution policy, discussion here will suggest that the lack of analytical clarity underlying these exploitation claims permits much scope for confusion, politicking and obfuscation of international norms.

Exploring Exploitation

At the outset, it is important to distinguish between the use of the term exploitation in its technical and normative senses. In its technical sense, exploitation means simply to make use of something or to ensure that something is not wasted. A person exploits the talents or resources at their disposal all the time in morally unproblematic ways (indeed, in some cases, it may be more morally problematic *not* to exploit them). Yet, there is also a separate (albeit related) sense in which we use the term exploitation, and here it takes on a pejorative connotation and a normative dimension. This second use usually comes into play when we are referring to the treatment, not of characteristics or things, but of people, and more specifically when we are referring to the relationships *between* people (Feinberg 1990, 177). When someone uses or takes advantage of another person in a way that serves their own ends, we frequently refer to this as exploitation. While not all such exploitation is necessarily blameworthy (a student may, for example, use their teacher as a means to passing his or her examinations without moral censure), where that use takes the form of a sheer, improper or unfair use, we tend to treat it as a kind of injustice (Wilkinson 2003, 38).

For the purposes of this discussion, it is this second, normative sense of exploitation that is of interest. But what exactly this entails is by no means uncontroversial. As Arneson reminds us, although we can all agree with a simplistic assertion that A exploits B when A takes unfair advantage of B, when we try to develop a fuller account, we will discover 'as many competing conceptions of exploitation as theories of what persons owe to each other by way of fair treatment' (Arneson 2001, 350). Debates have arisen, for example, over whether the objectionable essence of exploitation lies in the instrumental use of a person as a means to another's end or in the resultant outcome that one person gains disproportionately at the expense of another. Buchanan, on the one hand, adopts a Kantian conception which defines exploitation as involving 'the harmful, merely instrumental utilisation of (another person) or his capacities, for one's own advantage' (Buchanan 1985, 87; see also Buchanan 1979). Meanwhile, on the other hand, Levine asserts that exploitation occurs when there is an exchange 'in which the exploited party get less than the exploiting party, who does better at the exploited party's expense' (Levine 1988, 66). These different understandings of exploitation are characterised by Wilkinson as 'wrongful use' and 'disparity of value' respectively. While in the former, the exploitee is wronged by being used solely as a means (and so is objectified and instrumentalised inappropriately), in the latter, the exploitee is wronged more because she is *unfairly* used, with this unfairness typically consisting in the fact that her position of vulnerability is taken advantage of in order to under-reward her role within a given transaction. Although there may be situations in which both these types of exploitation operate, there will also be contexts in which only one is present and it is important to be sure about which is involved (Wilkinson 2003, 14).

Cutting across this distinction between the different genres of 'wrongful use' and 'disparity of value', moreover, are further debates about the relevance of harm. According to Wilkinson, most theorists who adopt a 'wrongful use' view of exploitation tend to consider some kind of harm or disadvantage to be essential and integral (Wilkinson 2003, 25). By contrast, however, theorists who adopt a 'disparity of value' approach tend to be more divided. On the one hand, for example, Tormey asserts the inevitability of harm by arguing that exploitation constitutes a 'zero-sum game' in which 'what the exploiter gains, the exploitee loses; or minimally, for the exploiter to gain, the exploitee must lose' (Tormey 1974, 207). But at the same time, other theorists have argued, to the contrary, that it is perfectly possible for a person to be exploited whilst simultaneously gaining in some way as a result of the transaction. Thus, Munzer, for example, has asserted that exploitation 'can occur in morally unsavoury forms without harming the exploitee's interests' (Munzer 1990, 171).

On first sight, this claim that it can be possible both to be exploited *and* to benefit from that exploitation may seem counter-intuitive. To understand this position, it is important to bear in mind that we are talking here about an 'all things considered' assessment. Indeed, as Wertheimer reminds us, there are negative elements in virtually all non-controversially beneficial transactions – even paying a fair price for a good that another is happy to sell entails some negative element in that it would have been better, for me at least, if I had been able to acquire the good for free. Similarly, it is perfectly conceivable that there will be situations in which, while a party gains less from a transaction than they would be entitled to under fair(er) conditions of exchange, they nonetheless benefit, since the transaction places them in a better position overall than they would have otherwise enjoyed. The question, then, is not whether a practice has harmful elements, but whether it generates a net harm overall.

Of course, the baseline against which this should be assessed is by no means obvious (see Wolff 1999, 113; Miller 1987). Wilkinson suggests three distinct possibilities – first, the 'pre-interactive baseline' which focuses on what would have occurred had the parties to the transaction never met; second, the 'closest possible world' baseline which focuses on what would have occurred if the exploitee had entered into the same kind of transaction but with someone other than the exploiter; and third, the 'normative baseline' which focuses on what the position would have been had the exploitee had the level of welfare she ought to have had. While Wilkinson prefers the normative baseline in most cases, he accepts this may not always be appropriate. In particular, he notes – and others have lamented – that this more expansive approach renders harmful many instances of 'disparity of value' exploitation in which the transaction involved, if compared to other baselines, would be regarded as mutually advantageous and harmless overall (Wilkinson 2003, 60–64).

These disagreements over whether harm must result from a practice or transaction in order for it to be exploitative, and how any such assessment of harm is to be made, relate in turn to a further debate over the relevance of consent. A number of commentators have argued that a party cannot be properly viewed as having been exploited unless the transaction in question was in some way forced upon her, or her apparent consent to it laboured under a crucial qualitative defect. Moore, for example, insists that exploitation entails not just an exchange under conditions in which there is an obvious discrepancy between the value of the goods/services provided and their cost, but also that 'one party to the exchange uses a substantial degree of coercion' to secure the other's compliance (Moore 1973, 53). Expressing a similar position, Arneson has argued that – put simply – 'without force or coercion, there is no exploitation' (Arneson 1981, 225). Meanwhile, other theorists, particularly those who subscribe to Marxist analysis, have pointed out that this coercion can be structural as well as personal in its operation. Thus, according to Reiman's 'force-inclusive' definition, 'a society is exploitative when its social structure is organised so that unpaid labour is systematically forced out of one class and put at the disposal of another' (Reiman 1987, 3).[2] By contrast, however, a number of other commentators have taken a quite different stance on the necessity of a link between exploitation and coercion. Thus, Munzer, for example, insists that there can be exploitation 'despite the exploitee's fully voluntary consent' (Munzer 1990, 171; also Wolff 1999, 113).

Of course, the critic may interject here that if we look more closely at the contexts against which such exploitative arrangements are apparently agreed upon, we will see that the quality of the exploitee's consent remains in some way defective – if not because of direct coercion or force, then because of either a dearth of alternative options afforded to her or a false consciousness which causes her to misconstrue her own will. To respond to these charges, it is necessary to go somewhat beyond this immediate analysis of exploitation and into the realms of consent theory itself. In his account of exploitation, Wertheimer takes steps in this direction, arguing that 'although B might prefer to have a different range of options available, B can make a perfectly rational decision as to the advisability of the various options' and so can give a meaningful token of consent to transactions under conditions of constraint (Wertheimer 1996, 27). I have argued elsewhere that there are reasons to be critical of this 'consensual minimalist' approach (Munro 2005b). But for current purposes, it is enough to accept, as I largely do, that there may be *some* situations in which, even though there are background conditions that obviate full and free choice, it is possible to exercise a meaningful degree of agency in entering into transactions. Moreover, in a context in which it has been argued, by some at least, that exchanges that are recognised as exploitative may nonetheless bring about a level of advantage to both parties (when compared against a pre-transaction baseline), the existence of conditions

2 Interestingly, as Wertheimer (1996) points out, while libertarians come to very different conclusions on the existence of coercion than Marxists, it is apparent that they too also adopt this 'force-inclusive' view of exploitation, since in their view, the fact that there is no coercion entails that there is also no exploitation. See Mayer (2002) for discussion of the relationship between Marxist and liberal (libertarian) perspectives on exploitation; and Roemer (1985) or Wolff (1999) generally on Marx.

of poverty and so on render entrance into those exchanges not only likely but also profoundly rational. Thus, while it might properly be argued that a background of hard circumstances may, in some cases, give rise to a defect in consent, this is by no means inevitable and it is important to be clear that the existence of such circumstances does not in and of itself constitute this defect (Wertheimer 1996, 270).

These debates, relating as they do to the merits and demerits of 'wrongful use' and 'disparity of value' interpretations, as well as to the relevance of both harm and consent, clearly go to the heart of our understanding, and condemnation, of exploitation. Despite this, however, it is submitted in this chapter that when claims to exploitation are invoked in the context of people trafficking, the complexity of these debates is rarely acknowledged. Mirroring pre-existing debates on prostitution, commentators have typically attributed their disagreements over the wrongfulness of, and most effective response to, trafficking activity, not in the meaning of exploitation itself but rather in the appropriateness of its application to specific contexts. This, in turn, has generated some highly polarised engagements, as well as a problematic tendency to presume inappropriately a coherence to the concept of exploitation that masks the extent to which it may in fact be deployed in legal responses in divergent (and often conflicting) ways. Building on this, discussion in the next section will chart the emergence of these claims to exploitation in anti-trafficking laws and policies. In particular, it will highlight the important but subtle ways in which, underneath the blanket turn to the concept of exploitation in international and national frameworks, lie divergent understandings of its remit and wrongfulness as between sex and labour trafficking.

Exploitation and Trafficking

While the phenomenon of cross-border trafficking in human beings is far from new to the international community, its contemporary incidence has become the focal point for renewed legislative, media and campaigning attention. Official documents condemning this activity have proliferated over the past decade, during which time national laws have also been developed that stipulate the components of this criminal offence and set out the options for the punishment of its perpetrators and the recompense of its victims (for discussion, see, for example, Askola 2007; Toepfer and Wells 1994; Hauber 1998; Corrigan 2001). There can be little doubt, moreover, that this modern variant of people trafficking exhibits a number of distinctive characteristics. Processes of globalisation and socio-economic displacement across Eastern Europe and the developing nations have promoted patterns of widespread migration (IOM 2002, 2005). This trend has typically been met with measured resistance by receiving countries; and their stipulation of stringent financial, training or familial criteria within immigration policy has ironically generated a large community of would-be migrants who, in the absence of avenues for legitimate entry, have increasingly had recourse to networks or individuals offering illicit alternatives.

At the same time, though, it is apparent that a significant number of those identified as contemporary victims of trafficking have not in fact entered the destination country illegally. In some cases, migrants may have entered entirely independently – for example, via a short term visitor or education visa – while in others, they will have been facilitated by illegitimate third parties who, not having been called upon to assist in the avoidance of detection at the point of entry, may instead finance the trip or provide employment on arrival in exchange for a fee. While the employment in question will often involve illicit or unregulated markets, in its contemporary guise, trafficking activity has also diversified into a range of industries in which there is an insatiable demand for cheap labour. There remains a high female representation within this migrant community and a strong relationship between migration and prostitution (Kelly 2002; UN 2006), but the trafficking of men, women and children into domestic, agricultural and factory work is a fast growing phenomenon (see, for example, Bales 1999; Anderson 2000; Dowling et al. 2007).

Against this backdrop, national and international law-makers have come under increasing pressure to define trafficking in distinction from the smuggling offences with which it is often conflated, and to offer thereby a transparent basis upon which to identify and respond to its migrant victims. In contemporary times, this has led to the increasing punctuation of anti-trafficking discourse with the claim that it is a practice that involves, by definition, the exploitation of persons. The UN General Assembly, for example, has defined people trafficking as 'the illicit and clandestine movement of persons across national and international borders' with 'the end goal of forcing women and children into sexually and economically oppressive and exploitative situations.' More recently, the UN Optional Protocol on People Trafficking has taken a similar, albeit broader approach, focusing on the combination of transportation and exploitation. Article 3 states, 'trafficking in persons shall mean the recruitment, transportation, transfer, harbouring, or receipt of persons … for the purposes of exploitation.' While this provision does not define exploitation as such, it does give some further guidance as to what it would, as a minimum, include in this context: namely, 'the exploitation of the prostitution of others or other forms of sexual exploitation, forced labour or services, slavery or practices similar to slavery, servitude or the removal of organs.' These definitions have also been adopted by the recent Council of Europe Anti-Trafficking Convention, which imposes on signatories more extensive victim support obligations than those set out under its UN counterpart.

Recent domestic anti-trafficking responses in the UK have, in turn, also mirrored this international and regional level focus on exploitation claims. The Sexual Offences Act 2003 brought into effect in England and Wales a series of domestic anti-trafficking offences targeting the movement of a person into, out of, or within the UK for the purposes of commercial sexual exploitation (ss. 57–9). Notably, no detailed consideration was given as to what exploitation might mean in this sexual context, with the apparent presumption being that the mere fact of having worked as, or having had it intended that one would work as, a prostitute would suffice. In line with Article 3 of the UN Protocol, moreover, there is no explicit mention here of the need for the trafficked person to have been coerced into prostitution. Thus, it would seem that the claim to sexual exploitation (that constitutes the trigger for this trafficking offence) can be made out even where the selling of sex has been consented to and even where, as is currently the case under UK criminal law, such selling of sex is perfectly legal.

But this position can be contrasted somewhat against the treatment afforded to labour exploitation more generally. Provisions under section 4 of the Asylum and Immigration (Treatment of Claimants) Act 2004 make it an offence to facilitate the transportation of a person into, out of, or within the UK for the purposes of labour exploitation. Although this provision, like its sex trafficking counterpart, lacks a clear definition of exploitation, steps have been taken here to provide an exhaustive list of circumstances in which exploitation will be established. These include where a person is subjected to force, threat or deception in order to compel her to provide labour, services or benefits. Thus, it seems that in this context, unlike in the context of sex trafficking, the existence of coercion or deception is in fact crucial to the exploitation.

As discussed above, there are certainly arguments to be made in favour of this kind of 'force-inclusive' account, but what is striking is that, in a context in which both national and international provisions purport to bring the divergent forms of sex and labour trafficking into closer alignment by uniting them under the nexus of being 'for the purposes of exploitation', it is clear that two quite different understandings of what exploitation entails are being deployed here. This inconsistency in approach can be seen to throw up some immediate and significant difficulties. For one thing, it is not clear, at least not without further investigation, why labour exploitation should entail *forced* work or services while there is no mention of such coercion in the context of sexual exploitation or organ removal. What's more, it might legitimately be objected that defining the exploitation in sex trafficking by reference to the exploitation in prostitution, without further clarification of the latter, is circular and largely unhelpful. The 'special relationship' to prostitution that has historically marked international anti-trafficking responses is preserved under the UN Protocol, despite its formal extension to trafficking for non-sexual purposes. In turn, recent UK legislation provides a vivid illustration of the ways in which the malleability of the concept of exploitation can be manipulated by destination states to enable the deployment of restrictive interpretations that accord sex trafficking a higher priority.

At the same time, though, the reasons behind this distinctive treatment of trafficking for sexual purposes may not be particularly mysterious. This policy level disinterest in force is supported by an abolitionist approach to prostitution, which sees the selling of sex as inherently exploitative, irrespective of the conditions under which such exchanges take place. While UK policy on prostitution has at times been difficult to classify, in recent times, during which sex trafficking has re-emerged as a concern, there has been an apparent preference for abolitionism (see, for example, Kantola and Squires 2004; Brooks-Gordon 2005; Munro 2005a).[3] This sentiment was clearly reflected, for example, in the words of David Blunkett, the then Home Secretary, when introducing to Parliament the commercial sexual exploitation proposals that preceded the Sexual Offences Act 2003. It was high-time, he argued, for modern British society, including its law-makers, 'to face up to the reality of that sub-world of degradation and exploitation' that is implicated in prostitution, since

3 For more specific discussion of some of the recent trends in policing of prostitution, see also Matthews (2005); and for a European comparative perspective, see Kilvington, Day and Ward (2001).

'from antisocial behaviour to mafia-style criminality, communities are bedevilled by this terrible trade.' Similarly, in his preface to the subsequent *Paying the Price* consultation, Blunkett asserted unequivocally that 'prostitution can have devastating consequences for the individuals involved', because as a practice it includes, amongst other things, 'the abuse of children and the serious exploitation of adults' (Home Office 2004, 5).

Whatever the basis for this distinctive treatment in the UK context, however, it is clear that this policy level disinterest in the force underpinning sex trafficking activity does not always translate into practice. Indeed, in an arena in which, to date at least, official discretion and *ad hoc* provision of services have dominated, interviews conducted with those personnel charged with responding to victims indicate a tendency to construct a hierarchy of exploitation in accordance with the levels of coercion or deception that preceded the commercial sexual activity (see Munro 2005a, 2006; and O'Connell Davidson 2006).[4] This tendency has been criticised by some for its 'victim-blaming' connotations, and for failing to properly appreciate the complex background conditions that render apparent consent dubious. However, others have welcomed this recognition of the possibility that some women may choose to sell sex, even where they do not make this choice from an unconstrained range of options and even though they may be left vulnerable by virtue of the conditions (of stigma, illegality, patriarchy, or poverty) under which they make such transactions. What's more, it has been argued that this approach, in bringing responses to sex trafficking in line with those adopted in trafficking for labour provision, also has the benefit of avoiding the problematic tendency to resort to moral disapprobation in the context of prostitution (or of the sex industry more broadly).

Diverting Traffic? Reflecting on the Role of Exploitation

While claims to exploitation have increasingly permeated national and international anti-trafficking laws, policies and discourse, it is apparent, then, that different understandings of what this entails are being deployed within these frameworks (at least at the level of policy) as between its sexual and labour variants. There is little doubt that this divergence can be attributed, in large measure, to the influence of the highly moralised and politicised contexts in which these claims operate. But it is submitted here that a lack of theoretical clarity regarding the concept of exploitation itself has also played a key role in enabling and perpetuating this divergence, and in permitting thereby a number of crucial (and difficult) questions to be left unaddressed. Against this backdrop, discussion in this section will reflect on the nature of the exploitation that may be involved in contemporary people trafficking activity, and will examine its implications for the development of a more coherent legal response.

---

4 This research was conducted with the support of a Nuffield Foundation Grant (ref. SGS/00745/G).

In the context of people trafficking, charges of exploitation could be targeted at either (or indeed both) 'wrongful use' or 'disparity of value' forms. Not only may a trafficked person find herself providing services for limited (or, in some cases, no) remuneration whilst third party 'employers' generate considerable financial profit, but she may be treated by those persons in ways that reduce her dignity, render her a commodity to be bought and sold, or instrumentalise her labour or sex in the service of their own gratification. At the same time, though, it is clear that in this, as no doubt in many other social contexts, these two forms of exploitation may inter-connect, overlap, support and even conflict with one another in various ways. Distinguishing the conditions under which our everyday (and often morally unproblematic) utilisation of others is wrongful demands identification of a threshold beyond which it escalates into something inhuman or degrading. While on the face of it, this invokes 'wrongful use' criteria, in the trafficking context, establishing this threshold may also require reliance on 'disparity of value' considerations that mark the point for condemnation wherever there is an intolerable gulf between value and reward. Equally, though, in a context in which – Marxist analysis of capitalist labour relations aside – there are clearly many vulnerable workers who are compelled by the instruction of those with power over them to work longer hours than they would like to, under worse conditions than they would hope for and for less pay than they deserve, claims that at first sight appear to rely solely on 'disparity of value' considerations will often also depend on a threshold claim to 'wrongful use', which marks the transition from tolerable acts of profiteering to intolerable exploitation at the point at which the worker is treated solely as an instrument to be exhausted in the name of maximisation.

At the heart of the exploitation claims that animate anti-trafficking discourse, then, there is a complex, and sometimes even circular, relationship between these different forms of its manifestation. This in itself is not necessarily problematic but the current failure of laws and policies in the trafficking context to be clear-sighted and conscious regarding the nature and remit of the exploitation claims that they invoke does raise concern. International documents that purport to define people trafficking have too often obfuscated their position on key debates over the relevance of harm and consent by embracing the concept of exploitation in all its vagueness. The UN Protocol, for example, while insisting that 'the consent of the victim of trafficking in persons to the intended exploitation shall be irrelevant' goes on to stipulate that this will only be the case where compliance is secured as a consequence of threat, coercion, fraud, deception, abuse of power, abuse of vulnerability, or the provision of payments or benefits to a controlling third party. Thus, in cases where consent is given because of familial pressures, emotional attachment to a 'boyfriend' figure, or lack of employment opportunity in the country of origin, it may remain operative, relegating the offence from trafficking to smuggling and obviating the need to provide victim support. In this context, it is no surprise to find – as research has done – that national legislators, official stakeholders and invested campaigners have interpreted the provisions in line with their own (polarised and politicised) agendas, privileging victims who can prove their coercion and discrediting those who cannot.

Of course, in the specific context of sex trafficking, an additional and arguably free-standing claim to wrongful use exploitation might also be lodged, under which a clear stance on the role of consent and harm has been taken. Drawing on the claim that any selling of sex, even under preferential value conditions, constitutes an exploitative act, this abolitionist sentiment has attracted considerable support from a range of diverse groups and may provide an (at least partial) explanation for the disparate treatment of sexual and labour trafficking at policy level. In this light, the rejection of the need to establish harm or coercion in the context of sex (cf. labour) trafficking emerges less as a recognition that exploitation can occur in their absence, and more as a presumption that they exist wherever there is prostitution. But this approach can also be seen to be problematic. The relationship between using a person as a means and failing to respect her personhood is not always straightforward; and, as we have seen, a closer inspection of the individual context is always required to assess whether the use is wrongful in any relevant sense. Too often, however, this kind of analysis has been jettisoned in favour of blanket assertions of coercion and harm in the act of prostitution itself, even in a context in which many have countered that the exact nature of the harm inherent in prostitution is elusive (see Bainham and Brooks-Gordon 2004; Lacey 2001; Dempsey 2005; Marhsall 1999), and in which empirical work with women trafficked for sexual purposes indicates divergent levels of agency, as well as varied experiences of, and conditions for, the selling of sex.

It is important to be clear here – none of this is intended to deny, necessarily, that coercion and harm are endemic in prostitution. It is, however, to insist that this needs to be examined and established, rather than simply posited, in the exploitation claims that underpin anti-trafficking initiatives. At the same time, it is to emphasise that even if it emerges that there is both consent and evidence of mutual advantage in some commercial sex transactions, this does not in itself remove the possibility that there is also exploitation, and nor does it necessarily obviate the need to intervene. After all, the differences that exist between overall harmful and overall harmless transactions, and between giving consent under conditions of constraint and under conditions of full freedom, need not be ignored, even in an account of exploitation that denies their definitional necessity. To the contrary, these considerations may be crucial in assessing the 'moral weight' of the exploitation, which will often, in turn, have an important bearing on its 'moral force' – that is, the upshots or reasons for action that the exploitation gives rise to (Wertheimer 1996, 28).

Thus, a finding of exploitation does not, as is often presumed, mark the end of the matter but represents the starting point for new debate about how we ought, legally and morally, to respond. This recognition, though often absent from policy debates around prostitution (and by extension, sex trafficking), is important for a number of reasons. For one thing, it offers a more explicit theoretical grounding for drawing out and evaluating some of the arguments that inform abolitionist sentiment. While some commentators have argued that exploitation in its pure, un-occluded form, without the moral amplification generated by our disapproval of harm or coercion *per se*, constitutes a 'free-floating evil' that cannot be prohibited in a liberal society without resort to dubious moralist or perfectionist principles (Feinberg 1990, 176), others have entertained the possibility that a case for prohibition may be found in a strategic argument that focuses on protecting the interests, not of the participants themselves, but rather of those third parties who can establish a legitimate interest in preventing the transactions. This is important in the context of prostitution, since here – as in pornography and commercial surrogacy – the argument has often been made that even if the transactions in question are not harmful, all things considered, for the women immediately involved, they nonetheless have a negative impact on the social standing of women as a collective, which has real and damaging consequences for all.

There can be little doubt that such arguments represent a significant departure from the normal basis on which we justify intervention in exploitative arrangements – after all, since the transacting party's interests are not necessarily at risk here, intervention is 'justified not because it helps the exploited party but in spite of the loss to the exploited party that such prohibition imposes' (Wertheimer 1996, 309). In reality, then, this approach entails sacrifice on the part of those who, often living in conditions that render unfair exchanges rational, would benefit from the arrangement, in the interests of those who are already better off (Wertheimer 1996, 120–21). While these harsh realities have rendered this approach unpopular with many commentators and campaigners, fresh consideration of the complex issues around exploitation, harm and consent may suggest that such strategic intervention, while requiring careful measurement and consideration, is not necessarily in itself illiberal (Munro 2007).

At the same time, though, this kind of consideration can also offer an alternative line of argument to those who wish to defend decriminalisation of the sex industry: an argument which depends not on an oppositional denial of the existence of exploitation but rather on emphasising that such exploitation (which need not entail harm or coercion and which can be situated on a spectrum with mundane labour relations in non-sex industries) does not always entail or justify prohibition. The law, as many of us know too well, is a notoriously blunt instrument and legal interventions sometimes emerge as counter-productive in their effects, even when they are devised out of the best of motives. In a context in which it has been argued that previous heavy-handed criminal law interventions into prostitution have had negative effects of dispersal, stigma and increased vulnerability, it is by no means clear that, even if sex work does entail exploitation, the fact of this alone justifies the law's imposition.

This is not to suggest that the law should stand aside as people are trafficked into conditions in which they experience considerable hardships. It is, however, to question the analytical and justificatory role that the concept of exploitation, un-occluded by aggravating but contestable concepts of harm or coercion, is currently performing in contemporary anti-trafficking policies that set it centre stage. It is also to lament the failure of those who have devised such policies, at both international and national level, to interrogate the core concept of exploitation, to crystallise the basis on which we condemn it, and to examine critically, and without unreflective moralism or paternalism, the links between sex, work and sex work in this context.

Conclusion

It is clear that the claim that trafficking involves the exploitation of its victims is one that has captured the political and moral imagination. In its favour, the concept of exploitation leaves scope for identifying harms that may not be so easily captured by pre-existing categories and offers the potential to think through more fully the relationship between sex trafficking and its labour variant. At the same time, though, it is clear that invoking a claim to exploitation in itself does little to avoid difficult questions about what constitutes wrongful objectification of another, about what conditions of work and levels of reward are intolerable, about what relevance we afford to the existence of coercion or harm, and about how we respond to instances of exploitation in a world in which global and gender power imbalances generate personal vulnerabilities and then limit the opportunities for alternative forms of repair.

The fact that posing these questions in the context of people trafficking generates complex and sometimes circular responses is not in itself necessarily problematic. But without greater elucidation, it does threaten to cloud our vision both of the exact nature of the problem of exploitation and of the source of our moral condemnation thereof. As Hill reminds us, one of the upshots of using exploitation to 'fill the vague conceptual gap between the pre-analytic intuition that there is something wrong with a bargain and the post-analytic determination as to what this something wrong is, exactly' is that the concept assumes 'the role of an omnibus moral catch-all category, a term with as many meanings as those who use it, and which is, precisely for that reason, a most mercurial charge to which to respond' (Hill 1994, 699). Being clear-sighted on these issues is important, then, not just in terms of analytical clarity but also in terms of practical consequences. After all, as a number of commentators have suggested, the current socio-political climate is one in which there is a complex engagement between, on the one hand, the imperatives of expansion, human rights and production, and, on the other, the spectre of globalisation, organised crime, uncontrolled migration and the expansion of vice. Against this backdrop, the malleability of the concept of exploitation presents the opportunity for anti-trafficking commitments to be interpreted narrowly by destination states, reducing the categories that qualify for victim status (and the support and protection this entails) through reliance on criteria of coercion and harm, and perpetuating the current prioritisation of sex trafficking over its equally significant labour counterpart.

Susan Marks has recently argued that, although exploitation as a concept is clearly associated with ideas that have a long history in international law – including slavery, forced labour and the denial of decent working conditions – it has been invoked with unease in the context of labour trafficking, suggesting a perception that 'it is too political, or too divisive, or simply too embarrassing'. This can be contrasted against its more comfortable and uncritical deployment in the context of sex trafficking within which traces of earlier panics about 'white slavery' and prostitution have placed 'morality at the centre of what is at stake' (Marks 2008). It is only by opening up the concept of exploitation to the kind of interrogation initiated here that the bases for this distinctive treatment can be uncovered and tested. On the one hand, this process might yield a stronger basis for the assertion that there is something unique, and uniquely problematic, in trafficking for sexual purposes. On the other hand, it might expose the extent to which differential responses are grounded primarily in squeamish unease at the commodification of sex or bewilderment at the blurring lines between wage labour and servitude. Either way, it seems that – particularly in a context in which legislative responses too often re-affirm this trafficking hierarchy whilst simultaneously purporting to recognise no substantive difference – this project must be undertaken, and must be undertaken as a priority.

References

Anderson, B. (2000), *Doing the Dirty Work? The Global Politics of Domestic Labour* (London: Zed Books).

Arneson, R. (1981), 'What's Wrong with Exploitation?', *Ethics* 91:2, 202–27.

Arneson, R. (2001), Entry in Lawrence Becker and Charlotte Becker (eds), *The Encyclopedia of Ethics* 2nd edn (New York: Garland).

Askola, H. (2007), *Legal Responses to Trafficking in Women for Sexual Exploitation in the European Union* (Oxford: Hart Publishing).

Bainham, A. and B. Brooks-Gordon (2004), 'Reforming the Law on Sexual Offences' in B. Brooks-Gordon et al. (eds), *Sexuality Repositioned: Diversity and the Law* (Oxford: Hart Publishing), 261–96.

Bales, K. (1999), *Disposable People: New Slavery in the Global Economy* (Berkeley, CA: University of California Press).

Brooks-Gordon, B. (2005), 'Clients and Commercial Sex: Reflections on Paying the Price', *Criminal Law Review*, 425–43.

Buchanan, A. (1979), 'Exploitation, Alienation and Injustice', *Canadian Journal of Philosophy* 9, 121–39.

Buchanan, A. (1985), *Ethics, Efficiency and the Market* (Totowa, NJ: Rowman and Allanheld).

Corrigan, K. (2001), 'Putting the Brakes on the Global Trafficking of Women for the Sex Trade: An Analysis of Existing Regulatory Regimes to Stop the Flow of Traffic', *Fordham International Law Journal* 25, 151–214.

Dempsey, M. (2005), 'Rethinking Wolfenden: Prostitute Use, Criminal Law and Remote Harm', *Criminal Law Review*, 444–55.

Dowling, S. et al. (2007), *Trafficking for the Purposes of Labour Exploitation: A Literature Review*, Home Office Report 10/07 (London: Home Office).

Feinberg, J. (1990), *Harmless Wrongdoing* (Oxford: Oxford University Press).

Hauber, L. (1998), 'The Trafficking in Women for Prostitution: A Growing Problem Within the European Union', *Boston College International and Comparative Law Review* 21, 183–99.

Hill, J.L. (1994), 'Exploitation', *Cornell Law Review* 79, 631–99.

Home Office (2004), *Paying the Price: A Consultation Paper on Prostitution* (London: HMSO).

IOM (2002), *New Challenges for Migration Policy in Central and Eastern Europe* (Geneva: IOM).

IOM (2005), *World Migration 2005: Costs and Benefits of International Migration* (Geneva: IOM).
Kantola, J. and J. Squires (2004), 'Discourses Surrounding Prostitution Policies in the UK', *European Journal of Women's Studies* 11:1, 77–101.
Kelly, L. (2002), *Journeys of Jeopardy: A Review of Research on Trafficking in Women and Children in Europe* (Geneva: IOM).
Kilvington, J., S. Day and H. Ward (2001), 'Prostitution Policy in Europe: A Time of Change?', *Feminist Review* 67, 78–93.
Lacey, N. (2001), 'Beset by Boundaries: The Home Office Review of Sex Offences', *Criminal Law Review* 3–14.
Levine, A. (1988), *Arguing for Socialism* (London: Verso).
Marks, S. (2008), 'Exploitation as an International Legal Concept' in Susan Marks (ed.), *International Law on the Left: Re-examining Marxist Legacies* (Cambridge: Cambridge University Press), 281–308.
Marshall, S. (1999), 'Bodyshopping: The Case of Prostitution', *Journal of Applied Philosophy* 16:2, 139–50.
Matthews, R. (2005), 'Policing Prostitution: Ten Years On', *British Journal of Criminology* 45:6, 877–95.
Mayer, R. (2002), 'A Walzerian Theory of Exploitation', *Polity* 34:3, 337–54.
Miller, D. (1987), 'Exploitation in the Market' in Andrew Reeve (ed.), *Modern Theories of Exploitation* (London: Sage), 149–65.
Moore, B. (1973), *Reflections on the Causes of Human Misery* (Boston, MA: Beacon Press).
Munro, V. (2005a), 'A Tale of Two Servitudes: Defining and Implementing a Response to Trafficking in Women for Prostitution in the UK and Australia', *Social and Legal Studies* 14:1, 91–114.
Munro, V. (2005b), 'Concerning Consent: Standards of Permissibility in Sexual Relations', *Oxford Journal of Legal Studies* 25:2, 335–52.
Munro, V. (2006), 'Stopping Traffic? A Comparative Study of Responses to the Trafficking in Women for Prostitution', *British Journal of Criminology* 46:2, 318–33.
Munro, V. (2007), 'Dev'l-in Disguise? Harm, Privacy and the Sexual Offences Act 2003' in V. Munro and C. Stychin (eds), *Sexuality and the Law: Feminist Engagements* (London: Routledge-Cavendish), 1–18.
Munzer, S. (1990), *A Theory of Property* (Cambridge: Cambridge University Press).
O'Connell Davidson, J. (2006), 'Will the Real Sex Slave Please Stand Up?', *Feminist Review* 83, 4–22.
Reiman, J. (1987), 'Exploitation, Force and the Moral Assessment of Capitalism: Thoughts on Roemer and Cohen', *Philosophy and Public Affairs* 16: 3–41.
Roemer, J. (1985), 'Should Marxists Be Interested in Exploitation?', *Philosophy and Public Affairs* 14:1, 30–65.
Toepfer, S. and B. Wells (1994), 'The Worldwide Market for Sex: A Review of International and Regional Legal Prohibitions Regarding Trafficking in Women', *Michigan Journal of Gender and Law* 2, 83–128.

Tormey, J. (1974), 'Exploitation, Oppression and Self-Sacrifice', *Philosophical Forum* 5, 206–21.

UN (2006), *Trafficking in Persons: Global Patterns* (New York: UN Office of Drugs and Crime), available at <http://www.undoc.org>.

Wertheimer, A. (1996), *Exploitation* (Princeton, NJ: Princeton University Press).

Wertheimer, A. (1997), 'Remarks on Coercion and Exploitation', *Denver University Law Review* 74:4, 879–906.

Wilkinson, S. (2003), *Bodies for Sale: Ethics and Exploitation in the Human Body Trade* (London: Routledge).

Wolff, J. (1999), 'Marx and Exploitation', *Journal of Ethics* 3, 105–20.

Chapter 6

Putting Trafficking on the Map: The Geography of Feminist Complicity

Sharron A. FitzGerald[1]

> All the people think that victim of trafficking is like some stupid girl from some small town. But mostly it is a very strong womens [sic] with a high education and the women decide to immigrate, to go to another country for a job, for a better economical situation for the future.[2]

Processes of globalisation, identified by increased flows of capital and people as 'global citizens', have transformed the globe. The driving force behind such transformation is the ideology of neoliberalism, which operates on the principles of equality and freedom for all through 'a single framework of global governance' in a so-called 'borderless world' (Ohmae 1991, xii–xiii). Movement has always been a key force for sociospatial organisation. But what sets this most recent phase apart is the scope of its geographical scales that range from the body to the nation state and beyond. During this time of international reorganisation, geopolitical disputes about the integrity of nation states and adjacent territories triggered the fall of the Berlin Wall, the collapse of the Soviet Union and the end of the Cold War. One of the key features of the post-Cold War era has been the diffusion of economic and political migrants from Soviet Bloc countries into the European Union (EU). More recently, as developing nations attempt to integrate and compete in the global economy, persistent inequalities force migrants from Africa and Asia to move in search of better opportunities (Castles and Miller 2004). Thus, in the twenty-first century, the sceptre of 'irregular' migrants at the borders of 'Fortress Europe' has led to the increased politicisation of EU immigration law and border control. Many Europeans perceive that globalisation challenges the authority of the nation state to determine domestic law and social policy (Balibar 2004). If, as Pred argued, such perceived threats to the future of European sovereignty are 'apt to be culturally and politically reworked as expressions of racism' (Pred 2000, 10), then, it could be argued that this racism is located in particular sociospatial relationships expressed in

1 I am grateful to Vanessa Munro, Marina Della Giusta and Andreas Philippopoulos-Mihalopoulos for their comments on an earlier draft of this chapter, and to Rolf Laber for his support through this process.

2 Anna Sverta is a former Latvian law student and a trafficked migrant. I took this quotation from an interview she gave in a documentary on human trafficking in the Netherlands, which featured on the BBC World Service as part the 'Global Perspectives: A World of Crime' in May 2006. I maintain its original orthography.

the European perception of a 'lack of social control of subjects who are not "in place"' (Stychin 2003, 98). It is the peculiarities of the state's production of knowledge of these migrant populations as 'out of place' in the EU that forms the backdrop of the discussion that follows.

Processes of globalisation have also produced a new kind of migrant. These migrants are young women and girls who hail primarily from the former Soviet Union and the developing world (Sassen 2002). Women enter migration circuits by responding to the Western demand for cheap labour. They also cite political and economic marginalisation, displacement and gender inequality 'at home' as reasons to move 'here'. Consequently, female migrants now form over half of the world's migrant population (Zlotnik 2003). Feminist research on the scale of female migration patterns adds complexity to our understanding of this phenomenon revealing that while most women move out of necessity, some move out of a desire to experience the world (Jordan 2002; Agustín 2005).

Nevertheless, in the post-9/11 era, stricter EU immigration law and social policy have curtailed possibilities for women to migrate legally to the West. The increased regulation of EU borders by domestic and supranational operations, such as Frontex (the EU border control unit based in Warsaw, Poland), means that the number of organised criminal gangs trafficking human beings into EU territory has proliferated. Although the precise number of trafficked migrants continues to elude authorities, the United Nations Office on Drugs and Crime (UNODC) estimates that organised criminals traffic hundreds of thousands if not several millions of men, women and children annually to the West. The UN claims that a disproportionate number of those trafficked are young women and girls who will potentially end up in the sex industry (UNODC 2006). Statements such as these are problematic on three counts. Firstly, they represent organised crime gangs as the only source of human trafficking. Secondly, it perpetuates the gendered myth that trafficking only affects women. Finally, it eschews the West's culpability in the conditions from which many migrants flee and ignores other forms of labour exploitation such as those experienced by agricultural or temporary migrant workers.

Thus, in the first decade of the twenty-first century the phenomenon of trafficking highlights a number of cross-cutting legal, political, socioeconomic and moral questions. This chapter focuses on feminist interventions on trafficking and the attendant issues of prostitution. Specifically, it analyses how the anti-prostitution Coalition Against Trafficking in Women (CATW), and its affiliate the European Women's Lobby (EWL), and the pro-sex-worker lobby the Global Alliance Against Trafficking in Women (GAATW) have influenced the state production of knowledge of female trafficked migrants in EU immigration law and border control. The chapter begins by outlining international anti-trafficking legislation namely, the United Nations (UN) Optional Protocol to Prevent, Suppress and Punish Trafficking in Persons, especially Women and Children (The Palermo Protocol) and two binding EU legal instruments on trafficking – the 2002 Framework Decision (and the attendant directive on temporary residence permits) and the 2004 The Council of Europe Convention on Action against Trafficking in Human Beings.

Secondly, the chapter problematises polarised feminist groups' use of idioms such as the 'global sisterhood' and 'trafficking as modern day slavery' as a form of identity politics. In the context of this discussion, I will assert that such discursive strategies both structure and define the material and immaterial spaces in which the debate occurs. What is of particular interest and will constitute the remainder of this section is how these discursive strategies have gained political purchase among female Members of the European Parliament (MEPs). Finally, in order to understand how feminist rhetoric infiltrates the production of knowledge about female trafficked migrants at the national level, I will interrogate two UK Home Office documents, namely the 2002 White Paper, *Secure Border, Safe Haven* and the 2006 Consultation Paper, *Tackling Human Trafficking: Consultation on Proposals for a UK Action Plan.*

From the outset, I wish to make it clear that it is not my intention to deny that human trafficking is exploitative. The question of *why* this is the case has been analysed by skilled researchers and needs no further elaboration here (Barry 1995; Hughes 2000; Kelly 2005; see also Munro in the previous chapter of this collection). My primary aim is to question *how* feminists and state parties manipulate respectively the *location* of the female trafficked migrant as a 'victim' of organised immigration crime into issues of higher political importance. To develop this argument, I draw on the theoretical insights provided by Michel Foucault's 'analytics of power' and link these to methodologies in my home discipline, namely feminist cultural geography. Situating my discussion in a methodology sensitive to the production of subjectivity at a variety of spatial scales and through multiple and simultaneous spatial configurations, I hope to move the parameters of the debate forward. Before proceeding, it will be useful to outline recent international legal interventions in prostitution and trafficking.

Situating the Debate: The Spatiality of Law

In December 2001, the UN released for ratification its two optional Protocols to supplement its Convention against Transnational Organised Crime. The first of these is the Palermo Protocol.[3] The second is the Protocol against the Smuggling of Migrants by Land, Sea and Air. During the drafting of the Palermo Protocol, the UN claimed that it wanted to break the conceptual link between trafficking and prostitution. Consequently, various stakeholders, including polarised feminist groups, lobbied the UN for definitional clarity on what constituted 'forced' or 'voluntary' prostitution and urged it to differentiate between human smuggling and trafficking. This is important because if state parties determine that a migrant consents to enter another country illegally, then they have been smuggled and not trafficked, and are thereby liable to immediate deportation.

3 Article 3(a) of the Protocol to prevent and suppress trafficking states: '"Trafficking in persons" shall mean the recruitment, transportation, transfer, harbouring or receipt of persons, by means of the threat or use of force or other forms of coercion, of abduction, of fraud of deception, of the abuse of power or of a position of vulnerability or of the giving or receiving of payments or benefits to achieve the consent of a person having control over another person, for the purpose of exploitation. Exploitation shall include, at a minimum, the exploitation of the prostitution of others or other forms of sexual exploitation, forced labour or services, slavery or practices similar to slavery, servitude or the removal of organs.'

Yet, an analysis of the Palermo Protocol reveals that definitional ambiguity surrounding migrants' initial 'consent' to be transported from one country to another continues to impede the Protocol's effectiveness as an anti-trafficking measure. Commentators remark that Article (3a) of the Palermo Protocol retains a 'special relationship' between trafficking and prostitution (Sullivan 2003). Ambiguity such as this provides states with ample legal and moral space to impose a narrow interpretation of consent, which in turn affects states' conception of their obligations to trafficked migrants, for example in the form of social advice and assistance (Munro 2005). As Askola reminds us, the continued ambiguity surrounding trafficking 'masks the reality in which the experience of exploitation resides within a rather more complex range of coercion and choice' (Askola 2007, 206). As will be discussed below, migrants' consent to 'exploitation' is relative to their particular circumstances. However, as discussed by Munro in Chapter 5 of this volume, and explored here at a later stage, the outcome of exploitative relationships can sometimes have beneficial net results. International anti-trafficking instruments and state parties rarely include this understanding. While the UN attempted to find consensus on the trafficking debate, a parallel debate evolved among EU member states. Extending this discussion, the next section addresses anti-trafficking legislation in the EU.

European Legal Spaces

International differences between EU member states combined with different definitions of trafficking and cultural responses to prostitution made the task of producing effective anti-trafficking legislation difficult. The EU Commission, which is responsible for drafting and enforcing EU legislation, tended to view trafficking as a law and order problem. It emphasised the apprehension and prosecution of traffickers and organised crime gangs, calling for increased cooperation on law enforcement among member states. Conversely, the Council of Europe, with its traditional concern for human rights, adopted a more 'victim centred' approach to trafficking. Taking the Council's lead in 2002, the Commission re-evaluated its position on trafficking under the 'Brussels Declaration', which combines the needs of victims of trafficking with the need to combat crime. It is interesting to note how the Commission maintained its focus on the regulation of specific populations through a directive on temporary and conditional residence visas for victims of trafficking and smuggling. These legal instruments are important because, unlike earlier initiatives, they required member states to modify their law and social policy on trafficking by a specific deadline, namely 1 August 2002. Finally, in 2003, the Commission convened an Experts Group on trafficking in human beings. Recommendations from the Experts Group structured The Council of Europe Convention on Action against Trafficking in Human Beings on 3 May 2005. The EU opened the Convention for signature in Warsaw on 16 May 2005, giving member states until August 2006 to comply.

A cross section of EU domestic anti-trafficking responses reveals that, while most member states have signed and ratified international anti-trafficking Protocols and Conventions, this does not correlate into justice once trafficked migrants enter European criminal justice systems. Despite their obligations under the EU Convention and the UN Palermo Protocol, French, German, Dutch and UK laws do not deal with trafficking via a dedicated statute but through adaptation and/or retention of pre-existing immigration and criminal law; and tend to focus on traffickers rather than on immigrants themselves. For example, prostitution is legal in France, Germany and the Netherlands but procurement of sexual services such as trafficking for the sex industry is not. While prostitution is not illegal in the UK, the 'condemnation of "prostitution as work" model continues to inform sexual offences provision' (Munro 2005, 103). This fundamental disapproval of all forms of sex work permeates the UK response to trafficking, but it has achieved its fullest form in the EU in Swedish law, where a zero tolerance policy on prostitution and human trafficking operates.

Although all EU member states condemn human trafficking as coerced sexual exploitation, there is evidence to suggest that state parties often use the 'problem' of trafficking and the attendant issue of prostitution to legitimise the regulation of the movement of specific populations through stricter laws on immigration, security and border control. To exemplify, researchers indicate that during the 2002 French presidential elections, the debate on transnational prostitution as a threat to public safety instigated by the then Minister of the Interior, Nicolas Sarkozy, became a ruse by a right-wing government to address the immigration issue as a law and order and national security issue (Allwood 2004, and Chapter 4 of this volume; Ticktin 2005). Extending this discussion, in later sections of this chapter I argue that EU member states' attempts to regulate non-Western female mobility by focusing on their so called 'exploitation' represents a racialised class and gender counter-narrative to neoliberalism, global citizenship and the narrative of a borderless world. In order to construct the theoretical framework, from which I will examine how this operates, I turn to the work of Michel Foucault.

The Spatiality of Power Relations

Foucault's theorisation on the sociospatial construction of knowledge and power relations is hardly new. Yet his concern with the construction of the 'social body' as a site for the regulation of specific populations and subjectivities has found new expression in geographical work that analyses the important role that racialised class, gender and sexual categories play in Eurocentric visions of the nation state (Foucault 1980, 95). In *The History of Sexuality, Volume 1*, Foucault argued that relations of power are 'matrices of transformations' (Foucault 1980, 99) and that the individual's experience of domination is an 'effect' of power rather than proceeding 'from a specific source of power' (Foucault 1980, 93). The pivotal point in Foucault's 'analytics of power relations' is that they are a 'complex reciprocal relationship' (Foucault 1980, 127) requiring us to understand the importance of the question of *who* exercises power simultaneously with *how* groups or individuals deploy it.

Spatialising Foucault

Foucault influenced feminist geographers' theorisations on how the individual's experiences of space are an effect of mobile power relations (McDowell and Sharpe 1999). Geographers broadly adhere to the understanding that 'space is created out of the vast … networks of relations at every scale from the global to the local. What makes a particular view of these social relations specifically spatial is their simultaneity' (Massey 1992, 80–81). Thus, contemporary feminist cultural geography concentrates on the interconnected processes and power relations that produce female subjectivity across a variety of spaces and at a number of scales. These spatial relationships determine whose bodies belong where, how different groups' subjective experiences of spatial relations vary according to context and what sorts of exclusionary and disciplining techniques are applied to specific bodies (Rose 1993; McDowell 1999; Bondi et al. 2002). Within this rubric, concepts such as the 'politics of location' and 'situated knowledge' conceive that positioned actors working in/between all kinds of locations always produce specific interpretations of events as an effect of shifting and negotiated power relations.

The negotiated nature of power relations and identities in those relationships leads me to a second interconnected theme, namely the geographical concern with the construction of spatial difference and how it coincides with the organisation of specific political agendas from the local to the global. Most existing geographical knowledge about the state and the scale of its physical and ideological borders is masculinist, and it eclipses racialised class and gender processes that are 'taking place in other sites' (Nagar et al. 2002, 260). Questions of mobility and migrant subjectivity prompted certain scholars to challenge the notion that spatial concepts such as scale spatially fixed entities (Walton-Roberts 2004). In the context of human trafficking, scale as an organising principle illustrates how dominant groups and institutions define the parameters of the debate.

My reasons for rehearsing these arguments here is that while geographers have been at the forefront of research on questions of the sociospatial production of subjectivity, knowledge, migration and territoriality, there is a lack of theoretical attention from a geographical perspective given to the regulation of the female trafficked migrant and the attendant issue of prostitution. Hubbard (1999) reminds us that as a rule, geographers have tended to avoid sustained critical explorations of prostitution. Where geographers make mention of prostitution, it tends to focus on either the economic, criminal and spatial distribution of prostitution in Western cities (Henderson 1999; Kumar 2005) or the regulation of sexuality and the politics of empire (Howell 2004; Phillips 2006). Recently, geographers have begun to examine trafficking in children from West Africa (Bass 2004; Robson 2005; Manzo 2005). Nevertheless, a spatially sensitive approach applies well to the material and immaterial spaces where state parties organise knowledge of the female trafficked migrant. Such an approach will add to feminist geographical and socio-legal research on trafficking by focusing on how trafficking operates at other crucial scales of analysis. The section that follows explores how Western feminists regulate the material and immaterial spaces of their political agendas on trafficking and prostitution through a strict adherence to geospecific identity politics. What is of particular interest to me is how feminists define the parameters of these ideological spaces against 'Other' interpretations. Therefore, in the following section I interrogate two interconnected tropes that permeate feminist and, in turn, state initiatives on human trafficking and sex work, namely: 1) the global sisterhood and 2) female trafficked migrants as modern day sex slaves.

The Topography of Trafficking

The Global Sisterhood

Since the 1970s, feminists have articulated their concerns about the globalising sex industry due in part to improved transportation and communication networks between the West and the developing world. Radical feminists in the anti-prostitution CATW emphasised the patriarchal roots of social dominance of women by men where time/space compression facilitated Western male consumers' exploitation of poor women for their sexual services (Barry 1979).[4] In light of these concerns, the anti-prostitution lobby asserted that trafficking is evidence of continued patriarchy which is most 'fully revealed in prostitution' (Barry 1995, 23). In this account, universal class domination of the 'sisterhood' by men 'is so pervasive that it actually invokes consent' (Barry 1995, 23–4). Thus, any discussion of women's informed consent to sex work under these conditions is mute (Enloe 1989; Raymond 1998). This standpoint dominated the political landscape on prostitution and trafficking until the mid 1990s when alternative voices such as the pro-sex-worker GAATW lobby emerged. The GAATW's platform revolves around the argument that the state must recognise the 'right' of adults who work as prostitutes of their own volition, and differentiate between these 'workers' and those who have been deceived or trafficked under duress (Sullivan 2003). The feminist move to reclaim the spaces of authority on human trafficking and the attendant issue of prostitution corresponds to an 'instrument of cartography' (Bell 1995, 148) that has the power to determine where and what constitutes appropriate feminist understandings of these issues.

An examination of policy statements by the anti-prostitution CATW/EWL reveals the importance of the concept of the 'global sisterhood' as an organisational tool used by the anti-prostitution lobby to define the scale of its response to trafficking. For example, 'factors that impel women to take the risk of illegal migration are … the resurgence of traditional discriminatory practices against women' (O'Connor and Healy 2006, 6). The CATW/EWL argue that trafficking is a vehicle for 'first world' domination disproportionately victimising 'third world' women (Ekberg 2002). Consequently, the CATW/EWL is grounded in the belief that any woman who has been trafficked is a victim of human rights violations (Barry 1995; Ekberg 2002). To give an example: 'legitimizing prostitution will thwart efforts towards reciprocal, equal, just and empowering relationships between women and men … and the individual and collective rights of women will be eroded' (O'Connor and Healy 2006, 26). This analysis permits the CATW/EWL to assert: 'we cannot dissociate prostitution from other forms of male violence against women … in all countries around the world' (O'Connor and Healy 2006, 27). Gender ideology based on the idiom of the universal female 'victim' of patriarchy understands, regulates and defines a geospecific cultural system that declares that prostitution and, by association, trafficking 'is always … degrading and damaging to women' (Anderson and O'Connell Davidson 2002, 8).

---

4 Time/space compression is a term used to describe processes that seem to accelerate the experience of time and reduce the significance of spatial distance during a given historical moment (Harvey 1989).

This understanding does not permit any consideration of the will or consent of the female trafficked migrant. Radical feminist ideology upholds that no woman would genuinely consent to engaging in prostitution when presented with an alternative (Wijers 2001). Fundamentally, the CATW/EWL positions itself as a force against those 'who promote the alleged "right to prostitute" and romanticises prostitution as "sex work," in essence defending the vested interests of the sex industry' (O'Connor and Healy 2006, 3). In this context, the anti-prostitution lobby's use of the location of the female trafficked migrant outlines the boundaries of representation within their feminist identity politics by defining the discursive formations in which appropriate female subjectivity may be grounded and the specific sites of its enforcement.

Despite the fact that the pro-sex-worker GAATW makes it clear that the link between trafficking and prostitution is socially and politically constructed, a comparison between the pro- and anti-prostitution lobbies also highlights how the pro-sex-worker lobby also deploys the ideology of the 'global sisterhood' to further its agenda. This occurs in the significance they place on the need to eliminate violence against all women as a causal factor of trafficking in all its forms. Consider the following statement from the GAATW: 'the gendered nature of trafficking derives from the universal and historical presence of laws, policies and customs ... that justify ... the discriminatory treatment of women and girls' (GAATW 1999, 3). However, a closer examination of these proposals discloses a protectionist rather than an inclusive project that draws on colonial stereotypes of the silent female 'Other' to make its case. Fidelity to the image of the 'global sisterhood' in trafficking as a tool to ensure universal women's rights reveals itself as follows:

> The historical linkage of 'women and children' has proven problematic in multiple ways. Linkages often encompass the treatment of women as if they are children and denies women the rights attached to adulthood, such as the right to have control over one's own life and body (GAATW 1999, 4).

Thus, the GAATW identifies the 'problem' of violence against women as one of state interference in all women's right to autonomy (GAATW 2007, 13). What is more troubling here is the way the GAATW couches the argument about women's rights to autonomy and bodily integrity by reactivating a neo-colonial narrative with the female trafficked migrant a victim of uncivilised and patriarchal cultures that perennially subordinate her. Here again is evidence of the West's failure to acknowledge difference among women, which in this instance would also include varied understandings of the concept of exploitation.

Once again, feminist identity politics ideologically rescale the material and immaterial spaces of the female trafficked migrants' subjective experiences as reflecting those of the 'global sisterhood'. These assertions activate the notion that all women experience issues of human rights, sexuality, mobility and structural inequalities under capitalism and patriarchy equally (Kapur 2005, 5). This approach eschews the centrality of geographical locations, cultural and class differences to women's situated experiences. Furthermore, such a claim operates on a false reciprocity of values that assumes that all women share the same understanding of their 'vulnerability' or situation. The concept of the 'sisterhood' does not reflect the reality of the geographies of inequality that often act as both 'push' factors or impediments to female migration in the first instance. It thus seems misplaced to argue in terms of universality when difference continues to organise the geographic effects of globalisation and the 'rights' that may or may not flow from it. This leads me directly to a second principal representational space where the female trafficked migrant appears in feminist guidelines on prostitution, namely the female trafficked migrant as the modern day sex slave.

Discourses of Slavery

Feminist geographers are interested in how the individual's experiences of the state production of modalities of racialised class, gender and sexual subjectivity coincide with 'material, symbolic and discursive constructions of space' (McDowell 1996, 41). Such sociospatial processes are of significance in discussions of how Western feminists have claimed the right to name the female trafficked migrant as a 'victim' of twenty-first-century slavery. Judith Butler (1999) reminds us of the dangers of discourses that operate according to one understanding of gender. Postcolonial theorists echo this concern and ask that Western scholars theorise heterogeneity so that the complex relationships between men and women, as well as between women themselves, will emerge (Spivak 1992; Mohanty 2003). Yet an analysis of the range of feminist discourses on human trafficking and the attendant issue of sex work reveals how feminists rework the female trafficked migrant's subjective experience to reconfigure the scale of the issue as a form of slavery in the service of the 'global sisterhood'.

Feminist anti-prostitution debates invoke the emotive and politically charged landscape of the nineteenth-century slave trade:

> Regulating prostitution is often viewed … as progress. However, we must remember that past debates over race slavery advocated regulating rather than abolishing slavery … Unfortunately, we are today having the same debate over sexual slavery (CATW 2004, 9).

The discourse of trafficking as slavery redefines the moral scale of prostitution where abolitionists liken women to 'merchandise' in organised crime gangs who will enslave them (O'Connor and Healy 2006, 10). 'Globalization of the economy also means globalization of the sex slave trade and the sex industry' (O'Connor and Healy 2006, 24). As a result, 'once in prostitution a woman … is the shared property of any male who can pay the price for sex and her body' (O'Connor and Healy 2006, 18). Hence, female 'victims' of trafficking 'must be "rescued" or – if they are not willing to accept the identity of victim – be made aware of their oppression' (Wijers 2001, 302).

An analysis of pro-sex-worker GAATW's objectives on trafficking uncovers entrenched geospecific stereotypes 'of this contemporary form of slavery' that take spatial form in the bodies of female trafficked migrants (GAATW 2004, 1). This position gains purchase when lobbyists situate it in debates on 'forced' and 'voluntary' prostitution, where 'victims of trafficking are treated as objects or commodities' (GAATW 1999, 3). Discursive shifts, such as these, purposefully rescale the definition of trafficking in non-Western sex workers' experience as 'slavery-like conditions of exploitation' (GAATW 1999, 5). What is interesting here is how the pro-sex-worker strategies focus on the conditions of coercion, in which trafficking violates women's human rights. The organisation asserts: 'the core elements of trafficking are the presence of deception, coercion or debt bondage … the victim may have agreed to work in the sex industry but not to be in slavery-like conditions' (GAATW 1999, 5). The pro-sex-worker lobby is careful to define the scale of sex work as legitimate labour when Western sex workers engage in it. Western sex workers are autonomous individuals who are fully in charge of their bodies and understand the ways of the world (Murray 1998). But a calculated rescaling of the same labour retrieves a colonial paradigm of non-Western women as naïve and passive victims of their circumstances, whose ignorance makes them especially prone to ending up 'in a situation analogous to slavery' (GAATW 2007, 12).

In many ways, globalisation and time–space compression have produced a 'politics of connectivity' (Desforges et al. 2005, 444) among feminists, evident in their sense of social responsibility for the female 'Other' beyond national territory. While this development offers the potential for an alternative politics and 'social justice', I suggest that feminist politics on trafficking and prostitution indicate some pitfalls with this approach. While I accept that the idea of global connectivity is important, I am concerned about how feminists deploy this conceptual framework to reinforce their international interventions from the platform of universalism. Furthermore, it reinforces a hierarchy of womanhood buttressed through colonial stereotypes of non-Western women. This neo-colonialism places Western feminists at the centre of the spaces of authority to advocate for all 'Others'. Therefore, I argue that, despite their claims to internationalism and the politics of differences, certain feminist activists work within a regional framework that is geospecific in character.

This comes into sharp relief when we consider other scales of analysis, namely in the spaces of political representation in the European Parliament (EP) and its associated fora. The following section focuses on how the anti-prostitution lobby has found purchase among feminist Members of the European Parliament (MEPs). It begins by giving some examples of how feminists invoke the idioms of the 'global sisterhood' and trafficking as slavery. These discourses, I will argue, form the basis of international and politically sophisticated policy initiatives that shape the contours of public knowledge of non-Western women within broader debates on equality. The section then proceeds to a discussion of how feminists summon the geographical history of slavery to frame the 'problem' of the sex trade as a threat to all women.

European Fora

The Global Sisterhood

At the same time as the debate on prostitution and trafficking gained momentum in the international feminist movement, women working across the spectrum of EU institutions organised around the same issues. During the last two years, the pro-sex-worker lobby has gained some ground among MEPs such as the Italian, Monica Frassoni, of the Italian Green Party. The abolitionist lobby, however, continues to dominate the spaces of representation at the centres of EU law and policy formation on trafficking and prostitution at the EP. Foucault's discussion of the regulation of the bodies of specific populations as a matter of public concern illustrates the spaces and scales at which feminist politicians debate and deploy discourses of the 'global sisterhood' in the EU. By conducting a discourse analysis of EP documents, it is clear that the anti-prostitution lobby helped to organise the female MEPs' stance on trafficking. Indeed, I argue that this is key to maintaining the legitimacy of their position on gender mainstreaming and equality. This they achieve by the rescaling of the link between prostitution and trafficking as an international women's issue.

Feminist MEPs working in the Committee on Women's Rights (CWR) emphasise specific sociospatial processes in their objections to trafficking in women within the EU territory. To give some examples, Christa Prets reported to the Committee on Women's Rights and Gender Equality (CWRGE): 'developing successful prevention strategies [for violence against women] should go hand in hand with addressing main causes of trafficking' (European Parliament 2005, 14); and Maria Antonia Aviles Peres, reporting to the CWRGE asserted that trafficking is representative of 'the general problems of violence against women' (European Parliament 2001, 14). Feminists' active participation in the discourse of 'protecting' the boundaries of women's rights across EU jurisdictions also refracts a method of inclusion and exclusion. The following quote from MEP, Sue Waddington, is representative of how feminists locate the 'problem' of trafficking and the attendant issue of prostitution: 'Trafficking feeds into a number of markets ... the majority of those trafficked are women ... for the purpose of sexual exploitation' (European Parliament 1997, 11). She states that trafficking is evidence of the continued 'unequal power and wealth relations between men and women' (European Parliament 1997, 13). Another example of this perspective is found in a statement made by MEP, Marianne Eriksson: 'it is undeniable that trafficking for sexual exploitation is directly linked to prostitution' (European Parliament 2005, 16). Addressing the Committee on Women's Rights and Equal Opportunities, Eriksson added that trafficking and prostitution both represent 'men's power in society and control over women's sexuality' (European Parliament 2001, 14). She expressed her concern about the impact of the sex industry on European lives when she argued: 'prostitution can never be reduced to a profession' (European Parliament 2001, 14). Similarly, MEP Christa Prets argued that trafficking cannot be eliminated unless state parties 'understand the importance of promoting gender equality' for all women (European Parliament 2005, 20).

Yet the feminist concern with gender equality and exploitation as it relates to trafficking is diluted when we understand it from a spatially sensitive perspective. The Eurocentric rescaling of trafficking as a problem of inequality is revealed 'in how gender inequality ... is still largely confined to the realm of the EC ... where the primary beneficiaries are EU citizen women' (Askola 2007, 204). What I have discussed above is not simply an ideological landscape but a form of territoriality. In this case, I do not deploy the term in its traditional political geography usage, but rather in the situated framework of feminist identity politics that define the scope and range of anti-trafficking action. The act of drawing borders around what constitutes an infringement on the female trafficked migrant's rights is representative of this process. With this in mind, the following section addresses how the process of boundary making around trafficking and prostitution emerges in discourses of trafficking as modern day slavery.

Trafficking as Slavery

The territoriality of feminist discursive strategies on trafficking and prostitution involves various attempts to establish a global narrative, in which the power and the 'right' to demarcate and name trafficking as modern day slavery revolves around a series of spatialisations. In so doing, feminists have reactivated and redeployed imagery from the early-nineteenth-century anti-slavery campaigns, mobilised through a twenty-first-century concern with the effects of processes of globalisation on women. With this in mind, consider the following quotations taken from EP debates on trafficking. Parliamentarian, Marianne Eriksson, claims that trafficking 'is one of the world's most lucrative industries' in which 'women have become a commodity' (European Parliament 1997, 12). She goes on to suggest that 'the sex trade harms first and foremost all the women who are exploited, but it creates a false image that everything can be bought for money' (European Parliament 1997, 12). A depiction of trafficking as 'modern-day slavery' also frames Sue Waddington's statement that 'these women are in effect imprisoned and enslaved' (European Parliament 1997, 13). At the same time, Eriksson supports the view that trafficking facilitates 'the sex slave trade and an increasingly aggressive marketing of the female body' (European Parliament 2004, 14).

This organisation of knowledge overlooks the multiple scales of non-Western women's subjective experiences (as homemaker, breadwinner, parent) and the decision, or a lack of any other alternative in their specific contexts for survival, that drives their migration. A sustained engagement with MEPs' stance on trafficking illustrates how they maintain the notion that all women operate from the same site of subordination, united in their neoliberal political support of women's equality and freedom. Indeed, the privileged spaces within EU institutions serve to promote the dominance of Western feminists and their political agendas. Scrutiny of feminist strategies on trafficking and prostitution illustrate how they operate from a spatially fixed premise. The feminist organisation of knowledge in the EU about the female trafficked migrant operates by appealing to a situated 'European identity' and to the EU as a 'community of values' united by shared norms and values that condemn trafficking as 'a slave-trade and violation of human rights' taking place 'on its [EU] territory and within its borders' (Locher 2002, 14).

Yet, in the spaces of representation within EU legal discourse and practice, non-Western women's voices remain silent. Feminist organisations, such as the CATW/EWL, deploy discursive strategies that infantilise the female trafficked migrant by denying her right to self determination, while simultaneously legitimising their right to set the parameters of the trafficking debate. This debate supports a hierarchy of womanhood where non-Western women are unequal partners. Thus, for female trafficked migrants from the developing world, the sisterhood and feminist theorisations on racialised class and gender categories do not correspond to the racialised gender realities that limit their mobility and discriminate against the rights of specific populations. While policy statements based on universal human rights and equal opportunities for all women and girls resonate with women across EU jurisdictions, in reality they have little bearing on the lives of female migrants from the developing world. Signifiers, such as the 'sisterhood' and trafficking as a form of modern day slavery eschew difference among women. It seems misplaced to argue in terms of universality among women when difference continues to organise the effects of globalisation and the rights that may or may not flow from it.

How then do we begin to extrapolate how the idiom of the enslaved female 'victim' of slave-like conditions has infiltrated EU member states at the domestic level? To answer this question, I will focus on the UK stance on 'irregular' migration. By examining policy on security, national identity and citizenship, in the remainder of this chapter, I hope to illustrate how the UK locates human trafficking within a broader programme of border control.

The British Context

In the first decade of the twenty-first century, immigration law and social policy are key avenues for state formation among EU member states. State formation produces a hierarchy of inclusion or exclusion that decides who is permitted to remain within the spaces defined as belonging to citizens of the nation state. In a world where many of us live in countries we were not born into, and increased governance and regulation are combined with the erasure of traditional understandings of spatial distance and scale, juridical rulings on mobility do not reflect these transformations. Yet these policies have implications for people worldwide. It is in the context of border control, ushered in through increased migration from the less developed world, that the British government locates its policies on trafficking in human beings and constructs knowledge about female migrants. From a geographical perspective, what is particularly interesting about this is how government authorities use extant ethnic tensions in national processes of place making, as well as anxiety about invading 'hoards' from the South, to validate increased regulation of British identity and citizenship. It is important, then, to analyse the nature of this campaign.

'The First Challenge Migration Poses is to our Concepts of National Identity and Citizenship'

In 2001, civil unrest in the ethnically mixed northern England towns of Bradford, Burnley and Oldham prompted the British government to address the issue of immigration, asylum and citizenship in the 2002 Home Office White Paper, *Secure Borders, Safe Haven.* This White Paper laid the groundwork for the Home Office's 2006 Consultation Paper, *An Action Plan for Human Trafficking*. In the 2002 White Paper, the then Home Secretary, David Blunkett, used the language of cultural incommensurability and spatial difference to argue that the root causes of the violence stemmed from the fact that 'ease of [international] movement has broken down traditional boundaries' (Home Office 2002, 3). For the British government, stringent control of 'citizenship and nationality policy' (Home Office 2002, 12) is necessary to counteract the detrimental effect to 'our sense of belonging and identity'

(Home Office 2002, 4). Close scrutiny of the micro politics of British immigration law reveals how government authorities secure their policies on trafficking in human beings. This occurs under the hegemonic umbrella of discourses of social control of specific populations, within and beyond national territory, in the interests of national security but also 'for their own good'.[5] I assert that British state parties, propped up by some prominent Western feminist initiatives on trafficking and sex work, construct knowledge about the female trafficked migrant through two simultaneous sociospatial ideological moves.

First, the state deploys racialised class, gender and sexual stereotypes of non-Western women and casts them as naïve and vulnerable to the vagaries of organised crime gangs who dupe and enslave them. Second, the state inserts the 'problem' of female vulnerability into a legal and social policy framework that justifies the regulation of their mobility and exclusion. How these discursive strategies develop and support British immigration and border control policy now forms the remainder of my analysis.

'Organised Crime is a Growth Industry'

A spatially sensitive analysis of Home Office documents reveals how British policy on trafficked migrants supports the CATW/EWL's anti-prostitution stance. The state prioritises 'detection and deterring … to disrupt the flows of people who do not qualify' to be here (Home Office 2002, 17). The idiom of the naive and sexually exploited female 'Other' is symbolically and materially important here. For example, in 2002, the Home Secretary stated: 'given the majority of those who are trafficked are women … we must prevent traffickers from taking advantage of others' desperation to move' (Home Office 2002, 88). By focusing on trafficking as organised immigration crime that preys on the 'vulnerable', state parties substantiate the argument that irregular migration must be dealt with by 'strengthening the law … tackling criminals, intelligence and enforcement operations' (Home Office 2002, 77). The rationale behind these measures is grounded in the following observation: 'It is clear that people who are in this country illegally are vulnerable to exploitation both by traffickers … and by a few unscrupulous employers' (Home Office 2002, 77).

This approach buttressed measures proposed by the Home Office in the 2006 trafficking Consultation Paper. The evidence suggests that state parties use the alleged threat posed by organised crime to justify schemes 'preventing trafficking at source' (Home Office 2006, 9). These schemes take sociospatial form in the racialised topography of immigration procedures designed to exclude specific non-Western populations and the powers embodied in the immigration officer. The emphasis in the 2006 Consultation Paper on 'other opportunities to prevent trafficking upstream' shows a clear focus on female vulnerability in order to justify its intention 'to build

---

5 I follow Antonio Gramsci's understanding of hegemony. Gramsci deployed the hegemony to describe 'the area of state action' in contexts, in which political leaders 'must claim to be ruling in the interests of the ruled in order to stay in power' (Showstack Sassoon 1993, 255–6). The current meaning of hegemony refers to the 'function of systems of ideas' in the maintenance and structure of the state 'and a particular society' (Showstack Sassoon 1993, 256).

capacity in source and transit countries' and to 'highlight the dangers of illegal immigration' (Home Office 2006, 9).

The document also reveals how female vulnerability has been used to authenticate the Foreign and Commonwealth Offices' initiatives that have funded work with the Turkish authorities to 'build detention capacity and raise awareness ... within the law enforcement community' (Home Office 2006, 9). This conflation is problematic because law and order responses fail to recognise how legal interventions, which continue to operate along dichotomies of 'here' and 'there' or 'us' and 'them', actually contribute to the production of clandestine migration flows in the form of human trafficking (Kapur 2005). The ways in which law and social policy respond to irregular migration flows prioritise border control over humanitarian concerns and push vulnerable people further underground, making them even more distrustful of the police (Kapur 2005). The urge to represent Britain's stance on its treatment of female trafficked migrants as humanitarian deflects public attention away from the root causes of non-Western women's movements. Furthermore, there is no acknowledgment that the promotion of regular migration channels for women would be a positive step in the fight to eradicate trafficking and exploitative practices in the first instance. This links directly to the second dominant British discourse on the female trafficked migrant, namely migrant as modern day slave.

'This is a Modern Form of Slavery'

The analogy between slavery and trafficking is powerful. It defines the key process through which the state deploys the patriarchal 'gaze' on the female trafficked migrant's body and behaviours (Agustín 2005). In the 2002 White Paper, *Secure Borders, Safe Haven*, the Home Office argued that its interventions in human trafficking occur on the understanding that 'those who can truly be described as trafficking victims have usually been treated as little more than a commodity' (Home Office 2002, 77). The British government's effort to regulate the movement of non-Western women 'for their own good' draws on the abolitionist argument that human trafficking, and the attendant issue of transnational sex work, is 'commercial sexual exploitation' (Home Office 2002, 77).

The 2006 Consultation Paper restores the ideological and moral link between slavery, trafficking, women and sex work where 'thousands of people are forced into slave-like conditions' (Home Office 2006, 2). A joint statement from British Parliamentary Under Secretary, Paul Goggins, and the Scottish Executive Minister for Justice, Cathy Jamieson, strengthens this point:

> The 1807 Parliament passed the Slave Trade Act ... 2007 will see the bicentenary of that landmark Act. We must recognise that there is another challenge facing us in today's modern world ... human trafficking (Home Office 2006, 2).

What retains our attention here are the sociospatial formulae by which the Home Office policies present this hierarchy of movement in a manner that does not appear to contravene women's universal human rights, but is all the while advantageous to those who govern. Aspects of the 2006 Consultation Paper reveal the racialised nature of British immigration policy. For example, the Home Office states that 'frontline personnel' such as airline staff and immigration officers look for specific 'characteristics' when they examine 'profiles of trafficking victims' among those travelling to the UK (Home Office 2006, 18). By invariably associating trafficking with women, the state perpetuates geospecific stereotypes that women from the developing world 'who move are implicitly suspected of crossing borders for the purposes of sex' (Kapur 2005, 4).

Embedded in the 2002 Home Office White Paper, *Secure Border, Safe Haven*, and the 2006 Consultation Paper, *An Action Plan for Human Trafficking*, are several discursive strategies state parties deploy to deflect public attention onto the bodies of female 'victims' of trafficking. Domestic anti-trafficking measures operate in ways that depend on the mobilisation of emotive and politically charged images that support institutionalised codes of morality on female sexuality. If unregulated migration challenges the spatial limits of Western liberalism and equality, then the female trafficked migrant who has perhaps participated in her own movement represents the outer parameters of the 'spatialised moral order' that remains the keystone of Western social mores. Thus the female 'victim' of trafficking fulfils a critical role in justifying the sociospatial and political marginalisation of 'Others' at a variety of spatial scales from the body to the state and beyond. Another key British response to trafficking in human beings has been to represent it as a sociosexual problem. This also suggests that, at this juncture, it is useful to explore the concept of institutional morality in tandem with racialised class, gender and sexuality.

'We have a Fundamental Moral Obligation which we will Always Honour'

British government strategies draw on imperialist notions of the West's moral obligation to guide and protect all 'Others' from exploitative organised immigration crimes, while simultaneously acting to exclude them from the centres of power and decision-making (Kofman 2005). This reflects not only 'the modern anxiety about human mobility but also states' desire to confirm their sovereign power over migration control' (Kostapoulou 2006, 350). As a result, the sociospatial impact of the state's deployment of discourses of morality concerning which forms of sexuality are desirable and 'normal' here is a mechanism of knowledge and power, but also of 'Othering' (Yeoh and Huang 1999; Walton-Roberts 2004; Kofman 2005). Typically, this underlying morality finds expression in the notion that certain sexual acts and identities, such as the female sex worker, are criminal or at the very least are morally wrong 'here'. Female sexual acts that serve women's sexual or economic interests are, within the context of moralising hegemony, represented as dangerous, immoral and indecent. Transnational sex workers occupy a space outside the 'normative' contours of appropriate female sexuality. Thus, the logical conclusion is to curtail their mobility or the right or need to earn a living in a manner they see fit. Indeed, polices that appear on the surface to be for the benefit of the victim often contribute to the further victimisation of female migrants across time and space. The approach that arises out of constructing women as victims undermines the reasons for their movement in the first instance, while the problems of abuse and inequality, the alleged purpose of these measures, go unaddressed.

Consider the following statement found in the Home Office's 2002 White Paper: 'in the short term … we are determined to close a loophole that allows foreign and EU nationals of whatever sex and age to be brought to the UK for the purposes of sexual exploitation' (Home Office 2002, 84). The encoding of a spatialised moral order is also evident in the 2006 Consultation Paper. Under the auspices of reducing demand for prostitution, but ostensibly to regulate non-Western women's mobility, the government stated that it wishes to 'address the harms caused by the prostitution market, in particular the harms to communities associated with on-street prostitution' (Home Office 2006, 9). Yet this last statement is problematic on two counts. First, initiatives to curb street prostitution in the long run have little bearing on the 'harms' experienced by trafficked women. Trafficked migrants tend to be located in off-street premises. In fact, the emphasis on repressive law enforcement in relation to prostitution feeds into exploitative practice such as detaining sex workers in dangerous environments against their will. Second, this statement illustrates that the UK maintains an ideological link between trafficking and prostitution. What is critically important is that this stance ignores other forms of exploitation such as that experienced by migrant caregivers. Such a singular and gendered understanding of trafficking prevents the development of successful policy initiatives sensitive to the multiple scales, contexts and sociospatial relations in which trafficking occurs.

Home Office proposals also infantilise female trafficked migrants because they fail to acknowledge their identities as consenting adults and the rights and needs that flow from this status, such as the right to choose to migrate and control one's life and body. Recent research provides evidence that refutes the metanarrative of the female 'victim' of trafficking (Jordon 2002). Far from viewing themselves as victims, many women view clandestine migration as an opportunity to improve their circumstances (Kofman 2005). This seemingly contradictory statement does not sit comfortably alongside state and certain NGO policy reports on trafficking and the attendant issue of prostitution. The sociospatial coordination of knowledge and practices of ruling over non-citizens involves the state erasure of the conditions in which women make the decision to move. I argue that the institutions of state and certain NGOs cannot accommodate the finer scales of ambiguity that characterise the status of female trafficked migrants in international migration circuits. To exemplify, female trafficked migrants often start their journeys as willing agents in specific places that are connected to processes of globalisation at a variety of scales (Nagar et al. 2002). However, sometimes they become victims or at other times they occupy places in between. The image of the exploited female trafficked migrant permits the UK government to occupy the moral high ground because it adopts a broad stroke definition of the concept of 'exploitation'. UK anti-trafficking policy tends to assume that all relationships in the process of trafficking are exploitative. This phenomenon links directly to Munro's critical interrogation of the concept of 'exploitation' in the context of sex trafficking (Chapter 5, this volume). Munro shifts the focus away from the circular pro- and anti-prostitution debates. Instead, she concentrates on the notion of 'consent' and whether its presence or absence makes trafficking exploitative. Such an approach leads us into fascinating and complex ideological and political terrain because it calls on us to accept that even in the most compromising circumstances, female trafficked migrants can exercise a level of self determination and may consent to exploitative situations when faced with no better alternatives. The notion that some people are willing to make such compromises, Munro argues, rarely appears in trafficking initiatives.

In fact, research reveals that while traffickers dupe some women, many enter into the arrangement aware of what lies ahead of them (UNODC 2006, 61). The UN report stressed that many women are prostitutes in their country of origin. This finding is also borne out by feminist research on transnational sex workers, which claims that, contrary to the image of the transnational sex worker as poor and naïve, many of these women are well informed and must have financial resources to pay traffickers (Agustín 2005). What state parties have yet to recognise is that mobility, and the capacity to be mobile are a significant part of women's strategy 'to stay at home' (Morokvasic 2004, 7). The remittances from their transnational labour in all its forms often support entire families where government initiatives have failed. In the postcolonial moment, 'these counter-geographies of globalization' reflect the ways in which mobility as a strategy has become an important resource and a tool for social innovation in non-Western women's migration circuits (Sassen 2002, 256).

Conclusion

Through a spatially sensitive methodology, the aim of this chapter has been to identify the ways in which the feminist production of knowledge, and its categorisation of female 'victims' of trafficking, influences debates on irregular migration at the EU and domestic level. I have argued that this is especially significant in how state parties incorporate differences about the nature of sex work, and specifically between forced and voluntary sex work, into supranational and domestic legal and social policy responses to 'irregular' migration. This occurs in two interconnected ways.

First, state parties make female migration the overriding concern and problem. Exploitation 'away from home' is conceptualised as a separate problem from exploitative socioeconomic and political power relations 'at home'. Exploitation comes to be identified with women's movements abroad and loses its moorings from the effects of the geography of inequality in processes of globalisation that make working abroad seem like a better option for many women in the developing world. By problematising migration itself, this approach leads us away from a discussion of the socially and culturally organised conditions of people's poverty and inequality. Second, at the international and domestic level, criminal and immigration law regulates female migration. However, it tends to silence non-Western women and overlook their desire or right to migrate. The logical conclusion is the curtailment of women's mobility or their entitlement to earn a living in a manner they see fit. Polices that appear on the surface to be for the benefit of the victim often contribute to the further victimisation of female migrants.

References

Agustín, L. (2005), 'Migrants in the Mistress's House: Other Voices in the "Trafficking" Debate', *Social Politics* 12:1, 96–117.

Allwood, G. (2004), 'Prostitution Debates in France', *Contemporary Politics* 10:1, 145–57.

Anderson, B. and J. O'Connell Davidson (2002), *Trafficking – a Demand Led Problem?* (Stockholm: Save the Children).

Askola H. (2007), *Legal Responses to Trafficking in Women for Sexual Exploitation in the European Union* (Oxford: Hart Publishing).

Balibar, E. (2004), *We the People of Europe? Reflections on Transnational Citizenship* (Princeton, NJ: Princeton University Press).

Barry, K. (1979), *Female Sexual Slavery* (New York: Avon).

Barry, K. (1995), *The Prostitution of Sexuality: The Global Exploitation of Woman* (New York: New York University Press).

Bass, E. (2004), *Child Labour in Sub-Saharan Africa* (Boulder, CO: Lynn Rienner).

Bell, D. (1995), 'Pleasure and Danger: The Paradoxical Spaces of Sexual Citizenship', *Political Geography* 14:2, 139–53.

Bondi. L. et al. (2002), *Subjectivities, Knowledges and Feminist Geographies: The Subjects and Ethics of Social Research* (New York: Rowman and Littlefield).

Butler, J. (1999), *Gender Trouble* (New York: Routledge).

Castles, S. and M.J. Miller (2004), *The Age Of Migration: International Population Movements in the Modern World* (New York: Palgrave).

CATW (2004), *Coalition Report* (Amherst, NY: CATW).

Desforges, L., R. Jones and M. Woods (2005), 'New Geographies of Citizenship', *Citizenship Studies* 9:5, 439–51.

Doezema, J. (1998), 'Forced to Choose: Beyond the Voluntary v. Forced Prostitution Dichotomy' in K. Kempadoo and J. Doezema (eds), *Global Sex Workers* (London: Routledge), 34–50.

Doezema, J. (2001), 'Ouch! Western Feminists "Wounded Attachment" to the Third World Prostitute', *Feminist Review* 67, 16–38.

Doezema, J. (2005), 'Now You See Her, Now You Don't: Sex Workers at the UN Trafficking Protocol Negotiations', *Social and Legal Studies* 14:1, 61–90.

Ekberg, G. (2002), 'The International Debate about Prostitution and Trafficking in Women: Refuting the Arguments'. Paper presented at a seminar on the effects of legalisation of prostitution activities, A Critical Analysis Organised by the Swedish Government, Sweden.

Enloe, C. (1989), *Bananas, Beaches and Bases: Making Feminist Sense of International Politics* (Berkeley, CA: University of California).

European Parliament (1997), 'Report on the Communication from the Commission to the Council and the European Parliament on Trafficking in Women for the Purpose of Sexual Exploitation' (COM (96) 0567-C4-0638/96) 27 November. Committee on Women's Rights (CWR).

European Parliament (2001), 'Report on the Consequences of Globalization for Women Immigrants from the Mediterranean Countries' (2000/2251) (INI) Committee on Women's Rights and Equal Opportunities (CWREO).

European Parliament (2004), 'Report on the Consequences of the Sex Industry in the European Union' (2003/2017) (INI) Committee on Women's Rights and Equal Opportunities (CWREO).

European Parliament (2005), 'Report on the Strategies to Prevent the Trafficking of Women and Children Who Are Vulnerable to Sexual Exploitation' (2004.2216) (INI) 14 December 2005, Committee on Women's Rights and Gender Equality (CWRGE).

Foucault, M. (1980), *History of Sexuality: An Introduction*, trans. Robert Hurley (New York: Vintage).

GAATW (1999), *Human Rights Standards for the Treatment of Trafficked Persons*, <www.inet.-co.th/org/gaatw/>.

GAATW (2004), 'A Rights Based Approach to Trafficking', *Alliance News* 22.

GAATW (2007), *Collateral Damage: The Impact of Anti-trafficking Measures on Human Rights around the World* (Bangkok: Amarin Printing and Publishing).

Goodey, J. (2004), 'Sex Trafficking in Women from Central and East European Countries; Promoting a "Victim-Centred" and "Woman-Centred" Approach to Criminal Justice Intervention', *Feminist Review* 76, 26–46.

Harvey, D. (1989), *The Condition of Postmodernity* (Oxford: Blackwell).

Henderson, T. (1999), *Disorderly Women in Eighteenth-Century London Prostitution and Control in the Metropolis, 1730–1830* (London: Pearson).

Home Office (2002), *Secure Borders, Safe Haven: Integration with Diversity in Modern Britain* (London: HMSO).

Home Office and Scottish Executive (2006), *Tackling Human Trafficking: Consultation on Proposals for a UK Action Plan* (London: HMSO).

Howell, P. (2004), 'Sexuality, Sovereignty and Space: Law, Government and the Geography of Prostitution in Colonial Gibraltar', *Social History* 29, 444–64.

Hubbard, P. (1999), *Sex and the City: Geographies of Prostitution in the Urban West* (Aldershot: Ashgate).

Hughes, D.M. (2000), 'The "Natasha" Trade: The Transnational Shadow Market of Trafficking in Woman', *Journal of International Migration* 53:2, 625–51.

Jordon, A.D. (2002), 'Human Rights or Wrongs? The Struggle for a Rights-Based Response to Trafficking in Human Rights', *Gender and Development* 10:1, 28–37.

Kapur, R. (2005), *Erotic Justice: Law and the New Politics of Postcolonialism* (London: Glasshouse Press).

Kelly, L. (2005), '"You Can Find Anything You Want": A Critical Reflection on Research on Trafficking in Persons within and into Europe', *International Migration* 43:1/2, 235–65.

Kempadoo, K. (2001), 'Women of Colour and the Global Sex Trade: Transnational Feminist Perspectives', *Meridians, Feminists, Race, Transformation* 1:2, 28–51.

Kofman, E. (2005), 'Citizenship, Migration and the Reassertion of National Identity', *Citizenship Studies* 9:5, 453–67.

Kostapoulou, D. (2006), 'Freedom, Security and Justice: Police and Judicial Cooperation in Criminal Matters' in J. Peterson and M. Shackleton (eds), *Institutions of the European Union* (Oxford: Oxford University Press), 231–51.

Kumar, M.S. (2005), '"Oriental Sore" or "Public Nuisance": The Regulation of Prostitution in Colonial India, 1865–1889' in L. Proudfoot and M. Roche (eds), *Displacing Empire: Renegotiating British Colonial Geographies* (Aldershot: Ashgate), 155–73.

Locher, B. (2002), 'International Norms and European Policy Making: Trafficking in Women in the EU', Centre for European Studies Working Paper No. 2002/6.

Manzo, K. (2005), 'Exploiting West Africa's Children: Trafficking, Slavery and Uneven Development', *Area* 37, 393–401.

Massey, D. (1992), 'Politics and Space/Time', *New Left Review* 196, 65–84.

McDowell, L. (1996), 'Spatialising Feminism: Geographical Perspectives' in N. Duncan (ed.), *BodySpace* (New York: Routlege), 28–44.

McDowell, L. (1999), *Gender, Identity and Place: Understanding Feminist Geographies* (Oxford: Blackwell).

McDowell, L. and J. Sharpe (1999), *A Feminist Glossary of Human Geography* (London: Edward Arnold).

Mohanty, C.T. (2003), *Feminism without Borders: Decolonizing Theory, Practicing Solidarity* (Durham, NC and London: Duke University Press).

Morokvasic, M. (2004), '"Settled in Mobility": Engendering Post Wall Migration in Europe', *Feminist Review* 77: 7–25.

Munro, V. (2005), 'A Tale of Two Servitudes: A Domestic Response to Trafficking of Women for Prostitution in the UK and Australia', *Social and Legal Studies* 14:1, 91–114.

Murray, A. (1998), 'Debt Bondage and Trafficking: Don't Believe the Hype' in K. Kempadoo and J. Doezema (eds), *Global Sex Workers* (London: Routledge), 51–68.

Nagar, R. et al. (2002), 'Localizing Globalization: Feminist (Re)readings of the Subjects and Spaces of Globalization', *Economic Geography* 78:3, 257–84.

O'Connor, M. and G. Healy (2006), *The Links between Prostitution and Sex Trafficking: A Brief Handbook* (Stockholm: CATW/EWL).

Ohmae, K. (1991), *The Borderless World* (New York: Harper Collins).

Palmer, B.D. (1990), *Descent into Discourse: The Reification of Language and the Writing of Social History* (Philadelphia, PA: Temple University Press).

Phillips, R. (2006), *Sex, Politics and Empire: A Postcolonial Geography* (Manchester: University of Manchester Press).

Pred, A. (2000), *Even in Sweden: Racisms, Racialised Spaces, and the Popular Geographical Imagination* (Berkeley, CA: University of California Press).

Raymond, J.G. (1998), 'Prostitution as Violence against Women: NGO Stonewalling in Beijing and Elsewhere', *Women's Studies International Forum* 21:1, 1–9.

Robson, E. (2004), 'Hidden Child Workers: Young Carers in Zimbabwe', *Antipode* 36:2, 227–48.

Rose, G. (1993), *Feminism and Geography* (Cambridge: Polity).

Sassen, S. (2002), 'Women's Burden: Counter-Geographies of Globalization and the Feminization of Survival', *Nordic Journal of International Law* 71, 255–74.

Showstack Sassoon, A. (1993), 'Hegemony' in *The Blackwell Dictionary of Twentieth-Century Social Thought*, (ed.) W. Outhwaite and T. Bottomore (Oxford: Blackwell Publishers), 255–6.

Spivak, G. (1992), 'The Politics of Translations' in Michele Barrett and A. Philips (eds), *Destabilizing Theory; Contemporary Feminist Debates* (Stanford, CA: Stanford University Press).

Stychin, C.F. (2003), *Governing Sexuality: The Changing Politics of Citizenship and Law Reform* (Oxford: Hart Publishing).

Sullivan, B. (2003), 'Trafficking in Woman', *International Feminist Journal of Politics* 5:1, 67–91.

Ticktin, M. (2005), 'Policing and Humanitarianism in France: Immigration and the Turn to Law as State of Exception, *Interventions* 7:3, 346–68.

United Nations (2000a), 'United Nations Conventions Against Transnational Crime', <http://www.odccp.org/crime_cicp_convention.html#final>.

United Nations (2000b), 'The Protocol to Suppress and Punish Trafficking in Persons, Especially Women and Children, Supplementing the United Nations Convention Against Transnational Organised Crime', <http://www.odccp.org/crime_cicp_convention.html#final>.

United Nations Office on Drug and Crime (UNODC) (2006), *Trafficking in Persons Global Pattern* (Vienna: UNODC).

Walton-Roberts, M. (2004), 'Rescaling Citizenship: Gendering Canadian Immigration Policy', *Political Geography* 23:3, 267–81.

Wijers, M. (2001), 'European Union Policies on Trafficking in Women' in M. Possilli (ed.), *Gender Policies in the European Union* (New York: Peter Lang), 209–20.

Yeoh, B. and S. Huang (1999), 'Spaces and Margins: Migrant Domestic Workers and the Development of Civil Society in Singapore', *Environment and Planning A* 31:7, 1149–67.

Zlotnik, H. (2003), 'The Global Dimension of Female Migration', *Migration Information Source*, <http://www.migrationinformation.org/Feature/display.cfm?ID=109>.

Chapter 7

Simulating the Impact of Regulation Changes on the Market for Prostitution Services

Marina Della Giusta[1]

This chapter introduces an economic approach to studying prostitution, critically assessing the current limitations of economists' contribution to this important policy debate and illustrating the relative merits of economic modelling for policy design. The first part of the chapter reviews the principal contribution to prostitution debates that have informed the formulation of the approach adopted here, and indicates how it differs from other social scientific approaches and from existing work addressing these issues in economics. Central to the approach is the recognition of the role of social stigma in determining the configuration of the exchange of paid sex, and the way in which it is in turn understood and affected by policy (for a discussion of the link between stigma and regulation see Sanders 2007). Drawing on an economic model of the market for prostitution services analysing the interaction between demand and supply for paid sex (Della Giusta, Di Tommaso and Stroem 2007), the second part of the chapter describes ways in which different regulatory regimes are chosen by policy-makers.

On the part of economists, and also to a large extent feminist economists, there has until recently been a curious reluctance to engage with prostitution as an area of socio-economic life that mobilises large numbers of people and vast amounts of financial resources internationally. This is all the more surprising since paid sex is, depending on its regulation, either formally or informally part of the entertainment industry, where issues of regulation and labour conditions, particularly given the importance of international migration to the sector, are all well known to economists. The failure to analyse systematically a form of exchange that has many of the features that much recent research in economics claims to want to understand is bewildering, given that the exchange of paid sex appears to incorporate rather obviously issues connected with information and power asymmetries in exchange,[2] the relationship between formal and informal markets, and the role of regulation in fragmented markets. In

1 I would like to thank Vanessa Munro and collaborators in the Supply/Demand Dynamic in Prostitution seminars for fruitful discussions, as well as the British Academy and the ESRC for funding the organisation of these meetings.

2 See the seminal work of Fred Hirsch (1977) and Pagano (1999), widely used among other fields in cooperative and non-cooperative bargaining models of the family.

addition, the dynamics of international labour mobility, the allocation of resources within the household, women's entrepreneurship, and pathways out of poverty and social exclusion are also implicated. There is an unfortunate parallel between the lack of acknowledgment of prostitution as a form of work in policymaking and in the economic discipline, which by neglecting areas of human economic activity, contributes to their delegitimisation. Given the relevance of the economic profession to policy-makers, there is a need for economic research addressing this neglected area of enquiry, learning from the evidence from the sex sector as well as the work carried out in other disciplines.

This chapter forms part of a broad economic investigation which was initially inspired by the publication of a contribution by economists to the prostitution literature that appeared to be based on very limited knowledge of the sex industry and on several rather unsatisfactory assumptions (alas, a common feature of our discipline) (see Edlund and Korn 2002). The aim is to contribute an economic understanding of the paid sex exchange that provides opportunities for discussion with other disciplines as well as with policy-makers. The discussion begins with an illustration of the main ideas underpinning the economic model contained in Della Giusta et al. (2007a), which is then enlarged to illustrate the choice of policy regimes by policy-makers.

Economics and Prostitution

The economic literature has traditionally approached prostitution either showing how it is similar to other markets, or studying it as a form of crime and analysing the costs and benefits of alternative regulatory regimes, generally agreeing that the main motivation behind supply is an economic one (for a review, see Reynolds 1986). More recent theoretical and empirical contributions have focused on modelling prices and supply characteristics (Cameron et al. 1999; Moffatt and Peters 2001; Edlund and Korn 2002; Cameron 2002), demand determinants (Cameron and Collins 2003), health risk and the effect of condom use on prostitute's earnings (Rao et al. 2001; Gertler et al. 2003), and, more recently, the evolution of paid sex markets and the ways in which urban spaces favour sexual transactions (Collins 2004). The latter collection is much broader in scope, with paid sex markets being studied as part of the wider sexual market in which people seek partners for reasons that include deficiencies in amount or range of sexual activities in which they participate, or diversification of sexual consumption (Collins 2004, 1634). Edlund and Korn (2002) have contentiously modelled prostitution as a highly paid, low skill female occupation alternative to marriage, explaining high wages in terms of a loss of position in the marriage market.[3] Cameron (2002) provides a more sophisticated explanation for high wages in terms of compensation for social exclusion, risk (assault, disease, arrest, punishment), front loading in wage profile (informal pension scheme or insurance), boredom and physical effort, distaste (potential psychological and physical costs), loss of recreational sex pleasure, anti-social and inconvenient hours, possible excess

3 For a detailed critique see Della Giusta et al. (2007a).

demand and prices used to screen quality, taboos and agent fees. Moffatt and Peters (2001) find that prices are affected by duration of the transaction, location and age of the prostitute, but that other factors affect client satisfaction. Stigma enters these models in the form of a barrier faced by prostitutes when wanting to enter other professions, but it is unrelated to the nature of the transaction between prostitute and client. Cameron and Collins (2003, 274) model male clients' decision to enter the market for prostitution services, where he has the choice to derive utility from one relationship partner and/or one paid sex partner. They distinguish between the motivations of men in relationships (variety, specific acts, frequency, outlet for stress) and single men ('relative search costs of finding willing sexual partners, or partners willing to engage in specific sexual activities in an ad hoc or formal social context, and in a given time period'). An econometric study of the characteristics of male demand for street prostitution services, with the aim of assessing the significance of different types of clients' motivations is contained in Della Giusta et al. (2007b). Garofalo (2002) is so far the only explicitly feminist contribution, and focuses on explaining the different prices paid in the different prostitution sub-markets in terms of the power asymmetries between contractual parties, discussing the role of female prostitution in the construction of male identity. The latter would be at least partly based on asserting control over women through the paid sexual transaction, thereby confirming one's gender identity through the relationship with the opposite one. This links quite well with the evidence from female clients, who exploit various existing 'Othering' mechanisms based on class and race to assert difference and, through the exercise of economic power, control over the male sex workers whose services they buy (see below). Della Giusta et al. (2007b) analyse empirically the role of control in demand for sexual services and find that the desire for control is indeed a significant component of demand.

Using an Economic Model of Prostitution to Investigate Policy Alternatives

The usefulness of economic modelling is that, as long as it is based on valid stylised facts (that is, recurrences encountered in empirical evidence), models can be an extremely useful tool for testing hypotheses, and one whose validity can continuously be checked against empirical evidence. This, of course, is as long as all simplifying assumptions (especially those relating to *ceteris paribus*, that is, the idea that no other factors affecting the model's variables, and not included in the model, will not change simultaneously with the policy parameters of interest) are borne in mind when discussing the policy implications stemming from the model's results. The economic model of prostitution developed in Della Giusta et al. (2007a) is in the standard rational action tradition (based on the idea that agents make decisions based on the information available to them and having evaluated possible alternatives), but differs in that it contains representative agents who are social beings interested, in varying degrees, in the effect of their actions on their reputations, which are socially constructed, both in the sense that they are ascribed rather than intrinsic characteristics, and in the sense that they are affected by what other agents do (so that the relative diffusion of behaviour makes it more acceptable). The economic sociology literature on embeddedness and social capital (Granovetter 1985; Bourdieu 1986; Coleman 1988; Putnam 1993; Mansky 2000) points to two distinct ways in which reputations matter to economic agents: first, because, as social beings, they derive utility (or satisfaction) from a positive evaluation by others in the social groups they belong to (Casson 1991), and secondly, because they are aware of the costs that social sanctions may impose on their material progress (Akerlof 1980; Arnott and Stiglitz 1991).

Reputation has thus both intrinsic and instrumental value: it is desired *per se* and can be used to access other earning opportunities. Stigma can thus be understood as a loss of reputation which affects social standing for both clients and sex workers, as well as pay and working conditions in the sex trade and access to services and other jobs for sex workers. The model also incorporates personal differences in concern for reputation depending on agents' personal characteristics and the specific moment at which they exercise choice (so that people are allowed to differ and also to be inconsistent in their choices). This is important in order to describe situations of individuals with high reputation who disregard the effects of their actions, which would be otherwise construed as irrational behaviour. The model considered both the case in which reputational endowments are exogenous (that is not affected by behaviour within the sex industry) and the situation when those endowments are considered endogenous, that is a situation in which if a higher quantity of prostitution is sold or bought in the economy the stigma effect decreases. The second key assumption of the model is that the demand for sex and the demand for paid sex are not perfect substitutes to reflect the fact that other motivations, such as desire for control (explored at the empirical level in Della Giusta et al. 2007b), underpin demand. Findings from empirical studies of clients suggest that personal characteristics (personal and family background, self-perception, perceptions of women, sexual preferences), economic factors (education, income, work), as well as attitudes towards risk (health hazard and risk of being caught where sex work is illegal), lack of interest in conventional relationships, desire for variety in sexual acts or sexual partners, and viewing sex as a commodity, are all likely to affect demand. For example, Pitts et al. (2004) surveyed a sample of 1,225 men and women in Australia[4] and found that 23.4 per cent had paid for sex at least once. They reported paying for sex to satisfy sexual needs (43.8 per cent), because paying for sex is less trouble (36.4 per cent), and because it is entertaining (35.5 per cent). Significantly, the researchers found that there were not many notable differences between men who had paid for sex and those who had not, except that the ones who had were on average older, less likely to have university education and to have had a regular partner in the previous year. The motivations of sex workers' clients in the UK (who were all males and appeared to be representatives of all sectors of society)

4 The sample was taken by distributing a survey to customers of a Sexpo exhibition held in Melbourne 2001. This is a commercial event hosting a wide range of exhibitors of products associated with sex; of 4,905 respondents, 1,225 received a version of the questionnaires with questions on sex workers. Among 1,225 respondents , 612 were men and 601 were women.

studied in the course of a programme[5] on the sex industry presented by Channel 4 appeared to convey the impression that a connection existed between the effort and costs associated with finding a sexual partner who would readily satisfy their sexual preferences, and the straightforward and readily accessible option of sex work. Similar findings are reported by Coy, Horvath and Kelly (2007) on buyers of sex in East London,[6] as well as by Campbell (1998) and Sanders (2008). This is confirmed by Thorbek and Pattanaik (2002), who draw a sort of 'psychological' profile of male sex tourists on the basis of their own descriptions of themselves and accounts of their experiences. This indicates that many of them are finding relationships with others very difficult (either because they do not have the time or the skills required to meet people) and choose sex tourism as an 'easier' alternative, which does not imply any responsibility towards the person providing the sexual service. As for the views they held of sex workers, it appears that both sexism and racism mix in determining a very marked distancing, which allow sex tourists to practically ignore and show no interest in the lives and working motivations of the sex workers whose services they buy. Wider phenomena connected to consumerism and globalisation are also clearly related to this industry, which reflects multiple power structures: Marttila (2003) concludes from her study of Finnish clients that, 'the sex business is first and foremost about gendered, economic, social and cultural – global and local – power structures (Marttila 2003, 8). Thus, different intersections of gender, race and class all contribute to the creation of 'Othering' mechanisms that serve to both distance the parties to an exchange and justify the assertion of economic power within it. This phenomenon is obviously not limited to paid sex exchanges, and has been widely documented across a range of personal services (see for example Ehrenreich and Hochschild 2003).

As stated in the previous section, gender is also not the only variable at play: women clients are also engaging in sex tourism, as documented both in Thorbek and Pattanaik (2002), and in Sanchez Taylor (2001). The latter, in particular, offers a more in-depth analysis of North American and Northern European women buying sex work services of young men in the Caribbean, in what they themselves describe as 'romance holidays'. Responses to her interviews suggest that, on the one hand, women clients are mostly reluctant to define what they engage in as prostitution, and, on the other, that their ideas about the young men whose service they buy are deeply rooted in racist ideas about black men and black men's sexuality. The theme of inequality appears to be at the core of the relationship: prejudices that allow the stigmatisation of another person as fundamentally 'different' and inferior to oneself appear again and again in customers' accounts (Ben-Israel et al. 2005; Pitts et al. 2004; Kern 2000; Blanchard 1994).

Given these assumptions, the model predicts that clients will participate in the 'market' for paid sex if their marginal willingness to pay for sex exceeds the price of paid sex, plus the marginal costs of a worsened reputation. The higher their reputation capacity (or ability to withstand stigma), the lower is the marginal cost

5 'Dispatches: Sex on the Street'; Channel 4 season *Prostitution – The Laws Don't Work*, Channel 4, September 2002.

6 <http://www.cwasu.org/displayAuthorsPublications.asp?author_key=51>.

from reputation effects of consuming prostitution, and the more likely it is that prostitution is consumed. Conversely, an individual will start to sell sex if the price of paid sex exceeds its opportunity cost, again in terms of reputation and alternative uses of one's time: the higher the price of paid sex, the more likely it is that an individual will supply prostitution; the lower the availability of alternative income, the more likely it is that the individual will take part in the prostitution industry; and the lower the effect of stigma on sex workers, the more likely it is that prostitution will be sold. The equilibrium amount of prostitution sold and bought in the market (S*) is a function of the exogenous parameters: reputation capacities of sex workers (R_p) and clients (R_c) and other sources of income for sex workers (H_p). Table 7.1 describes the changes in both quantity and price (W) of prostitution that result from increases in reputations and alternative earnings.

Column 2 shows that more prostitution is sold at a higher price to clients with a high reputation capacity, that is, individuals who are able to cover to a great extent their consumption of prostitution.

Column 3 suggests that if it is difficult to have one's reputation ruined by being found out as a prostitute, then a lot of prostitution will be sold at a low price. This is consistent with the evidence of some temporary immigrant prostitutes in Europe who aim to work in prostitution only for a limited amount of time to accumulate savings and then return to their country (see Thorbek and Pattanaik 2002; Corso and Trifirò 2003).

Column 4 states that the fewer the alternative earning opportunities (H_p high), the more prostitution is sold at a lower price. This is consistent with the evidence from Thailand and other sex tourism destinations where the lack of alternative livelihoods and the power structures within households are important determinants of supply.

In the light of the examples above, policies that were to recognise prostitution as a job and reduce the associated stigma would have the effect of increasing the marginal net gain of supplying prostitution, and increase the marginal willingness to pay for prostitution. This should, in a closed economy, have the effect of increasing the price of prostitution and, given the same availability of alternative earning opportunities (if there are constant intermediation margins), increase the quantity supplied. However, in an open economy, there is always immigration of illegal workers and out-migration of clients (sex tourism), which would help keep prices low. Policies that increase the stigma of being clients, conversely, increase the costs associated with being caught for clients. Here, the expectation is that the marginal willingness to pay for prostitution would fall, as would the quantity of prostitution

Table 7.1 Changes in supply and wages of sex workers resulting from increases in reputation capacities and other earning options

Change in	R_c	R_p	H_p
S*	+	+	+
W	+	-	-

sold and the equilibrium price. However, the evidence from countries that criminalise clients seems to suggest that the response is often a 'going underground' of the sex industry, which increases the risks to which sex workers are exposed and does not decrease demand (Sanders 2005), as illustrated by the evidence from community action and displacement of prostitution (Hubbard 1998).

Another strategy followed by intervention programmes has been that of increasing alternative earning opportunities for prostitutes. The effect of these policies will be felt only on that part of prostitution which is supplied for lack of earning alternatives. This implies a fall in part of the supply which will not affect demand and therefore, in an open economy setting, might simply generate displacement of demand, rather than less prostitution being sold at a higher price. Again, this is consistent with the immigration of sex workers operating in the informal sex market which exists in countries that have legalised and have permeable borders (the Netherlands).

Thinking About the Effect of Changing Social Norms

The effect of social norms on people's behaviour has been discussed in economics in the context of studying the ways in which social codes change depending on their degree of acceptance. In particular, Akerlof's theory of social custom (Akerlof 1980) incorporates reputation in individual's preferences, and discusses the range of possible market equilibria that exist depending on whether people tend to generally believe or disregard a particular social code within the range of existing ones. This theory was used in our model as a foundation to be able to discuss the ways in which prostitution is stigmatised in different societies. Following the approach of Akerlof, changing social attitudes towards prostitution can be expected to produce different market equilibria in terms of the amount of prostitution exchanged, and the price of the service. The reputation function in Akerlof depends on the individual's obedience to the social code and the proportion of the population who believe in that code. Given an increase in demand for sexual services (as documented for example by Day and Ward for the UK), following Akerlof's theory, one would expect that more people would find the exchange of paid sex acceptable, which would appear to be confirmed by data from the UK Survey of Sexual Attitudes. Similarly, Della Giusta et al. (2007a) investigated the effect of market size on stigmatisation of both customers and sex workers, and suggested different scenarios depending on the degree of independence of mores from behaviour. The rest of this chapter is concerned with another aspect of stigmatisation, namely the degree to which policy-makers' reputations are affected by the kind of prostitution policy they adopt.

Prostitution Policy

Introducing policy-makers in the simple framework outlined above is no simple matter, as the motivation for regulating this activity is as complex as society's attitude towards it. Furthermore, it has to be borne in mind that most policy regimes have evolved in piecemeal fashion over time, with legislation not explicitly addressing sex work having an important effect. Penal codes reform, public health, social insurance and taxation regimes all play a major part, and, more recently, concerns over immigration and public order and security are exerting a major influence on policies addressing the sex trade (see, for example, Allwood in Chapter 4 of this volume). Defining different 'regimes' should therefore not create the impression that there are coherent alternative models that policy-makers choose from. Nonetheless, it seems useful to distinguish between the main currently existing models and illustrate how an economic approach to discussing their relative merits would operate. Historically, the prevailing concern informing policies addressing prostitution has been moral and legal sanctioning of those involved in the trade, being directed in different mixtures at sex workers, their clients, or those who organise in a variety of ways the sex trade. The ways in which intermediaries have been addressed by policy is often used as an illustration of the failure to understand the complexity of this activity, with pimps being used as a catch-all term comprising anyone from people traffickers, to parlour managers and apartment owners, to pushers and sex workers' partners. Policies addressing prostitution directly or indirectly have also been influenced by women's movements and feminist discourses in varying degree, as illustrated by Outshoorn (2004). The welfare of workers in the sex industry has sometimes featured in the discussions, although this has often been accompanied by a rather one-sided understanding of their agency (a point repeatedly discussed in this collection).

In order to describe the main different regimes, Outshoorn's definitions are adopted (2004, 8). According to these, abolitionism describes the position whereby prostitution should be banned and third parties, but not prostitutes, criminalised. Prohibitionism indicates instead that all prostitution is declared illegal and parties are held liable to penalties. Finland, for example, moved from being a purely abolitionist regime, with no penalties for prostitutes and sanctions against pimps only, to a regime of strong prohibition which has outlawed prostitutes, clients and pimps (Holli 2004). As is often the case, the application of the law differs markedly from the intent of the legislator, and the local prostitution ban in Helsinki only resulted in criminalisation of prostitutes rather than clients. Regulation means that the state intervenes in the ways in which the sex industry is run: for example, Australia has seen a trend towards the legalisation of prostitution, with street-walking being legal in New South Wales and brothels and escort agencies being legal in a further four territories or states (Sullivan 2004). Most countries fall somewhere between these categories – for example, Austria's approach has been defined as simultaneously regulatory and prohibitive since the legislation on social insurance recognises prostitution as a form of work but one which is coercive and immoral (Sauer 2004). Prostitution is permitted in Vienna but not in the provinces, and regulated through the registration of prostitutes (although it is estimated that less than 10 per cent of prostitutes are registered and 85 per cent are migrant women) and zoning. Meanwhile, brothels are legal, but not bars and private apartments (although prostitution is legal in clients' apartments).

The further category of decriminalisation should also be included in the present discussion, since it has featured quite extensively in discussions in both Canada and the UK, particularly in responses to the consultation launched by the Home Office (Home Office 2004). This approach essentially entails minimal policing and non-intervention. Canada makes it legal to be a prostitute but prohibits all forms of communication for the purposes of prostitution and has dealt with it mostly as a public nuisance (Jeffery 2004). This is in spite of the attempt to decriminalise following the Fraser's committee recommendations in the late 1980s which went unheeded as the change to a conservative government meant renewed pressure to treat it as a law and order issue.

Recent reforms in the UK following the consultation by the Home Office (2004 and 2006) entailed a shift from a traditionally abolitionist to an almost prohibitionist regime. There are probably several underlying motives for a move which has discounted expert opinion from a range of scholars, activists and sex workers' organisations and pushed towards a stated policy of eliminating sex work by a mixture of exiting and repatriation of immigrant prostitutes, and the adoption of a punitive stance towards clients. Without entering into the (de)merits of the actual policy instruments that are being proposed and/or adopted in England and Wales (which are discussed at length by other contributors to this collection), it appears that beneath this change in attitude lies the desire to meet the demands of rather conservative voters (for whom no inconsistency may occur between anti-immigration and anti-kerb-crawling views and liberal sex attitudes). This is not surprising, being in line with many of the policies affecting civil liberties currently underway, and not inconsistent with the traditional description of policy-makers' behaviour, once their reputation and its effect on re-election chances is considered. Policy-makers are usually described in terms of the maximisation of a public welfare function (including costs and benefits to the public from different options) under constraints which describe both the relationships between the variables that are outside the policy-makers' control (such as the relationship between inflation and interest rates, or the process of expectations formation) and the incentives of the policy-makers (often associated with maintaining power).

To keep matters simple, let us assume here three different types of costs reflecting the discussion above: policing, administration and public health (indicated by c_p, c_a and c_h respectively). Policing costs include both the cost of monitoring and arresting, as well as the costs from crimes associated with the sex industry. These are assumed to be higher the more punitive the policy regime. Administration costs refer to those from supporting exit strategies in abolitionism (if this is done) and to those from licensing in the case of regulation, and they are assumed here to be the smallest source of costs and smaller than the tax gains from regulation. Public health costs include those associated with sexually transmitted diseases as well as those coming from the other physical and mental damages sustained by sex workers, who feature disproportionately amongst victims of violent crime. Evidence suggests that repressive regimes (prohibition and abolition) increase these costs by pushing prostitution underground and making it difficult for sex workers to protect themselves (see Sanders 2007). Let us also make no assumption regarding the relative magnitudes of policing and health costs.[7]

---

7 Note that we are not assuming any 'public nuisance' costs here, as the evidence reviewed by the author on regulated streetwalking areas suggests that the perceived sharp trade-off between safe neighbourhoods and streetwalking is largely a result of mis-representation: well managed street walking zones are overwhelmingly located away from residential areas, which tend instead

Let us also assume that policy-makers, like clients and sex workers, have reputations (indicated by R_G) which reflect their current rating by the general public, and can increase or decrease their rating depending on the policies they adopt, and whether these shift opinion in their favour. The point of the electoral cycle of course matters too: the relative importance of reputation will increase closer to term, since the policy-maker will at that time foster a greater interest in swaying votes in its favour (particularly those from swing voters). Switching between regimes will thus depend on the actual reputation enjoyed by the policy-maker and the proximity to elections. If swing voters tend to have views that are fairly conservative, they will be less impressed by liberal policies which may make the sex industry more acceptable and visible (such as regulated brothels), and more in favour of policies that curb it or at least make it less visible. This latter point is rather crucial, since some of the perceived inconsistency of government policy possibly reflects the attempt to achieve the latter goal, even when the former is stated in principle. It is useful to see, given the assumptions made, what overall incentives the policy-maker has to switch away from an existing policy regime. Looking at the separate components of the policy-maker's payoff first, and taking prohibition as the basic case, Table 7.2 suggests how these may be summarised, given the assumptions outlined above.

Thus, if all the above assumptions hold, a government wishing to increase public welfare whilst simultaneously preserving its chances of re-election would move towards less repressive regimes if elections are far away, as these options increase public health and reduce policing costs. However, the same government will not move away from prohibition if it is close to elections and wishes to maximise its reputation with swing voters. Extending this line of reasoning, a switch from less liberal to more liberal regimes will only occur if the government is either sure of re-election or far away from it. These results are based on social cost-benefit calculations, but little evidence exists that these are actually performed when deciding between policy options towards this sector, as in other 'morally contentious' policy areas (for example, drugs).

Table 7.2 Changes in policy-maker's payoffs when switching from prohibition to different regimes

Policy regimes	*Reputation effect*	*Taxes on sex work* T_s	*Policing costs* c_p	*Administration costs* c_a	*Health costs* c_h
Prohibition (baseline)		None		None	
Abolitionism	?*	0	0	+	0
Legalisation	?*	+	-	+	-
Decriminalisation	?*	0	-	-	-

?* = depends on public views.

to become used for soliciting in the absence of regulation (and often in association with repressive regimes). For a discussion of displacement see Collins and Judge, Chapter 8 in this collection.

Conclusions

The aim of this chapter is twofold. On the one hand, it hopes to show how economists can engage in discussions with other disciplines on the complex issues surrounding prostitution. On the other, it seeks to demonstrate how an economic approach can illuminate more clearly some of the outcomes of policy decisions on participants in the sex trade, and society more largely, and therefore help policy-makers to adopt more systematic approaches based on rigorous evaluation of the costs and benefits associated with different regimes.

At the centre of the approach adopted here is the recognition that stigma plays a role in prostitution, and the effect it has not just on the reputation of the parties directly involved, but on that of policy-makers too. On this basis, a very simple rational action model based on stylised facts from the sex trade would suggest liberal policies that maximise public welfare by lifting stigma associated with the sector. But, as has been demonstrated, the same rational action model also helps to illustrate why politicians adopt what has often been described as hypocritical behaviour, choosing more repressive regimes which demonstrably worsen the lives of sex workers remaining in the trade, as well as those of society at large.

Appendix

Formally, if the policy-maker maximises the following utility function incorporating both its own reputation and public welfare:

$$\text{Max } U\,(R_{G}, - C)$$

where C is a cost function increasing in all its components C (c_p, c_a, c_h) which has an identifiable minimum value, and reputation has a fixed component and a variable component r_G reflecting the effect of changing prostitution policy, whose relevance depends on the closeness to election $tr_G > 0$ with $0<t<1$ where $t=1$ is election time.

Thus, maximising the policy-makers' utility will require simultaneously maximising reputation and minimising costs, that is, satisfying the following:

$$tr_G = U_c'C'$$

if elections are far, that is $t=0$, then the policy-maker will switch to a regime that minimises costs. Conversely, at election time $t=1$ and if swing voters are relatively conservative, the policy-maker will switch to a regime that increases costs of an amount equal to the reputation increase that the policy-maker requires in order to attain re-election.

References

Aggleton, P. (ed.) (1998), *Men Who Sell Sex* (London: UCL Press).

Akerlof, G. (1980), 'A Theory of Social Custom – Of which Unemployment may be One Consequence', *Quarterly Journal of Economics* 94:4, 749–75.

Arnott, R. and J.E. Stiglitz (1991), 'Equilibrium in Insurance Markets with Moral Hazard', Working Paper No. 3588 (Cambridge, MA: National Bureau of Economic Research).

Ben-Israel, H. and N. Levenkron (2005), 'The Missing Factor: Clients of Trafficked Women in Israel's Sex Industry', unpublished manuscript, Hebrew University in Jerusalem.

Blanchard, K. (1994), 'Young Johns', *Mademoiselle* 100:5.

Bourdieu, P. (1986), 'The Forms of Capital' in J.G. Richardson (ed.), *Handbook of Theory and Research for the Sociology of Education* (Westport, CT: Greenwood), 241–58.

Bowles, S., M. Franzini and U. Pagano (1999), *The Politics and the Economics of Power* (London and New York: Routledge).

Cameron, S. (2002), *The Economics of Sin* (Cheltenham: Edward Elgar).

Cameron, S. and A. Collins (2003), 'Estimates of a Model of Male Participation in the Market for Female Heterosexual Prostitution Services', *European Journal of Law and Economics* 16:3, 271–88.

Cameron, S., A. Collins and N. Thew (1999), 'Prostitution Services: An Exploratory Empirical Analysis', *Applied Economics* 31, 1523–9.

Campbell, R. (1998), 'Invisible Men: Making Visible Male Clients of Female Prostitutes in Merseyside' in J.E. Elias, V.L. Bullough, V. Elias and G. Brewer (eds), *Prostitution: On Whores, Hustlers and Johns* (Amherst, NY: Prometheus), 134–54.

Casson, M. (1991), *The Economics of Business Culture* (Oxford: Clarendon Press).

Chapkis, W. (1997), *Live Sex Acts: Women Performing Erotic Labour* (New York: Routledge).

Chen, Z. and F. Woolley (2001), 'A Cournot-Nash Model of Family Decision Making', *The Economic Journal* 111, 722–48.

Coleman, J.S. (1988), 'Social Capital in the Creation of Human Capital', *American Journal of Sociology* 94, S95–S120.

Collins, A. (ed.) (2004), 'Sex and the City', *Urban Studies* 41:9.

Corso, C. and A. Trifirò (2003), *E Siamo Partite: Migrazione, tratta e prostituzione straniera in Italia* (Firenze: Giunti).

Coy, M., M. Horvath and L. Kelly (2007), '"It's Just Like Going to the Supermarket": Men Buying Sex in East London', London: Child and Woman Abuse Studies Unit, London Metropolitan University.

Della Giusta, M., M.L. Di Tommaso and S. Stroem (2007a), 'Sex, Power and Reputation: A Model of the Market for Prostitution Services', *Journal of Population Economics*, forthcoming (published on line from 6 April 2007, and available at <http://www.springerlink.com/content/k2v47x73u2n62604>).

Della Giusta, M., M.L. Di Tommaso, I. Shima and S. Stroem (2007b), 'What Money Buys: The Demand for Prostitution Services' *Applied Economics*, forthcoming (published on line from 12 December 2007, and available at <http://www.informaworld.com/smpp/content~content=a788424853~db=all~order=author>).

Dobbelsteen, S. and P. Kooreman (1997), 'Financial Management, Bargaining and Efficiency within Household: An Empirical Analysis', *De Economist* 145:3, 345–66.

Edlund, L. and E. Korn (2002), 'An Economic Theory of Prostitution', *Journal of Political Economy* 110:1, 181–214.

Ehrenreich, B. and A. Russell Hochschild (eds) (2003), *Global Woman: Nannies, Maids, and Sex Workers in the New Economy* (New York: Henry Holt and Company).

Garofalo, G. (2002), *Towards an Economic Theory of Prostitution* (Mimeo: University of Siena).

Gertler et al. (2003), *Risky Business: The Market for Unprotected Prostitution* (Mimeo: Cornell University).

Granovetter, M. (1985), 'Economic Action and Social Structure: The Problem of Embeddedness', *American Journal of Sociology* 91, 481–510.

Hirsch, F. (1977), *Social Limits to Growth* (London: Routledge and Kegan Paul).

Holli, A.M. (2004), 'Towards a New Prohibitionism? State Feminism, Women's Movements and Prostitution Policies in Finland' in J. Outshoorn (ed.), *The Politics of Prostitution* (Cambridge: Cambridge University Press).

Home Office (2004), *Paying the Price: A Consultation Paper on Prostitution* (London: HMSO).

Home Office (2006), *A Coordinated Prostitution Strategy and a Summary of Responses to Paying the Price* (London: HMSO).

Hubbard, P. (1998), 'Community Action and the Displacement of Street Prostitution: Evidence from British Cities', *Geoforum* 29:3, 269–86.

International Information Centre and Archives for the Women's Movement: <www.iiav.nl>.

Jeffrey, L.A. (2004), 'Prostitution and Public Nuisance: Prostitution Policy in Canada' in J. Outshoorn (ed.), *The Politics of Prostitution* (Cambridge: Cambridge University Press).

Kempadoo, K. and J. Doezema (eds) (1998), *Global Sex Workers: Rights, Resistance and Redefinition* (London: Routledge).

Kern, R.M. (2000), 'Prostitute Client Profiles: Indicators of Motivations for Prostitution Use', *Archives of Sexual Behaviour* 29:2, 165–77.

Lim, L.L. (ed.) (1998), *The Sex Sector: The Economic and Social Bases of Prostitution in Southeast Asia* (Geneva: International Labour Office).

Lundberg, S. and R.A. Pollak (1994), 'Non Cooperative Bargaining Models of Marriage', *The American Economic Review* 84:2, 132–7.

Lundberg, S. and R.A. Pollak (2003), 'Efficiency in Marriage', *Review of Economics of the Household* 1:3, 153–67.

Manser, M. and M. Brown (1980), 'Marriage and Household Decision Making: A Bargaining Analysis', *International Economic Review* 21:1, 31–44.

Mansky, C. (2000), 'Economic Analysis of Social Interactions', *Journal of Economic Perspectives* 14, 114–36.

Marttila, A.-M. (2003), 'Consuming Sex: Finnish Male Clients and Russian and Baltic Prostitution', paper presented at Gender and Power in the New Europe, the 5th European Feminist Research Conference, 20–24 August 2003, Lund University, Sweden.

McElroy, M. and M.J. Horney (1981), 'Nash-Bargained Household Decisions: Toward a Generalization of the Theory of Demand', *International Economic Review* 22:2, 333–49.

McKeganey, N. and M. Barnard (1996), *Sex Work on the Streets: Prostitutes and Their Clients* (Buckingham: Open University Press).

Moffatt P.G. and S.A. Peters (2001), 'The Pricing of Personal Services' (Mimeo: Royal Economic Society in Durham, April 2001).

Nussbaum, M. (1999), *Sex and Social Justice* (New York: Oxford University Press).

O'Connell Davidson, J. (1998), *Prostitution Power and Freedom* (Cambridge: Polity).

O'Kane, M. (2002), *Prostitution: The Laws Don't Work*, Channel 4 documentary, UK.

Outshoorn, Joyce (ed.) (2004), *The Politics of Prostitution* (Cambridge: Cambridge University Press).

Pagano, U. (1999), 'Is Power an Economic Good? Notes on Social Scarcity and the Economics of Positional Goods' in S. Bowles, M. Franzini and U. Pagano (1999), *The Politics and the Economics of Power* (London and New York: Routledge).

Pateman, C. (1988), *The Sexual Contract* (Stanford, CA: Stanford University Press).

Pitts, M.K., A.M.A. Smith, J. Grierson, M. O'Brien and S. Misson (2004), 'Who Pays for Sex and Why? An Analysis of Social and Motivational Factors Associated with Male Clients of Sex Workers', *Archives of Sexual Behavior* 33.

Putnam, R.D. (1993), *Making Democracy Work: Civic Traditions in Modern Italy* (Princeton, NJ: Princeton University Press).

Rao, V., I. Gupta, M. Lokshin and J. Jana (2001), 'Sex Workers and the Cost of Safe Sex: The Compensating Differential for Condom Use in Calcutta' (Mimeo: World Bank).

Reynolds, H. (1986), *The Economics of Prostitution* (Springfield, IL: C.C. Thomas).

Ryley, S. (1936), *A History of Prostitution form Antiquity to Present* (Delhi: Shubhi Publications), distributed by APH Publishing Corp., 1999. Reprint of the 1936 edition published by T.W. Laurie, London.

Sanchez Taylor, J. (2001), 'Dollars Are a Girl's Best Friend? Female Tourists' Sexual Behaviour in the Caribbean', *Sociology: Identity Politics in the Workplace* 35:3, 749–64.

Sanders, T. (2005), *Sex Work: A Risky Business* (Cullompton: Willan).

Sanders, T. (2007), 'Evidence to Local Government Committee on Prostitution (Public Places) Scotland Bill' from Dr Teela Sanders, University of Leeds, <http://www.scottish.parliament.uk/business/committees/lg/inquiries/ppp/lg-ppp-Sanders.pdf>.

Sanders, T. (2008), *Paying for Pleasure: Men Who Buy Sex* (Cullompton: Willan).

Sauer, B. (2004), 'Taxes, Rights and Regimentation: Discourses on Prostitution in Austria' in J. Outshoorn (ed.), *The Politics of Prostitution* (Cambridge: Cambridge University Press).

Schultz, T.P. (1990), 'Testing the Neoclassical Model of Family Labor Supply and Fertility', *The Journal of Human Resources* 25:4, 599–634.

Sharpe, K. (1998), *Red Light, Blue Light: Prostitutes, Punters and the Police* (Aldershot: Ashgate).

Sullivan, B. (2004), 'The Women's Movement and Prostitution Politics in Australia' in J. Outshoorn (ed.), *The Politics of Prostitution* (Cambridge: Cambridge University Press).

Thorbek, S. and B. Pattanaik (eds) (2002), *Transnational Prostitution: Changing Global Patterns* (London: Zed Books).

Tiggey, M., A. Harocopos and M. Hough (2000), 'For Love or Money: Pimps and the Management of Sex Work', Policing and Reducing Crime Unit (London: Home Office).

Chapter 8

Client Participation and the Regulatory Environment

Alan Collins and Guy Judge[1]

Informed by rational choice theory (Arrow 1987; Becker 1978), this chapter considers the issue of client participation and behaviour in paid sex markets that may operate under any particular regulatory regime. Specific consideration is also given to the issue of enforcement level variability within any such regime. Rational choice theory is essentially a framework for conceptualising and, if desired, even formally modelling human behaviour. The usual form of the maximand expressed concerns individual humans seeking to maximise their individual satisfaction or utility. Rationality is a common if not dominant assumption in much work in microeconomic analysis, but also in political science and some schools of sociology. Such an approach does not claim to provide a complete fit to reality in all cases but rather it does claim to help construct models which assist reasoning, large scale policy analysis and the generation of falsifiable hypotheses for subsequent empirical social enquiry.

In this chapter, there is also no linkage (explicit or implicit) in any way with an agenda that favours a specific path of market development, such as market elimination or sex worker exiting (the latter being one that Scoular and O' Neill [2007, and in Chapter 1 of this collection] view as a current tool of New Labour's attempt to increase social control under the rhetoric of inclusion, through 'techniques' of risk and responsibilisation). Nevertheless, if open-minded, and not tied to any specific moral agenda, governments can potentially learn from client behaviour to help design the demand side of regulatory policy in a way that balances the interests of sex workers, clients and community neighbourhoods.

In a rational consumer world, using prostitution services is viewed purely and simply as a consumption activity, albeit one that features to a greater, lesser or, in some cases, negligible extent, stigma or reputation costs (depending on location, prevalent social norms or the nature of any relevant peer group relations). Consumption of sex worker services also features considerable potential revelation costs in terms of disturbance to any existing personal relationship. For some individuals, recourse to the consumption of prostitution services serves also as an intrinsically time-saving consumption option. By this is meant the potential attribute of such services, whereby any desired amount or type of sexual contact can more reliably be scheduled in a

1 We are grateful for comments received at the Supply/Demand Dynamic in Prostitution seminars supported by the British Academy and the ESRC.

given allocated time slot, more or less on demand. For many, particularly wealthy individuals, it is the time constraint rather than any budget constraint which is far more important. Time is a commodity of which even the very wealthy cannot acquire or release more of without substantial changes to their existing work patterns and lifestyles.

The first part of this chapter briefly examines the economic literature that has explored the demand side of the market and then proceeds to consider the likely impact on consumers of alternative regulatory models. The latter part of the chapter takes the regulatory regime as given and then explores the likely effects of enforcement level variability (which arises for a whole raft of reasons) on client behaviour. Through a simple economic model, it is shown that such variability is likely to lead to consumption being subject to some spatial displacement. The implications of this phenomenon are then considered.

The Demand for Prostitution Services

In an early and somewhat curious theoretical economic paper on prostitution, Edlund and Korn (2002) asserted that client demand is purely a function of the price of commercial sex, the price of sex within marriage, male income, and the proportion of married and unmarried men. Their characterisation of demand also advances the view that the use of prostitution services by married men is less than that of unmarried men, mainly because married men tend to have less disposable income to spend in paid sex markets.[2] This particular aspect of the model contradicts a substantial body of evidence suggesting that a very large proportion (or in some cases the majority) of the clients (regular or otherwise) of both female and male sex workers are married men.[3] Potentially, this can be attributed to a desire for variety in demand preferences (Scitovsky 1976) and/or constraints and deficiencies regarding within-marriage sexual activity. Using a prostitute may address or satisfy all these needs without the need for any emotional complications, since the existing relationship may, in general, provide adequate companionship and emotional support. Indeed, unlike the heroine in the 1990 film *Pretty Woman*, prostitutes may well be able to treat sex as work and maintain emotional detachment from clients.

Since many consumers of prostitution services are in existing relationships, they are more likely to endure considerable social disapproval if discovered. Widespread realisation of this helps account for its harnessing in some city-wide policy initiatives, aiming to reduce any community nuisance arising from 'kerb-crawling'. An early spatial economic contribution shedding some light on such geographical variations found in regulating paid sex markets is provided by Reynolds (1986). She presents a detailed narrative explanation of the spatial variations found in prostitution markets and also provides a number of insights into the presence of prostitution activity in a

2 Cameron (2002) and Della Giusta et al. (2004) provide a more extensive critique of Edlund and Korn (2002).

3 See, for example, Morse et al. (1991); Heng et al. (1992); Havanon, Bennet and Knodel (1993); De Graaf (1996); De Graaf et al. (1997); Organista et al. (1997); Lawoyin et al. (2001); Brooks-Gordon and Gelsthorpe (2003).

given location using what may be considered a principally rational choice informed perspective. The study also describes the pattern of incentives and disincentives arising from different legal regimes in terms of the type of sex work that is engaged in and its location. A more extensive set of explanations for the urban concentration of much paid sex market activity can be found in Cameron (2004), Collins (2004) and Ryder (2004).

Regulatory Models in Paid Sex Markets

Men and women have been selling sexual (prostitution) services to each other for many centuries in wholly independent, state-owned or church-owned enterprises, or under various gradations and types of federal, state or municipal regulation. The legal status and degree of social stigma associated with prostitution since 1900 has exhibited enormous cross-country variation and even significant inter-regional or inter-urban differences. Over the course of the twentieth century, there have been social changes (for example, female emancipation and legalisation of homosexual activity) and public health concerns (primarily syphilis, gonorrhoea and subsequently HIV/AIDS) which have, in some locations, led to increasing liberalisation, and in others, encouraged even greater restrictions on paid sex markets.

In most countries, the more mainstream market in the early twentieth century comprised, as now, both street-based and off-street (brothel-based) prostitution. In 1902, New Orleans instituted Storyville (named after Alderman Sidney Story), which provides an early example of a sex work toleration zone. It was devised to help the city enjoy the economic benefits of this industry, but also to restrict 'nuisance' or 'disturbance' to the wider residential community (Tannahill 1990). The toleration zone was discontinued by the Federal Government around 1917, subsequent to a decree that all brothels within 5 miles of a naval base had to close. This event was at the tail end of a wave of bans and restrictions on prostitution in most states of the United States over the period 1910–1915, which were considered to be influenced by the actions of the Women's Christian Temperance Union.

At the dawn of the First World War, similar concerns to those of the US military were also evident in Germany. Yet closure of brothels was considered to be likely to affect adversely troop morale. Accordingly, mobile military brothels were a common feature behind fighting lines. Formal or informal military brothel operations have been a feature of the Japanese military in the 1930s, as well as the US military in connection with the Philippine occupation, and the Korean and Vietnam wars (Brock and Thistlethwaite 1996), and more recently in connection with United Nations troops in Bosnia.

The continued existence of paid sex markets remains subject to strongly contested views about the design of an appropriate public policy towards prostitution. Much argument is rendered less clear by the analytically unhelpful and often deliberately misleading conflation of the enormous range of prostitution markets into one single, seemingly homogeneous market. This means that paid sex markets involving, (a) minors, (b) the support of hard drug dependency, and (c) coercion and enslavement of sex workers are often considered (for reasons of political and lobbying strategy) in the same manner as prostitution markets that solely feature adult voluntary transactions devoid of (a) to (c). Yet even entirely consensual adult paid sex markets still ferment bitter rancour across the religious-moral-political spectrum, and even among some feminists.[4]

While legal changes are currently being advanced in England and Wales to permit brothels to operate with a cap on the number of workers (three being the upper limit) (BBC News 2006), more recent policy murmurings from the Labour Party are hinting at completely banning the purchase of (presumably both male and female) sex worker services. Nevertheless, regardless of the geographical context, it is likely that illegal sex workers and enterprises will still continue to operate in the same way that illegal traders operate alongside legal traders in countless other types of market. They may gain from tax evasion, offering banned (for example, under-aged sex) or higher risk premium services (unsafe sex) not permitted in the legal market (Cameron 2002). In those market contexts where regulation entails sex workers undertaking health checks for sexually transmissible infections, those who fail such checks may be under pressure to work illegally. Organised crime enterprises may also continue to attempt to use their coercion capital to 'manage' sex workers for generating third-party gains.

Arguably on the demand-side, the option of legal market participation is likely to erode significantly the client base from the much higher risk unregulated markets, reducing the illegal market demand to a residual hardcore client base. It is open to question whether this may be more easily targeted with the existing police enforcement resources. This might be expected given a potentially lesser required focus on the clients and suppliers in the mainstream legal market. Even with a permissive legal framework regarding prostitution, it is also likely that a jurisdiction may require the management and containment of prostitution activity (though not necessarily by police officers) to 'protect' nearby residents, or other elements of the community, from the real or perceived spillover effects from this activity. This generally means delimiting the hours of business and/or spatial margins of prostitution activity. These are limits that could apply to both on-street and off-street commercial sexual services. Without some credible enforcement effort, it is likely these limits of space and time would be challenged. If not subjected to legal interventions with a non-negligible probability, a custom of transgression may soon become established.

There is also a pragmatic consensus emerging around the world, formed in the light of decades of practical experience, that the basic guiding principles which should actually operate on the ground are feasibility of enforcement and harm minimisation in the community. In some mature industrial economies, however, market elimination or the gradual reduction of the numbers of working prostitutes remain as desired long-term objectives (Home Office 2004; Expert Group on Prostitution in Scotland [EGPS] 2004).

4 For a more detailed discussion, see Della Giusta et al. (2004).

Clients and Regulatory Regimes

Brief characterisations of a number of regulatory models found in various countries/regions are set out in Collins and Judge (2008a). These regulatory models are also given some stylised formal mathematical representation in order to support some economic policy focus on the nature and effects on client participation of alternative regulatory environments.

It is suggested that the key feature of such models is that the pattern of perceived client risk is more likely to be one where street-based unlicensed and illicit consumption feature the highest composite risk levels, while regulated off-street consumption is likely to present lower client risks. There is clearly some scope for debate as to whether licensed street-based consumption offers lesser or greater perceived client risks than off-street unlicensed consumption. Notwithstanding this caveat, it is asserted that the general pattern of perceived client risk moves from high to low as the consumption environment changes from illegal street-based consumption towards increasingly regulated off-street consumption. It seems likely that, were pro-legalisation regulatory changes to become manifest, then it should be expected that the extant volume of trade would increase, as clients previously deterred by higher risk consumption commence market participation.

From such a viewpoint, Collins and Judge (2008a) build on previous empirical work (Cameron and Collins 2003) suggesting that most clients are indeed responsive to risk level variations. They set out a theoretical model to depict the dominant market feature of normal risk responsive clients. The issue of risk loving individuals is recognised to be problematic. A persistent fraction of the client base will still hanker after greater utility from search and kerb-crawling, unlike the majority of clients. Nevertheless, given Collins and Judge (2008a) use a composite risk measure, it seems likely that even for some persistent nuisance kerb-crawlers, behaviour adjustment may still be elicited as a consequence of reductions in other categories of risk from other elements of the service experience.

Using such a framework, regulators can potentially harness clients' perceived risk responses to reduce harm on both sides of the market, as well as reducing the negative externalities of kerb-crawling (which are strongly associated with neighbourhood community nuisance). The crux of such a strategy by regulators seems to lie in the direction of genuinely greater liberalisation for some types of licensed sex service providers. These are likely to be characterised by market provision that is primarily off-street and probably in more distant locations from residential communities than is hitherto typically the case.

Clients in Paid Sex Markets and Variations in Enforcement Level

Police officers on the ground, as well as their senior officers, generally accept the view that arresting prostitutes and their clients is simply not as important as arresting many other types of 'offenders'. Police officer preferences and priorities will differ such that the discretion applied to the enforcement of paid sex market-related offences will vary geographically. Clients of prostitutes will also respond to such differences in the level of enforcement found across police and/or municipal jurisdictions at various levels. Analyses and debates on this topic have hitherto typically been guided by two key hypotheses that have emerged in the criminology and the economics of crime literature. Such work is often grouped around support or otherwise for the 'crime displacement' hypothesis[5] and the 'diffusion of crime control benefits' hypothesis.[6]

The crime displacement hypothesis asserts that crime prevention strategies that are built upon a greater profile to deterrence and 'clamping down' on specific criminal (target) individuals/groups in a given area are likely to be of limited effectiveness or completely ineffective. Such strategies, it is suggested, are subverted by the exercising of 'compensating behaviours' by those participating in illegal activity. Such behaviours may feature re-adjustment of offence participation in terms of one or more dimensions, namely, time, space and the focus/category of crime. Hence, should such re-adjustments take place in relation to a specific crime or group of crimes in a given place, the net welfare impacts to society as a whole becomes a somewhat open empirical question.

The 'diffusion of crime control benefits' hypothesis relates to crime prevention efforts in specific locations, and which are asserted to lead to crime problem improvements in adjacent areas. This hypothesis has provided a key theoretical driver to justify the implementation of 'zero tolerance' crime initiatives. These are characterised by the application of highly visible and persistently strong police (and other regulatory agency) enforcement, across virtually all categories of criminal activity (serious or otherwise). The standard popular explanation for such a strategy is often articulated in terms of 'the broken window principle'. This suggests that if even the results of minor visible crimes and/or physical dereliction (such as a broken window) are sustained, this acts as a signal. The message transmitted is one where the relevant community does not care about crime, and so more broken windows are said to be effectively invited and tolerated. This is considered to help foster a wider community malaise and to accelerate any predisposition to crime. Hence, the suggested solution is to clamp down heavily on all crimes and misdemeanours in a given neighbourhood to signal 'care' and 'interest' in the social and physical fabric of the community. A more detailed discussion on such initiatives is provided by, for example, Greene (1999) and Hubbard (2004).

The standard tools of microeconomic analysis can be applied to help re-frame some aspects of this 'crime' policy debate. What is often lost in such discussions is the possibility that prostitution services may be perceived by clients (in their more general guise as consumers) like other service goods, albeit those featuring some measure of risk in consumption. The presence of risk characteristics are, however, not unusual in many other goods and service markets. Thus, the enforcement level debate pertaining to 'crime displacement' or 'diffusion of crime control benefits' as applied to paid sex markets can also (and perhaps more usefully) be characterised as a simple consumer choice problem.

5 See, for example, Mehay (1977); Gabor (1981); Ratcliffe (2005).

6 See, for example, Smith (2001); Katz et al. (2001); Weisburd et al. (2006).

It is assumed throughout that any legislation applies equally across the jurisdictions, but for various reasons the law is not enforced to the same level in all areas. Consider two locations that are sufficiently close to each other so that a consumer in one location (A) can travel to the other (B), or *vice versa*, to satisfy part of their demand. Further suppose that there are risks of incurring a cost (or disutility) from the consumption of the good or service, at least some of which are location-dependent. If either the price of the good or service being offered, or the risks arising from the consumption of the good or service, go up in one of the locations but not in the other, then following standard consumer theory, one would expect to see, *ceteris paribus*, a shift in the demand away from the location where the price or risk has increased and towards the location where the price or risk has remained unchanged.

Intuitively, one could expect that some consumers who are concerned with revelation risks would be more likely to travel to a different area to consume such services. This tendency would be increased if there was a perception that the enforcement of the law was somewhat more relaxed in the other area. This would also have to be set against any additional travel costs and time loss incurred. The actual responsiveness to these different factors may vary. However, if people are in any way sensitive to revelation risks, there would likely be some cases where demand would switch between areas.

So if it is assumed that the price remains constant, and the same between the two locations at P*, based on the initial demand curves, there may emerge an equilibrium situation with demand at QA1* in location A and at QB1* in location B (see Figures 8.1a and 8.1b).

If consumers become aware of the fact that the law is not being enforced as strongly in location B as it is in location A, this may lead some consumers in location A to switch at least part of their demand to location B. The extent to which this will happen depends upon a number of factors including: (i) how much difference there is in their perception of the risk of being involved with the police in each location in the course of their consumption; (ii) the degree of disutility the consumers have as a result of any dealings they have with the police, both in terms of general inconvenience and, more seriously, revelation costs (or reputational effects) as these dealings become known to friends and neighbours [for some people these costs may well be trivial but for others they might be very significant]; and (iii) any travel costs that will be incurred if consumers feel it appropriate to move from location A to location B in order to consume sex services. A more formal mathematical analysis of the type of model sketched here is provided in Collins and Judge (2008b).

In summary, if the police in one area have a relatively relaxed attitude to enforcement, but those in a neighbouring area take a more stringent approach, such that the risk of incurring a possible disutility in the neighbouring area is increased, then a migration of demand towards the more relaxed policing area can be expected. This may be perceived as wholly acceptable on the part of the residents, voters and policing authorities in the less tolerant area. But quite clearly, those residents in the area where policing practices are more relaxed may feature considerable dissatisfaction.

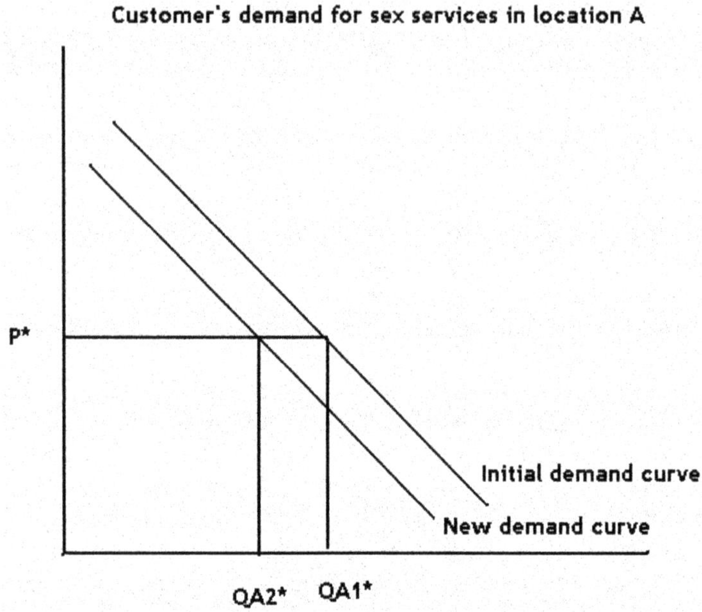

Figure 8.1(a) The shifts in demand resulting from a change in the perception of risk between two locations – the case of location A

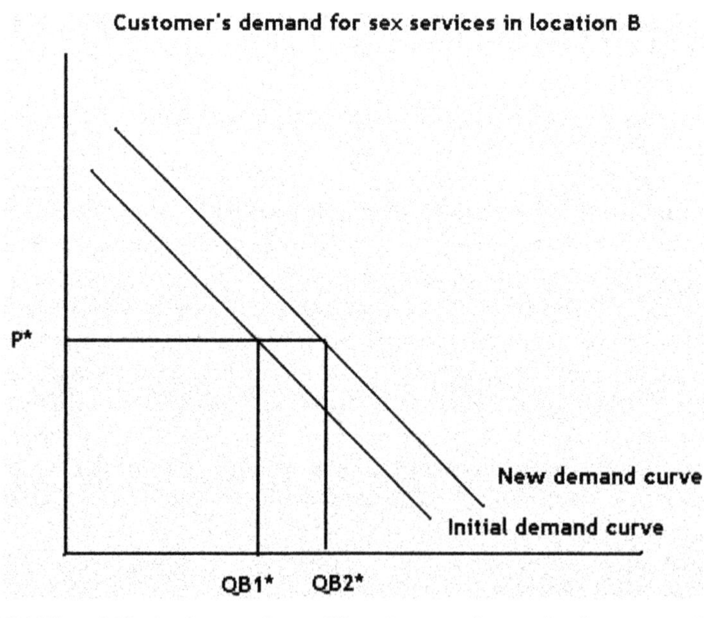

Figure 8.1(b) The shifts in demand resulting from a change in the perception of risk between two locations – the case of location B

The simple point to be made clear is that the kind of demand switching suggested in this study would be exacerbated even if law enforcement was merely *perceived* to be lower in a given location than elsewhere. Such switches may then lead to a number of (unintended) consequences. First, many of the residents of the area in which the demand was stimulated may experience additional nuisance costs. Second, the police in that area may find a surprisingly large number of complaints from residents about the increased sex services activity. Third, the police in the more tightly regulated area may experience a reduction in their typical number of cases as sex service consumers go elsewhere. Effectively, the nuisance costs and policing cost would be transferred along with many of the consumers from one area to another. Further, it may not be immediately obvious to all parties concerned what the root causes of these altered circumstances are.

It might reasonably be argued that this outcome is, in fact, a reasonable reflection of the different attitudes to the consumption of sex services in the different areas. It may even be argued that there are built-in correctional forces to produce movement to a suitable equilibrium. If residents in the currently light enforcement area feel strongly about what is happening, they would lobby for either more resources to be found for policing or for greater priority to be given to the policing of the sex services sector. However, if the intention of the national government was to have legislation in place that produces a common approach across all localities under their jurisdiction, then differential degrees of law enforcement would serve to obstruct this objective.

Surges of client and, in turn, supplier paid sex market migration might thus be expected in the face of differential enforcement. In principle, this could be reduced to some degree by a measure of enforcement coordination across police authorities. Yet, the extent to which this could in practice be genuinely sustained is more open to question. Police forces comprise individuals who will vary in work habits, social and moral disposition, religiosity and so on. This can influence their on-the-ground prioritisation of criminal offences in any given 'beat'.

If the enforcement regime differs across an adjacent national boundary, then similar effects can still be expected to be observed and their magnitude conditioned by the ease (or transaction costs) of border crossing. One such example is Sweden where the current government has criminalised the purchase of sex worker services, so that men cross the land border in larger numbers to participate in neighbouring country markets (Gould 2001; Kulick 2003; Ekberg 2004). This also has the effect of driving further underground any domestic market activity and making more economically viable the 'bussing in' of adjacent country sex workers to support highly profitable 'hit and run' market operations. Domestic prices are thus driven down in the face of greater competition and by domestic sex workers 'compensating' for the greater client risks from merely signalling themselves as potential consumers (Ostergren 2007). Some domestic sex workers may thus become so desperate for income that this could have a bearing on their ability to resist calls for unsafe sexual activities. It should also be noted that the Swedish policy does not seem to address the root problem of sex trafficking at all, as was heralded, since the experience so far appears to indicate that migrant sex workers are merely being deported.

The net effect of all this is, of course, also to make domestic clients more likely to be stressed and scared, with client evaluation necessarily being conducted in a more rapid manner. This raises the risk of many sex workers ending up with more dangerous clients than might otherwise be the case. Sex workers are seemingly more reluctant to seek help from the police regarding abusive clients and, given the more furtive nature of the market, domestic sex workers do not now have as comprehensive an informal social network to provide advance warnings on rogue clients (Ostergren 2007). There still appears to exist a real need for extensive, robust and independent quantitative field research to help assess in a more comprehensive and rounded way the full impacts of the Swedish 1998 legislation on the criminalisation of the purchase of sex worker services.

Such spatial adjustments also raise other equity issues. Figuring large among these will be the potential generation, over time and space, of a series of induced forced rider problems in adjacent jurisdictions. These arise because waves of paid sex market participants can potentially require swift and significant reactive changes to the composition of local public goods that feature in a particular jurisdiction. Inevitably, these may not be consistent with the current collective preferences and resource priorities of its voter-residents. The extent to which this is the case and the nature of any likely time path to some spatial equilibrium in this context is an open empirical question. There are, however, reasonable normative judgements to be made about the fairness of such outcomes to particular groups of voter-residents in particular locations. Alternatively, it may be argued that markedly divergent rates of offending behaviour, including that related to the consumption of prostitution services, are not intrinsically desirable. Hence, voter-residents who have historically enjoyed lower offending rates and now express dissatisfaction with any induced spending (to address a measure of displaced offending) are implicitly sustaining and helping to reinforce the existing spatial pattern of household socio-economic inequalities. In a national border setting, such regulatory regime differences can thus effectively mean activating and sustaining a policy that encourages the importing and exporting of sex work operations under conditions where work, health and trading standards are likely to be less visible.

References

Arrow, K.J. (1987), 'Economic Theory and the Hypothesis of Rationality', in J. Eatwell, M. Milgate and P. Newman (eds), *The New Palgrave Dictionary of Economics Vol 2*, 69–75.

BBC News (2006), 'New plan to permit small brothels', <http://news.bbc.co.uk/1/hi/uk/4619098.stm> [17 January 2006].

Becker, G. (1978), *The Economic Approach to Human Behavior* (Chicago, IL: University of Chicago Press).

Brewis, J. and S. Linstead (2000), *Sex, Work and Sex Work: Eroticizing Organization* (London: Routledge).

Brock, R.N. and S.B. Thistlethwaite (1996), *Casting Stones: Prostitution and Liberation in Asia and the United States* (Minneapolis, MN: Fortress Press).

Brooks-Gordon, B. and G. Gelsthorpe (2003), 'What Men Say When Apprehended for Kerb Crawling: A Model of Prostitutes' Clients Talk', *Psychology, Crime and Law* 9:2, 145–71.

Cameron, S. (2002), *The Economics of Sin: Rational Choice or No Choice At All* (Cheltenham, UK: Elgar).

Cameron, S. (2004), 'Space, Risk and Opportunity: The Evolution of Paid Sex Markets', *Urban Studies* 41:9, 1643–58.

Cameron, S. and A. Collins (2003), 'Estimates of a Model of Male Participation in the Market for Female Heterosexual Prostitution Services', *European Journal of Law and Economics* 16:3, 271–88.

Collins, A. (2004), 'Sexuality and Sexual Services in the Urban Economy and Socialscape', *Urban Studies* 41:9, 1631–42.

Collins, A. and G. Judge (2008a), 'Client Participation in Paid Sex Markets under Alternative Regulatory Regimes', *International Review of Law and Economics* (forthcoming).

Collins, A. and G. Judge (2008b), 'Differential Enforcement across Police Jurisdictions and Client Demand in Paid Sex Markets', *European Journal of Law and Economics* (forthcoming).

De Graaf, R. (1996), 'Segmentation of Heterosexual Prostitution into Various Forms: A Barrier to the Potential Transmission of HIV', *AIDS Care* 8:4, 417–32.

De Graaf, R., G. Van Zessen, I. Vanwesenbeeck, C.J. Straver and J.H. Visser (1997), 'Condom Use by Dutch Men with Commercial Heterosexual Contacts: Determinants and Considerations', *AIDS Education and Prevention* 9:5, 411–23.

Della Giusta, M., M.L. Di Tommaso and S. Strom (2004), 'Another Theory of Prostitution', Discussion Paper N13-2004, Centre for Institutional Performance, Reading University Business School.

Edlund, L. and E. Korn (2002), 'A Theory of Prostitution', *Journal of Political Economy* 110:1, 181–214.

Ekberg, G. (2004), 'The Swedish Law that Prohibits the Purchase of Sexual Services', *Violence Against Women* 10:10, 1187–218.

Expert Group on Prostitution in Scotland (2004), *Being Outside: Constructing a Response to Street Prostitution* (Edinburgh: Scottish Executive).

Gabor, T. (1981), 'The Crime Displacement Hypothesis: An Empirical Examination', *Crime and Delinquency* 27:3, 390–404.

Gould, A. (2001), 'The Criminalisation of Buying Sex: The Politics of Prostitution in Sweden', *Journal of Social Policy* 30:3, 437–56.

Greene, J.A. (1999), 'Zero Tolerance: A Case Study of Police Policies and Practices in New York City', *Crime and Delinquency* 45:2, 171–87.

Havanon, N., A. Bennet and J. Knodel (1993), 'Sexual Networking in Provincial Thailand', *Studies in Family Planning* 24:1, 1–17.

Heng, B.H., H.P. Lee, L.P. Kok, Y.W. Ong and M.L. Ho (1992), 'A Survey of Sexual Behaviour of Singaporeans', *Annals of the Academy of Medicine Singapore* 21:6, 723–9.

Home Office (2004), *Paying the Price: A Consultation Paper on Prostitution* (London: Home Office). Available online from <http://www.homeoffice.gov.uk/docs3/paying_the_price.html>.

Hubbard, P. (2004), 'Cleansing the Metropolis: Sex Work and the Politics of Zero Tolerance', *Urban Studies* 41:9, 1687–702.

Katz, C.M., V.J. Webb and D.R. Schaefer (2001), 'An Assessment of the Impact of Quality-of-Life Policing on Crime and Disorder', *Justice Quarterly* 18:4, 825–76.

Kulick, D. (2003), 'Sex in the New Europe: The Criminalization of Clients and Swedish Fear of Penetration', *Anthropological Theory* 3:2, 199–218.

Lawoyin, T.O., U. Larsen, H. Osinowo and M.E. Walker (2001), 'Sexual Behaviour Risks of Married Men in Oyo State, Nigeria', *International Journal of STD and AIDS* 12:1, 63–4.

McKeganey, N. and M. Barnard (1996), *Sex Work on the Streets: Prostitutes and Their Clients* (Buckingham: Open University Press).

Mehay, S.L. (1977), 'Interjurisdictional Spillovers of Urban Police Services', *Southern Economic Journal* 43:3, 1352–9.

Morse, E.V., P.M. Simon, H.J. Osofsky, P.M. Balson and H.R. Gaumer (1991), 'The Male Street Prostitute: A Vector for Transmission of HIV Infection into the Heterosexual World', *Social Science and Medicine* 32:5, 535–9.

O'Connell Davidson, J. and I. Sanchez Taylor (1996), *Child Prostitution and Sex Tourism: Costa Rica*, ECPAT International Research Report. Department of Sociology, University of Leicester.

Organista, K.C., P.B. Organista, J.E. Garcia de Alba, M.A. Castillo Moran and L.E. Ureta Carillo (1997), 'Survey of Condom-Related Beliefs, Behaviours and Received Social Norms in Mexican Migrant Laborers', *Journal of Community Health* 22:3, 185–98.

Ostergren, P. (2007), 'Sex Workers Critique of Swedish Prostitution Policy', <http://www.petraostergren.com/content/view/44/67/> [date accessed 1 January 2008].

Ratcliffe, J.H. (2005), 'Detecting Spatial Movement of Intra-Region Crime Patterns Over Time', *Journal of Quantitative Criminology* 21:1, 103–23.

Reynolds, H. (1986), *The Economics of Prostitution* (Springfield IL: C.C. Thomas).

Ryder, A. (2004), 'The Changing Nature of Adult Entertainment Districts: Between a Rock and a Hard Place or Going from Strength to Strength?', *Urban Studies* 41:9, 1659–86.

Scitovsky, T. (1976) *The Joyless Economy* (Oxford: Oxford University Press).

Scoular, J. and M. O'Neill (2007), 'Regulating Prostitution: Social Inclusion, Responsibilization and the Politics of Prostitution Reform', *British Journal of Criminology* (forthcoming).

Smith, M.R. (2001), 'Police-Led Crackdowns and Cleanups: An Evaluation of a Crime Control Initiative in Richmond, Florida', *Crime and Delinquency* 47:1, 60–83.

Tannahill, R. (1990), *Sex in History* (London: Book Club Associates).

Weisburd, D., L.A. Wyckoff, J. Ready, J.E. Eck, J.C. Hinkle and F. Gajewski (2006), 'Does Crime Just Move around the Corner? A Controlled Study of Spatial Displacement and Diffusion of Crime Control Benefits', *Criminology* 44:3, 549–92.

Chapter 9

Criminalising the Use of Trafficked Prostitutes: Some Philosophical Issues

David Archard

The Proposal

On 25 April 2006, the *Guardian* reported that '[m]en who knowingly have sex with trafficked prostitutes will be prosecuted for rape' (Muir and Taylor 2006). Again in September 2007, the *Guardian* reported senior members of the present UK government to be sympathetic to the idea of criminalising the purchase rather than sale of sex (Branigan 2007). The original proposal formed part of the launch of Operation Pentameter, a nationwide campaign in England and Wales, supported by the Association of Chief Police Officers and the Home Office, to tackle the illegal trafficking and exploitation of human beings. The philosophically interesting question raised by the proposal is whether a justifiable part of any such campaign is the prosecution of those who play no part in the trafficking of women for sexual exploitation but who nevertheless have sex with the women.

In what follows, I write as a moral philosopher trying to identify and evaluate one important question, namely whether – in order to eliminate or significantly ameliorate a very great social wrong – there is merit in punishing those who contribute to the wrong but who do so unwittingly and, in consequence, arguably innocently. In what follows, I therefore take as read the wrongness of trafficking women for sexual exploitation. In doing this, I do not want to ignore the complexity of matters, or discount the social scientific writing that seeks to make this complexity apparent (O'Connell Davidson 1998). The simple-minded question I address is this: if we grant that the trafficking of women for the purposes of prostitution is an awful wrong, is society justified in punishing the clients who use trafficked prostitutes unaware that they are trafficked and who played no part in their trafficking?

Since the proposals quoted presume that an attack on the so-called demand side of prostitution suffices to undermine the practice, I will have call towards the end of this chapter to say more about that presumption. Otherwise, my assumptions are idealising ones and serve the purpose of keeping the principal issue under review. I also leave to one side the general question concerning prostitution that has previously largely preoccupied philosophers, namely whether the uncoerced sale of sex is morally permissible. To repeat, my concern is narrowly with the permissibility of prosecuting those – the clients of trafficked prostitutes – who are, in some important sense, innocent and rightly not held responsible for the ills of trafficking.

Trafficked Prostitution as Involuntary

I start from a view that even liberal defenders of prostitution endorse: namely that prostitution is certainly wrong if the prostitutes only offer their sexual services because they have been forced to do so. Coercion, like deception and incompetence, vitiates the freely given consent that is presumed by liberals to underpin the putative moral and legal permissibility of prostitution. I thus assume that women who have been trafficked into prostitution do not offer their services freely. The coercion in question is two-fold. Women have been forced into prostitution, and subsequently forced to remain prostitutes. Someone could enter into a course of action or career under serious threat but continue that action or career freely once the threat had been removed. However, trafficked prostitutes are trafficked by force into their place of work, and then forced to continue working by real and terrifying threats. Indeed the threats are highly efficacious – and make the criminal prosecution of traffickers difficult – because they are aimed at those families the women have left behind at home, and are thus ill-placed to help.

The claim that trafficked prostitutes are coerced into sex does not, it is important to add, entail the correlative claim that non-trafficked prostitutes are *not* coerced into sex. It is obviously possible to argue that *all* prostitution is coerced sex. That seems to me to be an implausibly strong claim. But I do not need here to take a view on it. For my starting assumption is that trafficked women provide clear and indisputable cases of involuntary commercial sex.

It is the involuntariness of their activity which lies at the core of the wrongness of trafficking. It, thus, will not help to speak merely of their 'sexual exploitation'. Documents sometimes refer to those who are trafficked into prostitution in terms of their 'sexual exploitation' whilst speaking of other forms of compulsory work as 'forced labour' (UNODC 2006, 33). A practice is exploitative where circumstances are such that one party to an exchange unfairly gets more than they should and the other gets less than they should. However, that need not be sufficient reason to think that the practice is wrong on balance. Indeed, exploitative practices may be beneficial to all parties and represent an improvement for all on what otherwise would happen (Wertheimer 1996; see also Munro, Chapter 5 in this volume). Most pertinently, persons can freely enter into exploitative arrangements. In other words, it does not follow from the fact that A is exploited by B that A's exploitation is involuntary. Trafficked prostitutes, by contrast, do not freely engage in prostitution. Their labour is forced and the fact that their work is sexual does not affect the truth of this claim. Trafficked prostitutes are sexual slaves.

The Case for the Prosecution

Let me now spell out the strongest possible case for criminalising the use by men of trafficked prostitutes. To repeat, the argument from this point on makes idealising and simplifying assumptions about the nature of trafficking in order to allow an evaluation of a particular contentious claim. Here is the argument. The trafficking of women for what is nothing other than sexual slavery is an appalling wrong. It involves sustained brutalisation, the infliction of great pain and psychological torment, degradation, and the extensive loss of liberty and self-esteem. Such trafficking is deliberately organised, systematic and appears – despite the difficulty of securing accurate figures – to be growing. There is, then, a clear imperative to do everything possible to prevent such trafficking. This imperative binds individual states and is formalised in various international protocols.

Criminalising the use of trafficked prostitutes directly tackles the demand side of such trafficking by seeking to end, or at least seriously to constrain, the markets in trafficked persons. If men, for fear of prosecution, do not make use of and pay for trafficked prostitutes, then those who would traffic women for the purposes of prostitution have no, or at least a significantly reduced, financial motive for doing so. It would obviously be ideal to prosecute those on the supply side who coerce and deceive women into prostitution. However, there are acknowledged difficulties in identifying and successfully prosecuting traffickers, especially as their criminal activities cross national borders. There are familiar difficulties in combating organised international crime: both at the juristic level in agreeing binding international law and at the level of cooperative policing between distinct authorities. It is, by contrast, much easier on the whole to identify and legally to pursue the conviction of users of prostitutes within a single well-defined jurisdiction. Such is the strongest possible case for prosecuting those who make use of trafficked prostitutes.

The Case for the Defence of Clients: Reasonable Beliefs

The biggest single moral obstacle to prosecution lies in the objection that the users of trafficked prostitutes should not be prosecuted for unwittingly using women they do not know to be coerced into prostitution. They could not, for instance, be prosecuted for rape. The government proposal cited at the beginning of this chapter stipulated that '[m]en who knowingly have sex with trafficked prostitutes will be prosecuted for rape'. They would have to be prosecuted under the Sexual Offences Act 2003 whereby a man commits rape if he intentionally has sex with a woman who does not consent and if he does not reasonably believe that she consents. Lack of reasonable belief in consent can be shown if the man knows that any of a number of specified circumstances obtain. These are listed in section 75 of the Act and, of relevance, include the use of violence against, the fear of the use of violence against and the unlawful detention of the woman.

These legal provisions offer a very plausible account of circumstances in which a prostitute is coerced into sex, and all of them are extremely likely to obtain in the cases of trafficked prostitutes. Importantly, it is not necessary for a charge of rape that the man having sex with the woman is the very same man, or one amongst a group of men, using or threatening violence against or unlawfully detaining the woman. It is enough that the man having sex knows that the woman is or has shortly beforehand been subject to violence or the threat of violence, or is unlawfully detained, as it may be, by others.

It might be argued that a man cannot be guilty of having sex with a woman *by means of* coercion if he himself does not coerce the woman. However, he is still guilty of having sex *that is coerced*. It is surely just as wrong for a man to hold a gun to a woman's head in order that he should have sex with her against her will as that he should have sex with her whilst, with his clear knowledge and perhaps contrivance, his friend holds the gun to her head. That he does not himself directly coerce her to have sex is beside the point; he has sex with her knowing that she is coerced into such sex.

The trafficked prostitute is coerced into sex with her clients and, by the terms of the Sexual Offences Act 2003, is raped. However a man using a trafficked prostitute can only be guilty of rape if he knows that he is having sex with a woman under circumstances where it would be unreasonable of him not to infer that she is coerced into sex. Indeed, where any user of a prostitute knew that the prostitute was forced into sex then he could and should be prosecuted as a rapist. However, if a man who uses a prostitute can sincerely and plausibly attest that he does not know that she is coerced or that any of those circumstances obtain in which he ought to conclude that she is coerced, then he cannot be charged with an unreasonable belief in her consent. The user of a trafficked prostitute need not be guilty of rape if his ignorance of her coerced circumstances is such that he is not unreasonable in believing that she is freely selling her sexual services.

Of course, there have to be circumstances in which a client's belief that a prostitute is offering her services free of coercion is clearly unreasonable. It would be unreasonable, for instance, if the man using the prostitute was made directly aware of how she came to be a prostitute, or of the conditions under which she continued to work as a prostitute, or if he witnessed her being subject to violence or coercive threats. On the whole this is unlikely. Nevertheless might he come to know of her trafficked status indirectly if he learned certain specific facts? In these circumstances would his belief that the prostitute is acting freely be unreasonable?

Let us grant some facts that are often quoted in reportage of trafficked prostitution: that the overwhelming majority of women providing 'off-street' prostitution – in massage parlours, peep shows and brothels – are from Eastern Europe, and trafficked from there, against their will, to work in the United Kingdom. Someone who knew these facts could in principle conclude that an Eastern European prostitute working within a brothel is very probably trafficked, and thus working only as a result of coercion. However, the acquisition of this knowledge and the execution of the required deductive steps to the conclusion presume a great deal of the average client. Amongst other things, it takes successful identification of a prostitute as from Eastern Europe, knowledge of a statistical regularity, and an appreciation of what is involved in being trafficked into sexual slavery. Why would it be reasonable to expect a normal everyday man to know all of that? A man who used a trafficked prostitute need not be acting on an unreasonable belief that she was offering her services freely.

The provisions of the Sexual Offences Act 2003 are interesting precisely because they seek to make knowledge of some kinds of fact sufficient for a lack of reasonable belief in consent. This is estimable inasmuch as it may thereby acquit courts and juries of the vexed task of deciding what is and is not a reasonable belief. All they need to do is satisfy themselves that the accused men did know certain relevant facts. But the kinds of facts that can be cited in this context – and from which fault on the part of the men can reasonably be imputed – are ones having to do with the direct coercion of the women – the use or threat of violence against them, and their unlawful detention. A man who knows only that a woman is from Eastern Europe is a long, long way from knowing facts that could demonstrate a culpable ignoring of a woman's consent.

It is, of course, beyond dispute that some men do know that a prostitute is trafficked but are not disconcerted by that fact. It is also true that some men do not bother to inspect the available evidence that she might be. Some men would simply ignore or discount any such evidence they might be provided with. Such men behave appallingly. However, what is true of some men need not be, and is probably not, true of all men. A general law must apply to the actions and dispositions of all within its scope. We are thus still a long way from being able to show that any man using a prostitute in a brothel behaves unreasonably in virtue of falsely believing or simply presuming that she is working freely.

Could we not expect clients to ask prostitutes to confirm that their services are being offered freely, and to report to the police or relevant authorities their suspicions to the contrary? The requirement that individuals report a suspected crime, if they can do so at no unreasonable cost to themselves, is defensible. But even if men did ask prostitutes whether or not they were working of their own free will, it is very far from clear that they would obtain an honest answer. The fact is that the women in question have most likely already been subject to quite dreadful levels of violence – or made subject to credible threats of violence against those close to them – intended precisely to ensure cowed acquiescence. Needless to say, it is hardly likely in these overall circumstances that trafficked women, within closely supervised brothels, are going to respond honestly to a man's inquiry as to whether or not they are working there freely.

In summary, the obtaining of certain observable facts – that the woman has an accent and a certain appearance, and works in a brothel – does not provide any man using a prostitute with a reasonable assurance that the prostitute he is using is subject to coercion and unlawful detention. He might reach this conclusion if he had access to facts about the provenance of trafficked women and the circumstances of trafficking. However, his failure to know these facts or to draw certain probable conclusions from their obtaining would not be sufficient to indict his belief in the prostitute's voluntary service as unreasonable.

To get a clearer sense of what *can* be thought of as an unreasonable belief in a woman's consent to sex it helps to be reminded of the *Morgan* case (*DPP* v. *Morgan* 1976), and the jurisprudential debate surrounding it. In the *Morgan* judgement, the British House of Lords permitted as a defence to the charge of rape the holding by a defendant of a sincere but unreasonable belief that the woman did consent to sex with him. In the particular circumstances of this case, the defence in question was that a group of men could give credence to the claim by the woman's husband that his wife liked 'kinky' or rough sex with numerous men and that they should therefore ignore any protests or resistance she offered. Morgan's wife was dragged from her bed and multiply raped despite repeated and anguished protests.

Clearly, the belief on which the *Morgan* defendants might have rested their defence was wholly unreasonable and evidently false. It is unreasonable both in respect of being held despite the victim's clear, repeated and unambiguous protests, and in relying wholly on the word of someone other than the woman, namely her husband. I have argued elsewhere that unreasonableness in this context consists precisely in the defiance by men of the authoritative voice of the only person in a position to give or to withhold consent, namely the woman (Archard 1999). I also think it unreasonable for a man simply – and in the absence of clear expressions of agreement or in the presence of expressions of dissent – to rely on what are sometimes described as conventions whereby women give their consent to sex with a man (Husak and Thomas 1992). The conventions in question are argued to regulate behaviours which, taken in themselves, fall short of express agreements to have sex but which may nevertheless be taken under the convention to betoken such agreement. Needless to say, the existence and force of such putative conventions is a matter of deep disagreement. It should also not be possible for a man to allege that a woman's explicit dissent is outweighed by the assent which her behaviour, interpreted within such a convention, nevertheless signifies.

Thinking about the *Morgan* case allows us to develop a plausible standard of unreasonableness in respect of beliefs as to a woman's consent to sex. It consists in the discounting of any possible expressions of dissent and reliance upon something other than the woman's own voice – such as a disputed convention or the views of another. By this standard it is hard to see how believing a trafficked prostitute to be consenting might be unreasonable. In the case of trafficked prostitutes, we can assume that the women in question give no indication to the men that they are unwilling to trade sex. They do not by any word or deed protest at the transaction, nor do they resist. We can also assume that the man who uses a prostitute is reasonable in taking verbally agreed terms of payment for a particular sexual service as normally implying willing agreement by the woman. Needless to say, if the prostitutes do resist or protest, their clients have a strong obligation both to discontinue the transaction and to report their suspicions to the relevant authorities.

This overall conclusion, of course, is warranted provided that we repeat the following caveat: if a man is in possession of information about the fate of trafficked prostitutes and can reliably identify the prostitute he is with as trafficked, then any belief on his part that her agreement to trade sex is willing is unreasonable. However, as before, we should continue to think that a man who can be expected to know this much is not, as matters stand, the ordinary or average male to whom the law appeals for its understanding of reasonableness. Indeed, he is surely very much the rare exception.

Nevertheless it may still be too quick and easy to conclude that the absence of protest or dissent on the part of the trafficked prostitute acquits the man of any fault. A trafficked prostitute agrees to the sale of sex only because she has been brutalised, imprisoned and lives in fear of significant harm or death to herself or to those close to her. Her agreement to sex is feigned – and presumably must be feigned if she is to escape further ill-treatment at the hands of her traffickers. Nevertheless, it has been argued by many that it is in the very nature of sex that the absence of consent by one party could not but be detected by the other. Duff (1981), for instance, argues that 'in ordinary sexual contexts there is no logical space for either doubt or mistake about the consent of either party.' Telling (1983) similarly asserts that 'if a man is having, or is about to have intercourse with a woman … it is virtually impossible for him to fail to appreciate whether or not she is consenting to what he is doing or is about to do by the very nature of the exercise.' It would follow from the truth of Duff's and Telling's claims that a man using a trafficked prostitute could not but notice that her fearful agreement to trade sex is not willing. He must, thus, be guilty of intending nevertheless to have sex with her, or of being reckless as to her probable non-consent, and consequently guilty of rape.

The claim on which this charge rests seems to me too strong. Duplicity and error in sexual interactions – as to intentions, the particular nature of the sex, pleasure given and received – is neither unheard of nor rare. It is not impossible, then, that a man should fail to notice that agreement to sex was contrived. Moreover, the encounter of client and trafficked prostitute is not one of those 'ordinary' sexual contexts that Duff speaks about. If there are situations in which it is not 'virtually impossible' to fail to recognise the absence of consent, then surely the case of the trafficked prostitute, fearfully and strenuously disguising her servitude, is one of them.

Nevertheless, we might still argue that a man who fails to notice that she does not consent displays, as Huigens (2005) asserts, an 'extraordinary and troubling insensitivity'. Such insensitivity is not, Huigens concludes, sufficient to warrant prosecution of the man. Moreover, in 'ordinary' sexual contexts, such a failure – even if judged a reasonable one – might indeed bespeak a brutish inattentiveness. But, once again, this is not an ordinary sexual context. Such insensitivity as a user of a prostitute displays is not blameworthy to a degree that would justify the imposition of criminal penalties. It would be naïve to deny that the nature of prostitution is such as to make a mutual and reciprocated considerateness between parties highly unlikely. The sex between prostitute and client is of a kind, and normally expected to be of a kind, in which the attentiveness to one's partner, which is characteristic of non-commercial sex, is simply and probably totally absent. A man using a prostitute is not sensitive to the prostitute's wishes and needs, and moreover knows that he is not presumed or expected by her to be so. If a man using a prostitute does display insensitivity in not noticing that her agreement to sex is feigned, then such insensitivity is certainly not of the magnitude or kind characteristic of a failure to notice in other 'ordinary' sexual contexts.

I conclude at this stage that no good grounds for prosecuting men for having sex with trafficked prostitutes have yet been provided. In particular, there are no such grounds which are consistent with how we do, and how we should, understand culpability for rape or sexual assault. At most, I think we are entitled to say that such culpability would obtain in a very small number of cases, or could only be established following a massive, systematic official education programme and a sea-change in the attitudes of ordinary men who make use of prostitutes. The small number of cases would be those where a man is perfectly aware of the situation of trafficked prostitutes and of the fact that the particular prostitute he is using is trafficked. The education programme would need to be such that no man could, save at the cost of holding an unreasonable belief, believe that the prostitute he was using was not trafficked or, as such, was willingly trading sex with him.

A Suggested Principle

Given that the continued trafficking of women for prostitution is a dreadful wrong, and that preventing men from using trafficked prostitutes is one obvious way to tackle the problem, are there nevertheless any other grounds for prosecuting such men? Here is a tentative suggestion. We should appeal to and act upon the following principle: where (a) some number of persons benefit from something (by participation in a practice, or from availing themselves of a service, and so on) whose continued availability necessarily involves very great wrong (major harms to other individuals or serious injustice); and (b) this would cease to exist, or be significantly reduced in scale, if those persons were discouraged from making use of it, with the consequence that the great wrong were eliminated or at least seriously lessened; then (c) this gives us a good reason to deter those persons from using it. This is so even if the persons only derive unwitting benefit from what occasions the great wrong, since they are unaware that this is the case.

In order to make the scope of my suggested principle clear, I will add the following assumptions and qualification. First, I am going to assume that people would desist from using the service or participating in the practice if they knew that doing so had the terrible consequences that it did. In this way, we do not need to think that the individuals concerned are possessed of vicious characters or that their actions are culpable in a direct and immediate fashion. The behaviour of the individuals is presumptively 'innocent'. Each of them does not intend to bring about the wrong in question; nor does he even recklessly or negligently cause the wrong. Thus, if someone really genuinely does not know, and has no reasonable way of discovering, that he is making use of a trafficked prostitute, and we nevertheless prosecute him for doing so, then the offence in question would be a strict liability one.

I am also, second, going to assume that we could not hope, at any reasonable cost and with any reasonable expectation of success, to educate or inform every prospective user of prostitutes as to a way of reliably identifying trafficked prostitutes and of knowing their situation. In effect, then, we think of criminalising the use of trafficked prostitutes as a last resort, the only effective means left to us if we are to eliminate or significantly reduce the great harms of trafficking. This, of course, does not mean that we could not or should not institute educational programmes directed at men who are likely to use prostitutes. Targeted educational and awareness-raising public programmes might play some part in reducing the demand for prostitutes.

Importantly, third, I distinguish between what one might call incidental and essential beneficiaries. Someone is an incidental beneficiary of a practice if the practice would continue even if he, and others, derived no benefit from it. For instance, a war photographer earns his living by taking pictures of the carnage and suffering of warfare. But wars were fought before the invention of photography and will continue, regretfully, to be prosecuted even if there are no photographers around to record them. Most war photographers – even those whose careers rest upon their recording of conflicts – would, it is to be hoped, insist that they would prefer that there should be no further wars. By contrast, someone is an essential beneficiary of a practice if its continuance is dependent upon the derivation of benefits. Traffickers would not supply trafficked women if there were no men willing to and desirous of using them. I thus qualify the suggested principle as one that apples only where individuals are both unwitting and essential beneficiaries of the practice or service.

What is there to be said in favour of and against the suggested general principle? In the first instance, the principle has more plausibility the greater the evil prevented. If the trafficking of women is an appalling wrong then the principle applies. There is no simple criterion for determining what counts as a sufficiently serious evil to warrant application of the principle. However, the following suggests itself as a plausible precept: if the wrong or harm done is such that its knowing commission would be a major crime punishable by a lengthy custodial sentence, then it is such that those who unwittingly benefit from its commission should, by the terms of the suggested principle, be deterred from doing so.

What is to be said against the principle is, in the first instance and most centrally, that it offends against a jurisprudential tenet of fairness. Criminal liability presupposes fault, and normally this obtains in the presence of clear intention, recklessness or negligence. But the suggested principle applies where someone does not know, and further is not unreasonable in not knowing, that he is deriving benefits from a practice that has evil consequences. The crime of unwittingly using a trafficked prostitute would be a case of a strict liability offence, and such offences are thought to be unfair.

Even in the absence of standard fault conditions, we might nevertheless be justified in punishing those actions whose performance displayed a vicious character. But I do not think that we can say that even this much is true in the case of the user of prostitutes. As argued earlier, the users of trafficked prostitutes do not display vicious characters, even if we can at least say that the revealed dispositions are without redeeming moral merit.

A Modified Liberty Principle and an Extended Harm Principle

Could we then suggest that the law within liberal jurisdictions does indeed serve to protect the freedom of individuals, but that the liberty of using prostitutes is a liberty to engage in a morally worthless activity? Great care is needed here. Liberals who favour state neutrality in legislation will be loath legally to proscribe any activity on the basis of a moral judgement concerning its value. Dworkin (1981), for instance, defends a right to moral independence which is the right of citizens not to be disadvantaged 'in the liberties permitted to them by the criminal law' on the ground that the lawmaker thinks their 'opinions about the right way for them to lead their own lives are ignoble or wrong'. The use of prostitutes, we might say, is properly judged by most right thinking citizens as morally valueless, as base even. However, a liberal state should not prosecute some of its citizens simply for doing what others judge ignoble.

If a strict liability offence of the kind envisaged is to be justified, then it would have to be on the basis that its prosecution would secure a public good of sufficient significance to outweigh concerns about their unfairness. The principal function of the criminal law is the prevention of substantial harms. There can be no doubt that the trafficking of women for prostitution involves very considerable harms to large numbers of individuals whom the liberal state has a duty to protect. Here, then, is the principal case for prosecuting even the unwitting users of trafficked prostitutes. We thereby prevent or significantly reduce great harms. We do so at the moral cost of unfairly treating those who do not know that their actions are responsible, indirectly, for these great harms. Nevertheless, this cost is warranted given the scale of the harms prevented and given the proper function of the criminal law.

I have spoken of the user of the trafficked prostitute as acting unwittingly to cause, indirectly, great harms. Might we not then still hang on to some version of the liberal harm principle in order to justify the limitations on the freedoms of prostitute users? One way to do so has been argued to lie with an extension of the harm principle to encompass 'remote' harms. Hirsch (1996) defends the extension, and Madden Dempsey (2005) makes interesting use of this approach precisely to justify the criminalisation of prostitute use in circumstances where some prostitutes are coerced into their provision of commercial sex.

In certain situations my otherwise innocent actions may risk serious 'remote' harms. For Hirsch, the harms are remote not in any literal sense of their temporal or spatial remove but rather in the sense that they depend upon certain contingencies, and chiefly the actions of others. For instance, if I dump rubbish in a river my actions contribute to an endangerment of those who use the river only if others, and sufficient of them, also dump rubbish. My actions, such as carrying a gun, encourage or induce others to the performance of harmful actions, such as using their own gun, only if they choose to act so. My overtaking on a blind bend only endangers other road users if another car is in fact travelling from round the bend. Dempsey thinks that the use of prostitution can be fitted into Hirsch's category of 'abstract endangerment', whose critical feature is as follows: the riskiness of the conduct 'depends on the existence of a contingency, but where it is not known or knowable to the actor *ex ante* whether that contingency will materialise in the particular situation' (Hirsch 1996, 263). The risky overtaking manoeuvre clearly fits into this category.

Presumably, the thought is that when a man uses a prostitute he cannot know whether or not she is in fact a trafficked prostitute. Thus, the harm he risks – that of having sex with a woman whose compliance is coerced – depends on a contingent fact, namely whether or not she has been trafficked. However, note an important difference. In the case of the trafficked prostitute, the contingent fact – that she has been trafficked – obtains at the time the man has sex with her. In the case of the dangerous driver, his action takes place before the threatened harm – the car being driven from beyond the blind bend – can materialise. Whereas it is indeed true that the driver cannot know *ex ante* whether there is another car coming, a man could in principle know in advance whether the woman he is about to pay for sex with is trafficked. In practice, as I have been arguing, it is not normally reasonable to expect him to know this fact. The materialisation of the harm to the trafficked prostitute is a result of events that pre-date the purchase by the man of sex with her. The materialisation of the harms to the drivers is a result of a contingency, which is both spatially and temporally 'beyond' the present action of the one who makes the dangerous choice to overtake.

Perhaps this difference does not make any real moral difference. The point is that the overtaking driver risks a serious crash just as the man who uses a prostitute risks having sex with a woman who does not consent to the sex. In both cases, the materialisation of the harm depends upon the actions of others – in the case of the prostitute, those of the trafficker; in the case of the driver, those of another car user. In both cases, then, an action risks a harm whose materialisation is down to the contingencies of others' deeds. Does it matter greatly that in one case the deeds are anterior to the risky action whereas in the other they are posterior?

It may not since Hirsch's worry is how, in the case of remote harms, fault can fairly be imputed to the actor. If I only harm another, or risk harming another, if and when others act in certain ways that I cannot foresee or know, how can I be said to be liable for the harms? But then there is a difference in the reasonability of the respective lacks of knowledge. We can see how an agent ought reasonably to be expected to know that another car might be travelling in the opposite direction, even if he cannot know for certain that it will; or that others might also discard rubbish in the river, even if he cannot know that they will; or that others might follow one's example but both carry and use a gun, even if he cannot know that they will. We can see how these agents might reasonably anticipate the risks of harm much more easily than we can see how a man might know that the prostitute he intends using has been trafficked and is only agreeing to sex with him from fear of terrible consequences. Thus, although the harms a prostitute-user risks causing are very serious, he does not seem to be at fault for actually causing them in the way that the dangerous driver or casual rubbish dumper is for the consequences of their actions. If that is so, and the prosecution of prostitute-users is indeed for a strict liability offence, then my suggested principle, and not an extension of the harm principle, appears to be its only plausible justification.

Demand-side Strategies

The full case for the application of the suggested principle I have defended would require a demonstration that the criminalisation of the purchase of sex would have a significant impact on trafficking. I have thus proceeded on the assumption that prostitutes would not be trafficked – or at least would not be trafficked in the alarming and growing numbers that sadly they are – if there was a significant reduction in the number of men using them. This assumption rests on the twin claims that traffickers traffic women because there is a huge amount of money to be made from trafficking, and that men facing prosecution for using trafficked prostitutes would be deterred from doing so.

This assumption underpins a demand-side strategy for dealing with prostitution. It seeks to eliminate or diminish the incidence of prostitution by bringing about a reduction in the demand by men for the use of prostitutes. A demand based strategy can obviously complement, supplement or, most radically, supplant a supply based strategy. This latter seeks to eliminate or reduce the incidence of prostitution by lowering the number of women who offer their services as prostitutes. Thus, for instance, a policy of criminalising the purchase but not the sale of sex, such as was adopted in Sweden in 1998, would be a classic case of a demand-side only strategy.

But note that criminalisation is only one way of implementing either a demand- or a supply-side strategy. Thus, the assumption I am making – that prosecuting men for the use of prostitutes would significantly reduce trafficking – in fact comprises two assumptions: first, that in general terms a demand-side strategy in respect of prostitution is effective, either as an alternative to or in conjunction with a supply-side strategy; and, second, that men are deterred from using prostitutes by criminal sanctions. The latter may be open to doubt (Coy, Horvath and Kelly 2007).

There is, thus, an important and essentially empirical question to be addressed of whether men would be as effectively deterred by measures other than criminal prosecution. Moreover, any full evaluation of the merits of a strategy of prosecuting clients must take account of two sets of consequences: those of the criminalisation of the use of prostitutes and those of other measures short of criminalisation. Prosecuting clients might deter them from using prostitutes, but other measures might do so at least as well and without the other unwelcome effects of criminalisation.

The prosecution of clients of trafficked prostitutes would deter men, if it did deter them, from using *any* prostitute. This is wholly consonant with the earlier claim that men do not act unreasonably in failing to recognise that some women are trafficked. If some women derive important benefits from being able to enter into prostitution, then the general impact of criminalisation on prostitution is a reason against it.

If there are effective means other than criminal prosecution of deterring clients, they too need to be evaluated. An obvious candidate scheme is that of 'naming and shaming', widely publicising the identities of those detected using prostitutes by, for instance, publishing their names and photographs on a website, billboards and so on. There are obviously essentially empirical questions as to whether such shaming does deter. However, the principal normative question is whether shaming is open to fundamental and disabling moral criticism. The most obvious form of such criticism – well articulated recently by Nussbaum (2004) – is that shaming works by humiliating persons and thus offends against the principle that a decent liberal society should protect the dignity of all of its citizens.

In sum, a full evaluation of the merits of criminalising the use of prostitutes demands – apart from the defence of the suggested principle – a careful evaluation of both the likely effects of criminalisation and of the alternatives. In turn, these effects must be established by extensive empirical study.

Concluding Thoughts

My purpose in this chapter was a straightforward one. I made a number of simplifying assumptions – about the nature and wrongness of trafficking women for sex, and about the efficacy of various strategies to combat it – in order to consider what would be wrong with criminalising the use of prostitutes. The proposal to prosecute men who use prostitutes has been made by policy-makers concerned at the scale of the problem of trafficking. My concern was not with whether or not the proposal would work, but with whether it could be justified morally.

I argued that clients who use trafficked prostitutes cannot be regarded as rapists even if the women have been coerced by others into selling sex. They cannot be so regarded because the men do not have unreasonable beliefs about the women's consent. I do not think that the users of trafficked prostitutes can be regarded as exercising a liberty not worth protecting; nor as causing 'remote' harms in the way in which dangerous drivers can. Their actions thus do not fall outside the liberty principle protecting individual actions or under an extended liberal harm principle warranting criminalisation.

I argued that the prosecution of the clients of prostitutes could in principle be justified by using a principle of the following form: even those who are the unwitting beneficiaries of an evil practice which survives because of their participation may permissibly be deterred by criminal sanctions from continued participation. In effect, this principle offers a justification of strict liability offences.

I conclude with a brief comment about methodological approach. Orthodox philosophical discussions of the moral and legal permissibility of prostitution have, very largely, addressed the practice as essentially an aggregate of discrete commercial exchanges between individuals – a prostitute and her client. Key to understanding its permissibility has thus been a consideration of questions of individual consent, the proper objects of sale, and whether the law may interfere with the freely chosen actions of its citizens. However, trafficking prostitutes is a systematic organised crime across national borders. Hence, one can only judge what should be the proper response of the law by seeing prostitution, not as a matter of individual bilateral exchanges, but as a structured practice whose appalling effects may not be known to one half of the individuals involved.

References

Archard, D. (1999), 'The *Mens Rea* of Rape: Reasonableness and Culpable Mistake' in K. Burgess-Jackson (ed.), *A Most Detestable Crime: New Philosophical Essays on Rape* (Oxford: Oxford University Press), 213–29.

Branigan, T. (2007), 'Men Who Buy Sex Could Face Prosecution', *Guardian*, 10 September 2007, 1.

Coy, M., M. Horvath and L. Kelly (2007), 'It's Just Like Going to the Supermarket: Men Buying Sex in East London', Report for Sale Exit (London: Child and Women Abuse Studies Unit).

DPP v. *Morgan* [1976] AC 182.

Duff, A. (1981), 'Recklessness and Rape', *Liverpool Law Review* 3, 49–64.

Dworkin, R. (1981), 'Do We Have a Right to Pornography?', *Oxford Journal of Legal Studies* 1:2, 177–212.

Hirsch A. (1996), 'Extending the Harm Principle: "Remote Harms" and Fair Imputation' in A.P. Simester and A.T.H. Smith (eds), *Harm and Culpability* (Oxford: Clarendon Press), 259–76.

Huigens, K. (2005), 'Is Strict Liability Rape Defensible?' in R.A. Duff and S.P. Green (eds), *Defining Crimes: Essays on the Special Part of the Criminal Law* (Oxford: Oxford University Press), 196–217.

Husak, D. and G. Thomas (1992), 'Date Rape, Social Convention, and Reasonable Mistakes', *Law and Philosophy* 11, 95–126.

Madden Dempsey, M. (2005), 'Rethinking Wolfenden: Prostitute-use, Criminal Law, and Remote Harm', *Criminal Law Review*, 444–55.

Muir, H. and D. Taylor (2006), 'Police Target Customers of Trafficked Prostitutes', *Guardian*, 25 April 2006, 5.

Nussbaum, M. (2004), *Hiding from Humanity: Disgust, Shame, and the Law* (Princeton, NJ: Princeton University Press).

O'Connell Davidson, J. (1998), *Prostitution, Power and Freedom* (Cambridge: Polity).

Telling, D. (1983), 'Rape – Consent and Belief', *Journal of Criminal Law* 47, 129–39.

UNODC (United Nations Office on Drugs and Crime) (2006), *Trafficking in Persons: Global Patterns* (New York: UNODC).

Wertheimer, A. (1996), *Exploitation* (Princeton, NJ: Princeton University Press).

Chapter 10

Why Hate Men who Pay for Sex? Exploring the Shift to 'Tackling Demand' in the UK

Teela Sanders and Rosie Campbell

The title of this chapter was inspired by a 2007 poster campaign by Wolverhampton City Council with the slogan 'Wolverhampton hates kerb crawling. So get out and stay out.'[1] Such strong language and imagery was perplexing to us as researchers and symbolised a new phase in prostitution policy and management in the UK. One of the five key elements of the national Home Office prostitution strategy for England and Wales (2006) is 'tackling demand'. The strategy identified 'reducing demand' for street sex work as vital, alongside 'reducing supply', in achieving the strategic objectives of eradicating street prostitution and challenging the view that street prostitution is inevitable. The strategy formally endorsed measures such as prosecutions under the kerb-crawling legislation, local media campaigns including 'naming and shaming' and 'kerb-crawler re-education programmes'. Some areas in England and Wales have already embarked with vigour on crusades to eradicate street sex work via a strong focus on enforcement of kerb-crawling offences under the Sexual Offences Act 1985 – that was later strengthened under the Criminal Justice and Police Act 2001 – which made the offence arrestable and now the courts have the power to disqualify drivers. Whilst this chapter focuses on England and Wales, it is important to note similar shifts have happened throughout the UK. In October 2007, the policing Minister in Northern Ireland announced that kerb-crawling would be introduced into law as a specific offence. In Scotland, the Prostitution (Public Places) Scotland Act 2007 came into force in October 2007, which criminalised 'loitering or soliciting in any public place for the purpose of obtaining the services of someone engaged in prostitution'. Whilst the Home Office strategy and other home nation policies have tended to focus on measures which target men who make contact with sex workers on the street, and have not criminalised paying for sex *per se*, some ministers, MPs and SMPs have called for paying for sex to be made a crime.[2]

This chapter reflects on the shift in policy to an increased focus on tackling demand in relation to street sex work, the associated wider vilification of men who pay for sex and the emergence of support, amongst some politicians, for the wider

1 See, <http://www.wolverhampton.gov.uk/policing_safety/crime_law/street_sex_trade/campaign/default.htm>.

2 See, <http://news.bbc.co.uk/1/hi/uk_politics/6188203.stm>.

criminalisation of paying for sex. We argue this is shaped by an abolitionist radical feminist sectional lobby, which places particular emphasis on an area of social and economic relations where sexual services are exchanged, creating thereby a bias of analysis of sex work as a generator of the objectification of women and defining all sex work as violence and involuntary. Forced prostitution, particularly trafficking, has become part of this debate with supporters arguing that making it a crime to pay for sex will prevent trafficking. In such abolitionist analysis, the hostility towards men who pay for sex is visible. This can appeal to politicians with moral opposition to sex work and also to those with sympathy for policies that purport to address gender inequality and violence against women in society. We argue that beyond these interests, there is no apparent significant public campaign or support for such an approach to the sex industry in the UK or for such levels of hostility to all men who pay for sex. Yet, we acknowledge that ambivalent attitudes to the sex industry, sex workers and their clients means that they are easy targets, indeed scapegoats, for those who want to generate hostility towards them. It is easier to generate such hostility than develop an understanding of the personal, social, cultural and economic conditions that shape the lives of people involved in the sex industry, including those who pay for sex. It is arguably easier to pass symbolic legislation that has a moral message than to tackle the complexities of the sex industry, and to put resources into finding a more long term solution to a regulated market.

In this chapter, we argue that those supporting policies for further criminalisation of clients fail to address the impact of such policies on sex workers themselves, their rights, social inclusion and safety. This means there are contradictions between such shifts in policy and other objectives of policy which are supposedly intended to reduce the victimisation and vulnerability of sex workers. Hopefully, policy-makers will recognise that to criminalise paying for sex would mean that sex workers would have no legal clients, compounding the much documented stigma and marginalisation faced by sex workers and creating an even more illicit and informal industry. It is difficult to see how sex workers can seek to have their rights respected in a criminal industry. Hence, we argue for the regulation of a legal industry, ensuring rights for sex workers, and leaving scarce policing resources to focus on exploitative practices. Police resources, intelligence-gathering activities and investigations could be directed at exploitative practices relating to those who manage and control sex work premises and sex workers. Women who experience coercion into the sex industry against their will, or who have little or no control over working conditions, which clients are accepted, which sexual acts are sold, or the amount of money they keep, are those women who need assistance, support and protection. As Nussbaum (1998) argues, irrational beliefs about the wrongs of prostitution that are fuelled by prejudice and misunderstanding mask where the true problems lie in sexual exchanges for money.

We also argue that policy-makers should not only pay more attention to the research that exists which shows the diversity of experiences of people in the sex industry but should also explore the experiences of men who pay for sex and the social and cultural context they inhabit. Understanding the reasons why men buy sex and the function of commercial sexual services makes it more difficult to 'hate' men who pay for sex and avoids promulgating simplistic policies which rely on demonising a group of people rather than offering workable, balanced, evidence-based policies.

'Tackling Demand' and 'the Problem of Men': The Development of Policy Targeting Men who Pay for Sex in England and Wales

In 2004, the government announced a review of the prostitution laws because many were considered to be 'outdated, confused and ineffective' (David Blunkett in Home Office 2004, 5). Stemming from a wider New Labour agenda of focusing law, policy and resources on addressing social exclusion, civil renewal, anti-social behaviour and criminality, the *Paying the Price* document prioritised 'prevention', 'protection and support' and 'justice' aspects of prostitution. Criticisms were waged against the starting point for the review, due to a lack of acknowledgement of the historical legal context of the management of prostitution in the UK, namely the Wolfenden Report and its legacy (Soothill and Sanders 2004). Other criticisms against the review stated that it ignored the fact that selling sex can be voluntary under certain circumstances, that not all women involved in prostitution were victims and that the criminalisation of sex workers through increased arrests and Anti-Social Behaviour Orders increases women's health and safety vulnerabilities (Cusick and Berney 2005; Sanders and Campbell 2007). Relevant to men who buy sex, Brooks-Gordon (2005) argued that minimal research and evidence had been collated and applied to the review, and that there was generally a negative and unfair view of men who buy sex. For instance, the language of the document firmly states the position of the government: men who buy sex are referred to as 'the user' (Home Office 2004, 16). The position of men who buy sex was immediately equated with exploitation, danger, violence and generally an activity that should not be tolerated, debated or accepted in modern society. However, this perspective on men who buy sex was vastly at odds with Home Office research that suggests the 'user' is a 30-year-old male who is married, in full time employment and has no criminal record (Hester and Westmarland 2004, 143). By the end of the consultation process, Phoenix and Oerton (2005, 77) note that prostitution had been re-framed as a 'social problem', and that this had been achieved by crafting and promoting a specific attitude towards men who buy sex so they became part of a wider 'problem of men' discourse evident in New Labour's social and criminal justice policies (Scourfield and Drakeford 2002).

The criticisms from experts in the field on the evidence and perspectives delivered in *Paying the Price* generally went unnoticed by ministers and the outcome of the review, the *Coordinated Prostitution Strategy* published in 2006, presents a negative scenario where sex workers are criminalised and sex markets remain unregulated. The strategy, now the national blueprint on prostitution, indicates to police, local authorities and other partnerships the five priorities of prevention, developing 'routes out' for sex workers, ensuring justice, tackling off-street prostitution and tackling demand. The full implications of the *Coordinated Prostitution Strategy* on the safety of women involved in sex work have been well documented (see Boynton and Cusick 2006; Sanders and Campbell 2007). Here the implications of 'tackling demand' will be detailed.

The overriding emphasis of the strategy is to 'disrupt the sex markets' (Home Office 2006, 1). This objective has produced a two pronged approach. First, the key objective is to criminalise street sex workers. This is done by supplying avenues for 'exiting' alongside the criminal justice system and endorsing prosecution and sanctions, such as the use of Anti-Social Behaviour Orders (ASBOs). These civil orders were introduced in 2001 and soon applied to sex workers to ban them from certain streets. Often the conditions of the order are unrealistic and curfew women from important places, such as drug clinics and their own communities, leading to breaches which then turn into criminal offences. Research on the use of ASBOs has resoundingly identified how they are flawed and do not assist women to leave the sex industry but instead involve women in the criminal justice system further, leading to an increase in prison sentences and exclusion (Sagar 2007). Second, there is a re-emphasis on enforcing laws against kerb-crawlers. 'Deterring punters' was included in the strategy to achieve the wider objectives of removing the demand, supply and opportunity for street prostitution to take place (Sagar 2007, 2). Concerns about kerb-crawling from local communities were prioritised resulting in a 'new focus on the enforcement of the law of kerb-crawling' (Sagar 2007, 33). Yet the concerns of a minority of residents who consider street prostitution a nuisance is not reflective of the other communities who do not necessarily consider street prostitution a problem that should be tackled with enforcement (Pitcher et al. 2006). The focus on 'kerb-crawlers' includes a staggered approach leading to prosecution: informal warning letters to men spotted in 'red light areas'; court diversion through kerb-crawler re-education programmes (see below); prosecution using existing financial penalties, including disqualification from driving; and 'naming and shaming' tactics through the local media. However, astonishingly, this policy is not driven by informed empirical information: 'anecdotal evidence suggests that these warning measures and enforcement of the law against kerb-crawlers have a deterrent effect' (Pitcher et al. 2006, 7). At the Home Office's own admission, the success of these enforcement approaches is not evidence based and there is no empirical background that 'tackling demand' in these ways is vaguely successful.

Momentum for Legal Powers and Controls Over Men who Buy Sex

This formalisation within national strategy of the centrality of kerb-crawling legislation and 'shaming' tactics was a manifestation of a powerful anti-men discourse that had developed over the past two decades. Momentum to gain greater legal powers and controls over men who buy sex, in particularly kerb-crawlers, can be traced back to the 1980s. Brooks-Gordon (2006) maps out the changes to kerb-crawling laws, highlighting that the debates behind the emphasis on criminalising men who buy sex have been about sexuality, morality, public order and, more recently, immigration. Kantola and Squires (2004) note from parliamentary debates on prostitution in the late 1980s and 1990s that concerns over the public nuisance of the kerb-crawler overshadowed any other discussions of the sex industry. The 'kerb-crawler as nuisance' discourse was tightly connected with a concern for prostitution linked to organised crime and 'trafficking'. In addition, concerns with HIV and AIDS, public protection, 'sex offenders' and community cohesion have also been at the backdrop of anxieties about men who buy sex. As a result of these dominant discourses amongst the powerful, including residents who had access to decision-making people and processes, there was a steady 'uptariffing' of legislation against kerb-crawlers (Brooks-Gordon 2006, 21).

The Sexual Offences Act 1985 marked the first piece of legislation to include the offence of kerb-crawling and introduced two offences. First, that of 'kerb-crawling', that is, soliciting another person from a 'motor vehicle' or 'in a street or public place' that is 'likely to cause annoyance to the person … or nuisance to the other persons in the neighbourhood' (s.1 Sexual Offences Act 1985). The second offence is that of 'persistent soliciting', which captures a man who solicits another person in a public place for services of a prostitute (s.2 Sexual Offences Act 1985). This offence only carried the severity of a level 3 fine (approximately £400) and was not arrestable but arranged through a letter ordering the accused to attend the magistrate's court. However, the guidelines issued in the *Coordinated Prostitution Strategy* encourage arrest, and in practice the burden of proof may well be eroded to less compelling evidence of kerb-crawling because individuals will accept a charge in order to avoid going to court.

Since then, there have been regular calls from the Association of Chief Police Officers for forces to utilise kerb-crawling law more effectively and to address the apparent gender imbalance by which soliciting laws were utilised much more frequently than kerb-crawling legislation. Legislation has continued to increase the powers of arrest against men arrested for kerb-crawling and finally, under the Criminal Justice and Police Act 2001, kerb-crawling was made an arrestable offence. Some forces had pointed to the lack of a power of arrest as one of the reasons police forces found it harder to target kerb-crawlers effectively. Whilst annual statistics always showed more soliciting than kerb-crawling cautions and convictions, some force areas did place a greater, or at least an equal focus, on men paying for sex on the streets. The Powers of the Criminal Courts (Sentencing) Act 2000 gave magistrates the power to remove driving licenses from persistent kerb-crawlers and driving disqualifications were introduced as a sanction in January 2004. After rejecting a bill for toleration zones in 2003, Scotland followed the trend to target men when kerb-crawling was made an offence under the Prostitution (Public Places) (Scotland) Act 2007, sending the clear message that the state will not tolerate the sale or purchase of street sex.[3]

This 'uptariffing' of laws against kerb-crawlers has been paralleled with some other punishment tactics. During the late 1980s and 1990s a number of forces, supported by their community safety partnerships, utilised 'shaming' tactics by drawing attention in the media to men convicted of kerb-crawling, placing their names and photographs in local newspapers. A smaller number of forces experimented with 'John's Schools', most noticeably West Yorkshire, as the first to pilot this approach in the UK, and Hampshire (Southampton), who have one of the most sustained programmes. It is to these programmes, and recent high-profile anti-kerb-crawling campaigns, that we now turn to examine their attitudes towards men who pay for sex.

---

3 See, <http://news.bbc.co.uk/1/hi/scotland/7044063.stm>.

Vilifying Men who Pay for Sex: Rehabilitation and Shame

In the national strategy for England and Wales, we see shaming and rehabilitation of men who pay for sex with street sex workers formally endorsed. This, we argue, is shaped by a discourse which constructs men who pay for sex as abusive, immoral, unrespectable and deviant (Sanders 2008). In the strategy, the rigorous enforcement of the law includes a rehabilitation element for those men who are arrested for kerb-crawling. The Hampshire Change programme is heralded in the strategy as a success: a one-day programme funded by the arrestee (£200) 'designed to challenge their behaviour'. Success is measured crudely: of 304 attendees, only four have re-offended. The policy review has been criticised for recognising 're-education programmes' as a 'coherent approach' when no objective assessment of the programmes was undertaken or any recognition given to the dangers, costs and implications of the schemes (Brooks-Gordon 2005, 436). Yet this lack of an actual 'evidence' base from these programmes is one more example of non-evidence-based policy in the field of sex work. The 'rehabilitation' emphasis suggests the attendees are offenders in need of 'treatment', the programmes use intensive resources for limited outcomes and have not been evaluated against objective criteria.

There is generally a lack of balanced information and perspectives regarding the legalities of some sex markets and the voluntary nature of some sex work (Campbell and Storr 2001). Evaluations and assessments of the re-education programmes in the United States and North America unanimously state that there is little evidence to support the effectiveness of re-education programmes. 'Re-offending' is a poor outcome measure due to displacement of many different kinds (Monto and Garcia 2001). Deterrence may not be because of the programme, as recidivism may be related to other causal factors (Kennedy et al. 2004; Wortley et al. 2002). The 'voluntariness' of the programmes is doubted and there are concerns that offering men who are arrested the 'choice' of either court or a rehabilitation programme brings 'due process' into doubt (Brooks-Gordon 2005, 436).

There is support from the government for 'naming and shaming' those arrested for prostitution related offences. Sex workers have frequently had their personal details, including age and address, displayed in the local media when arrested, and more recently men arrested for kerb-crawling are treated with the same disrespect. Ignoring the lack of efficiency of the 'naming and shaming' policies which cannot produce positive outcomes (Pawson 2002), there are theoretical and moral reasons why using humiliation tactics is flawed as a method of punishment. Nussbaum (2004) presents powerful philosophical arguments why disgust and shame should not be invoked as the basis for criminalising an act or part of criminal law, in particular because the ideas pander to ideological images of how humanity should act rather than how it does act. Yet the search for a mythical utopian state, in this case where men do not buy and women do not sell sex, underpins continued calls to criminalise men who buy sex. Harriet Harman, Labour MP for Brent, who is at the forefront of calls to criminalise men who buy sex in the UK, used arguments that draw on ideals of a perfect humanity by stating: 'just because something has always gone on, doesn't mean you just wring your hands and say, "Oh well there's nothing we can do about it.""[4] Such simplistic arguments that induce shame and embarrassment (what Nussbaum (2004) calls 'primitive shame') penalise individuals for human imperfections.

The acceptability of shaming and social humiliation as a punishment tactic is evident in other ways. Priorities to enforce the law to 'tackle demand' and the general principle of deterrence accumulated in a 2007 Home Office 'pilot' campaign, entitled 'kerb-crawling costs more than you think', which ran across seven towns and cities (Middlesbrough, Peterborough, Southampton, London, Bristol, Bournemouth and Leeds).[5] These areas utilised Home Office produced materials to promote a 'marketing message' at 'potential' kerb-crawlers. These messages were promoted through posters in the media and radio 'warnings'. Listeners were told that kerb-crawling will result in an arrest, a court appearance, letters sent to their home, a £1,000 fine, a driving ban and shame to their families and employer. Beer mats were distributed and contained the text: 'turn over to find out how much it costs to pick up a prostitute', with the answer on the reverse: 'Your driving licence. Your job. Your marriage. A £1,000 fine.' The slogan 'kerb-crawling costs more than you think' that punctuates all of these promotional materials was intended as a deterrent and a moral message that buying is wrong and will be punished through the law and by society. In some of these areas, the pilots were accompanied by heightened targeted policing operations in areas of street sex work to enforce the kerb-crawling and, generally, the soliciting legislation. To date, no results from the evaluation of the pilot have been published. Indeed, it is unclear if there was any evaluation of this pilot deterrence campaign. Nonetheless, other cities have developed their own such promotion campaigns in efforts to 'clean up the streets'.

Perhaps one of the most strident and high-profile anti-kerb-crawler media campaigns to date in the UK is that launched by Wolverhampton City Council in 2007. This provides a clear case of repulsion for kerb-crawling, expressed in the language and imagery contained in the campaign. The poster used in the campaign declares; 'Kerb crawlers belong behind bars. Wolverhampton hates kerb crawling', and is part of their 'get out and stay out' campaign to eradicate street prostitution.[6] The poster depicts a white man under the bars of a gutter grate, sending the visual image of men who buy sex as dirt and rubbish that come from the dregs of society. This image has appeared as a billboard on key routes into Wolverhampton. This is indicative of a decade of growing hostility to kerb-crawlers in the UK, continuing the discourse utilised by some involved in the 1999 West Yorkshire kerb-crawler rehabilitation programme. These recent official messages and hostilities towards men who buy sex suggest that beyond the strategy, which chose not to make buying sex illegal, a fever of hatred has gathered amongst officials, and moral attitudes are at the forefront of this emergent policy and practice.

---

4 See, <http://news.bbc.co.uk/1/hi/uk_politics/7153358.stm>.

5 See, <http://www.crimereduction.homeoffice.gov.uk/publicity_catalogue/product_info.php?cPath=96_100&products_id=266&osCsid=c9676e79df6d9ff>.

6 See, <http://www.wolverhampton.gov.uk/policing_safety/crime_law/street_sex_trade/campaign/default.htm>.

Campbell and Storr (2001) questioned whether the language used to describe clients in reportage associated with the Kerb Crawler Rehabilitation Programme (KCRP) was helpful in enabling policy discussions about clients to move beyond mythology and stereotypes. For example, an article written by one of the KCRP's organisers appeared in *The Independent* newspaper under the title 'Out of the Gutter' (and was reprinted in *Trouble and Strife* with the title 'Flushing the Johns' (Bindel 1998)). Campbell and Storr (2001, 98) cautioned that 'a discourse which constructs clients as dehumanised, dirty and animalistic gets us no nearer to an informed debate about clients, and perpetuates stereotypes which obscure the complex social, economic and cultural relationships in which commercial sex takes place.' Atchison et al. (1998) described how research on clients had shifted from early work which treated the client as an abnormal deviant, through to more recent research which locates the client within cultural, gendered and economic relations. Much of the media discourse which surrounded the original KCRP in the UK, as well as the language and imagery we are seeing in the current anti-kerb-crawler campaigns, take us back to the construction of the client as an abnormal deviant, but also 'dehumanised' and 'unrespectable', in need of punishment and treatment.

The Canadian academic researcher John Lowman (2000) utilises the concept of the 'discourse of disposability' to describe enduring negative attitudes towards sex workers, often perpetuated by policy-makers aiming to 'eradicate prostitution'. This discourse constructs sex workers as disposable, not worthy of the protection of full citizenship, and hence contributes to a cultural context which condones violence against sex workers. Sanders (2008) describes a 'discourse of disrespectability' that is aimed at men who buy sex from the street. The majority of men who buy sex from indoor sex markets (such as independent escort services, massage parlours or saunas) are not targeted by policies, campaigns or general discourses of disgust, as their activities are hidden and considered less disruptive to society and communities. Instead, the visible street kerb-crawler is warned that his distasteful activities are contrary to expectations of his (often) middle-class status and 'respectability'. These class expectations become the butt of moral messages and direct policing. This discourse is part of the ideological narratives which are necessary to keep alight calls to make it a crime to pay for sexual services. In the field of sex work, where feelings often run high and emotive issues are discussed, it is vital that policy-makers use language responsibly and carefully assess policy proposals, rigorously examining all their implications and impacts. The 'discourse of disrespectability' and the clumsy demonisation that accompanies it, is a simplistic, deterministic analysis of the sex industry which obscures good practice in policy development on sex work in the UK.

The Swedish Model and Recent Calls to Criminalise Paying for Sex

Post-Strategy calls to criminalise men in the UK (see below) are tied to the changes that have occurred in Sweden. Swedish contemporary legislation that began in the 1980s was based on arguments that selling sex was essentially 'the commercialization of women's bodies', 'counterproductive to equality', and showed 'contempt for women' (Svanstrom 2004, 230). There was little room in the debates for anything other than an analysis that proposed prostitution as a violence against women, and the definition of prostitution moved from that of individual to structural violence against women (Leander 2005, 118). The political movement to introduce protective legislation to resist violence against women was equally matched by an overwhelming desire from a majority of political parties to introduce radical legislation against men who buy sex and to 'criminalise the john' (Scoular 2004). Outshoorn (2004) has documented how the climate and organising of the women's movement in Sweden since the late 1980s was very dominant in the Social Democrat party and explicitly favoured making it a crime to pay for sex.

In 1999, the Act Prohibiting the Purchase of Sexual Services was introduced by the Swedish government. Gould (1999) notes that this extreme law was introduced as a result of the success of the prohibitionists that used evidence relating to violence, drug use, and the problems faced by sex workers in a one-sided and unproblematised way. Exaggerated problems, a lack of an informed response about the different types of experiences and relationships sex workers have with clients, were some of the criticisms of the punitive law. Significant for the debates in the UK is the outcomes of the law since it has been implemented. Leander (2005, 122) produces figures for 2004 that show only 156 men had been charged with the crime of purchasing sexual services and that only 48 (31 per cent) had been convicted. Ekberg (2004, 1195), who praises the new law for its success, reports that 734 men have been arrested in five years from 1999 to 2004, generating 140 convictions, most of which resulted in a fine. Commentary since the Swedish law was introduced suggests that the law has been merely symbolic – an expression of what is acceptable sexual behaviour – in deterring men who may be interested in seeking commercial sex (Kaspersson 2006). Morally driven legislation and administration that serves no practical result or achieves little or no change is arguably not the purpose of legal statutes. Further, as Nussbaum (1998) states, maintaining negative social meanings around the use of the sexual body that enters into a contract only perpetuates stereotypes based on gender, race and prejudice rather than reason.

The fact that such small numbers of men have been punished through the criminal justice system confirms that the legislation was largely symbolic, designed to send a normative message about right and wrong types of sex. Reports from outreach and women's groups also indicate that there has been an increase in internet-based sex work, as well as men visiting neighbouring countries to buy sex, merely suggesting displacement of the markets.

In the UK, the legal changes born of dominant moral discourses amongst decision-making individuals and processes during the 1990s (see Kantola and Squires 2004), together with the development of a new national strategy, have meant that in 2007 we are faced with a dramatically different (legal and moral) landscape in relation to the men who buy sex. The *Coordinated Prostitution Strategy* did not include criminalising paying for sex. It stated that a significant number of respondents expressed some support for the Swedish approach (to make buying sex illegal), but stated that 'the magnitude and complexity of street prostitution here suggests that a more comprehensive and coordinated Strategy is required' (Home Office 2006, 7). Yet, other ministerial and political voices in government have been heard calling to make the purchase of sex illegal. Some of these calls have been centred in particular on the Criminal Justice and Immigration Bill 2007. This bill contains proposals to remove the term 'common prostitute' from the soliciting legislation and to create a 'rehabilitation order' intended to act as an alternative to fining people charged with soliciting. Both of these reforms were also contained in the national strategy, and some politicians have used the introduction of this bill as a platform to argue for new, and more expansive, legislation to criminalise paying for sex.

The most vocal have been female ministers or ex-ministers who are outside the Home Office, although some have been previously involved with the development of the policy. A small group of Labour MPs have vehemently called to criminalise men who buy sex as a direct effort to address 'trafficking' of women and children to the UK. The *Guardian* (10 September 2007) reported that ministerial campaigners were calling for criminalising clients as a means of assisting women who work in brothels and on the streets, as well as sending a stern moral message that paying for sex is not acceptable. The idea that legislation should be a tool of moral symbolism seems to be gaining momentum as wider concerns about more serious and sinister human rights issues are connected directly to the sex trade. The government Minister for Justice (MP for Camberwell and Peckham), Harriet Harman has proclaimed her support for the Swedish model as a means of addressing trafficking. On Wednesday 28 November 2007, Fiona McTaggart, supported by the Poppy Project, held a meeting 'Prostitution and the Damage it Does' to 'provide an opportunity to consider if lessons can be learnt from Sweden's work in the field, criminalising men who pay for sex'. The former special advisor to the Swedish government on trafficking in human beings was the key speaker. On 3 December 2007 the *Guardian* reported that the government was again reviewing prostitution laws and this would include an examination of the effects of Sweden's policy of prosecuting men for buying sex: 'Home office minister Vernon Coaker has told MPs he will travel to Sweden and the Netherlands in the new year to study how different regimes have affected demand, amid growing pressure for radical action to curb the growth in sex trafficking.'[7] These calls for criminalisation seem far removed from the recommendation in the *Coordinated Prostitution Strategy* that the government should look at re-defining the terms of a brothel to enable women to work together safely and within the law.

Trafficking Anxiety

For those supporting criminalisation, targeting 'demand' is tied up with the concerns that women and children are increasingly trafficked against their will into the UK for purposes of prostitution. These arguments make no distinction between the voluntary sex industry and trafficking, which is, on a number of levels, creating several problems for sex workers in the UK currently. There is no established evidence base that shows that criminalising paying for sex addresses trafficking. Recent efforts have seen high-profile attention to trafficking amongst UK police forces and the

7 See, <http://www.guardian.co.uk/society/2007/nov/30/homeaffairs>.

media. 'Operation Pentameter 2' was launched in October 2007 and set about to arrest those involved in the organised crime aspect of prostitution.[8]

This recent policing initiative is the second phase of an earlier anti-trafficking operation, 'Operation Pentameter', which was launched in February 2006 and ran until June 2006. This was heralded as the first ever national campaign against trafficking for sexual exploitation and the first policing operation to involve all the UK's police forces. The key objectives of Pentameter were: to recover victims and reduce harm caused to the individual and the UK; to increase the opportunities for partnership working to tackle trafficking in people; to raise the national awareness of the issue of trafficking and to identify the scale of the problem; to encourage UK police areas that maintain 'passive' approaches to off-street sex work to adopt a 'turn the stone' policy, and an operational focus on the organised crime groups involved; to improve the national and local intelligence knowledge base on the organised crime groups involved in trafficking and related immigration crime issues; to obtain a comprehensive baseline intelligence picture of people trafficking in the UK; and to secure evidence and convictions against exploiters and asset recovery. Home Office Minister, Vernon Coaker, announced on 21 June 2006 that, under the umbrella of Pentameter, the police had visited 515 premises nationwide and arrested 232 people.[9] By early July 2006, 134 people had been charged. It was reported that 84 women and girls, who it was believed had been trafficked, were 'rescued' during the operation. Twelve of the victims identified were girls aged between 14 and 17 years. In total 188 'victims' were rescued, hence 102 were not confirmed as victims of trafficking. The concerns and anxieties about 'trafficking', despite small numbers, appear to be at the forefront of direct policing initiatives in the sex industry and government policy on prostitution. Given that the majority of people involved in the sex industry are not in this category of 'trafficked', it seems that the real, ingrained issues relating to the sex industry remain un-reviewed and unregulated.

Simplistic associations – made without evidence – between the 'demand' for sex and women moving to the UK to become involved in industries including the sex trade are following similar paths as those that formed the momentum for Sweden to change the law. Kulick (2005) identifies how the Swedish laws were the result of greater fears relating to the national identity of Sweden in a time of European nation state and boundary re-configuration, and the fear of 'flooding' from immigrant women moving from Eastern European countries to the most affluent and stable Scandinavian countries. Similarly, the calls in the UK to drag men who buy sex into court for buying sex confuses the issues of forced and migrant sexual labour (Agustín 2007) and assumes that women enter into the sex industry only because of 'demand'. Such a simplistic assumption ignores the detailed theories on why women migrate, the relationships between globalisation and migration and the external and international economic forces that affect the sex industry, known as the 'push' and 'pull' factors (see Agustín 2007). The feminisation of poverty locally and globally, the links between drug and sex markets, the favourability of sex work compared to other unskilled forms of labour and the female based networks that are part of the sex

8 See, <http://www.pentameter.police.uk/>.

9 See, <http://www.pentameter.police.uk/docs/pentameter.pdf>.

industry are important factors that provide vital explanations as to why the industry is perpetuated. The supply/demand chain is not a simple equation but is situated within local and global economic, social and political patterns that are related to both gender inequalities and 'market' opportunities.

Envisaging What Outlawing Purchasing Sex Would Look Like

So, what if the supporters of criminalisation were successful and a law was passed which criminalised paying for sex? What would be the impact in the UK? Whilst it is always difficult to predict the impact of new legislation, we suggest a number of realities would arise. The few currently legal markets would become illegal. Escorts could not have legal clients and establishments working within the current law would become criminal; there would be no incentive to obey other laws such as tax or Inland Revenue responsibilities. Advertising and contact methods are likely to become much more illicit. We are likely to see a displacement of markets and there is likely to be a growth in internet markets which would be increasingly unaccountable and difficult to police. Hence, the sex industry goes further underground. This has a range of damaging and very serious consequences. The police and authorities would have less idea about where and who sex workers are. Sex work support projects would have to operate in an even more challenging context, which would have unquantifiable effects on health and harm prevention (Cusick and Berney 2005). Culturally, the 'discourse of disposability' would be strengthened as sex workers would be given fewer rights.

The social and economic conditions that currently lead to street sex markets, for example social disadvantage and drug dependency, will remain untouched by criminalisation. Many street sex workers have the least resources and opportunity to move to new markets. Men who pay for sex on the streets will remain the most visible to police authorities and hence the impacts of criminalisation on the dynamics of street sex work will continue to sustain it as the most dangerous sector to work in. The current research base on why men pay for sex would suggest that apart from a small section of men, the majority would continue to pay for sex, but more surreptitiously (Campbell 1998; Kinnell 2006).

Another reason for not adopting the criminalisation of men who buy sex is the difficulty of enforcing such a law. The amount of sex that is sold and purchased in the UK is an unknown quantity. There are indications of the levels in the population who have bought sex. For instance, in the UK, Ward et al. (2005, 468) compared results from a survey of men aged between 16 and 44 in 1990 (n=6000) with a survey in 2000 (n=4672). This comparative study showed that there had been a significant increase in the prevalence of buying sex over the decade with 8.8 per cent of men in 2000 admitting to buying sex in their lifetime, compared to 5.6 per cent in 1990. In Scotland, Groom and Nandwani (2006) reviewed 2665 retrospective case notes of male attendees of a sexual health clinic and found 10 per cent had reported paying for sex. Both these recent empirical studies suggest that the numbers of men who buy sex in the UK is significant. Given the prevalence and nature of selling and buying sex in the UK markets, even a police force that had unlimited resources could not police the sex markets as they stand. The trajectory of arrests of men who buy sex in the UK has remained at low levels: 726 (2000), 856 (2001), 993 (2002), 884 (2003) and 808 (2004) (Home Office 2006, 33). These figures are largely relating to men who are arrested for kerb-crawling offences on the street, as currently men who buy sex from indoor premises are within the law. Kinnell (2006) questioned the practicalities and logic of introducing and enforcing such a law in the UK:

> Estimates of the numbers of clients, based on the numbers of sex workers and the amount of business they do, indicate that at least 11% of the adult male population pays for sex fairly regularly. The level of resources that would be required to police the behaviour of such a large proportion of the population is unthinkable. Police and allied agencies tasked with apprehending and monitoring violent sex offenders are already over-stretched. To require them to chase after more than 2 million men who pay other consenting adults for sexual acts, which would be legal if no money changed hands, is absurd.

Making it a crime to pay for sex undermines initiatives to promote the safety of sex workers, it communicates that paying for sex is a criminal act, hence creating stigma. Most dangerously, it rules out initiatives to promote responsible and respectful client conduct, it diverts police attention from focusing on preventing and investigating actual violent crimes against sex workers by making all men who pay for sex criminals. Kinnell (2006) has argued very convincingly that the claim that making it a crime to pay for sex will address violence against sex workers is, quite simply, a red herring.

Further criminalisation of sex markets should really worry people concerned about trafficking. Illegal and unregulated markets generally increase opportunities for organised crime and the potential for trafficking. Police resources would be stretched further as all men who pay for sex become criminals, rather than directing limited resources to targeting exploitative and violent men and those who traffic and smuggle people against their will into the UK and the sex industry. It is also difficult to see how criminalisation would provide a fruitful context for sex workers to have their employment and other rights respected. Sex workers in any sector of the sex industry would be in a position of working in a shadow sector of the economy where their clients are criminal.

If such a law was introduced, where would the definitions of 'buying sex' stop? If the basic premise for such an abolitionist law is that 'buying sex is wrong' and should not be tolerated, there is no logic to state that buying sex from the street is wrong but buying sex from indoor locations is acceptable. Therefore, such a law would logically need to apply to all markets and commercial sexual relationships where direct sexual services are sold. Including escorting, brothels, massage parlours and other outlets (see Agustín 2005 for a comprehensive list of sexual service sites) would widen the net of sex venues far beyond the capacity of any police force. The number of such establishments, given both the prevalence and fluid mobility, is very difficult to estimate. Given that a significant part of selling sex takes place in private spaces initiated by entrepreneurial sex workers who work alone (from hotels, their own home, rented apartments, and in other leisure venues), finding and arresting those involved would move policing from the public realm to the private. If consensual adults who voluntarily agreed a contract that exchanged money for sexual services were arrested, then this would mean that adults in conventional relationships such as marriage or casual relationships would also be culpable. Marriage, as an economic institution sanctioned by the state and religion, is essentially a voluntary agreement where financial sustenance (usually by the husband) is supplied in exchange for types of emotional and physical labour and sexual labour (usually by the woman) as part of the conjugal roles. Prasad (1999) argues that, as a cultural practice, prostitution, as a commodity exchange that takes place in a 'market', lacks the 'ambiguity, status-dependence, and potential hypocrisy' that occur in the 'gift exchange' that is the basis of romantic sexual relationships. It is in this regard that the question needs to be asked – what the real differences are between sexual relationships that are based on 'love' (and other such obligations) and those that are based on an agreed monetary transaction?

Conclusions: Legal Economy Not Illegal

A key problem for sex work in the UK is that there is no framework for regulating markets, no governance of commercial sex and no encouragement for responsibly managed establishments or practices. The working conditions of sex workers in terms of age, rights and conditions of employment within an establishment are left to the unregulated market. Employers, owners and managers of sex work venues remain unscrutinised and even those who want to work within the law are prevented from doing so. The failure of government to regulate creates conditions where people are more vulnerable to forms of exploitation and further marginalised from services and trade unions. Coy et al. (2007) argue that legalisation contributes to normalisation which in turn increases the likelihood of paying for sex. Yet there is no evidence that in countries where legalisation exists, more men purchase sex. New Zealand or provinces in Australia where brothels are legal do not show any greater prevalence of men who purchase sex, and where there is any statistical difference, this is likely to be affected by methodological procedures capturing legal rather than illegal populations.

As much as those supporting criminalisation of 'demand' may argue they want to support sex workers and stress that in the Swedish model it is not a crime to sell sex, there is no avoiding the reality that criminalisation would penalise women involved in the sex industry. In one legislative blunder, all the clients of sex workers become criminals. Hence, any current markets that can operate legally become illegal. Sex workers have no legal clients. This creates a new crime which will compound the much documented stigma and marginalisation of sex workers. How can voluntary sex workers seek their rights in a criminal industry? Those who support the Swedish model rarely acknowledge voluntary sex work but, in doing this, they can ignore thousands of people who would be detrimentally affected by the introduction of such legislation. This blanket policy does not differentiate between forced and voluntary workers and 'good' and 'bad' management. If law is passed that criminalises men who buy sex, the moral message of commercial sex as 'wrong' will be based on the force of change and not evidence or fact (Weitzer 2007).

References

Agustín, L.M. (2005), 'New Research Directions: The Cultural Studies of Commercial Sex', *Sexualities* 8:5, 618–31.

Agustín, L.M. (2007), *Sex at the Margins: Migration, Labour Markets and the Rescue Industry* (London: Zed Books).

Atchison, C., L. Fraser and J. Lowman (1998), 'Men Who Buy Sex: Preliminary Findings of An Exploratory Study' in J. Elias, V. Bullough, V. Elias and J. Elders (eds), *Prostitution: On Whores, Hustlers and Johns* (New York: Prometheus Books), 172–203.

Bindel, J. (1998), 'Flushing Out the Johns', *Trouble and Strife* 38, 35–6.

Boynton, P. and L. Cusick (2006), 'Sex Workers to Pay the Price', *British Medical Journal* 332 (28 January), 190–91.

Brooks-Gordon, B. (2005), 'Clients and Commercial Sex: Reflections on *Paying the Price: A Consultation Paper on Prostitution*', *Criminal Law Review*, 425–43.

Brooks-Gordon, B. (2006), *The Price of Sex: Prostitution, Policy and Society* (Cullompton: Willan).

Campbell, R. (1998), 'Invisible Men: Making Visible Male Clients of Female Prostitutes in Merseyside' in J. Elias, V. Bullough, V. Elias and G. Brewer (eds), *Prostitution: On Whores, Hustlers and Johns* (New York: Prometheus Books), 155–71.

Campbell, R. and M. Storr (2001), 'Challenging the Kerb Crawler Rehabilitation Programme', *Feminist Review* 67 (Spring), 94–108.

Coy, M., M. Horvath and L. Kelly (2007), '"It's Just Like Going to the Supermarket": Men Buying Sex in East London', London: Child and Woman Abuse Studies Unit, London Metropolitan University.

Cusick, L. and L. Berney (2005), 'Prioritizing Punitive Responses over Public Health: Commentary on the Home Office Consultation Document *Paying the Price*', *Critical Social Policy* 25:4, 596–606.

Ekberg, G. (2004), 'The Swedish Law that Prohibits the Purchase of Sexual Services: Best Practices for Prevention of Prostitution and Trafficking in Human Beings', *Violence Against Women* 10:10, 1187–218.

Gould, A. (1999), 'Punishing the Punter: The Politics of Prostitution in Sweden', Department of Social Science, Loughborough University.

Gould, A. (2001), 'The Criminalisation of Buying Sex: The Politics of Prostitution in Sweden', *Journal of Social Policy* 30:3, 437–56.

Groom, T. and R. Nandwini (2006), 'Characteristics of Men Who Pay for Sex: A UK Sexual Health Clinic Survey', *Sexually Transmitted Infections* 82:5, 364–7.

Hester, M. and N. Westmarland (2004), *Tackling Street Prostitution: Towards a Holistic Approach* (London: Home Office).

Home Office (2004), *Paying the Price: A Consultation Paper on Prostitution* (London: HMSO).

Home Office (2006), *Coordinated Prostitution Strategy* (London: HMSO).

Kantola, J. and J. Squires (2004), 'Discourses Surrounding Prostitution Policies in the UK', *European Journal of Women's Studies* 11:1, 77–101.

Kaspersson, M. (2006), 'The Problem with Symbolic Legislation and Deterrence: The Case of the Swedish Prostitution Law', British Society of Criminology, Glasgow.

Kennedy, M.A., C. Klein, B.B. Gorzalka and J.C. Yuille (2004), 'Attitude Change Following a Diversion Program for Men Who Solicit Sex', *Journal of Offender Rehabilitation* 40:1/2, 41–60.

Kinnell, H. (2006), 'Clients of Female Sex Workers: Men or Monsters?' in R. Campbell and M. O'Neill (eds), *Sex Work Now* (Cullompton: Willan), 212–62.

Kulick, D. (2005), 'Four Hundred Thousand Swedish Perverts', *GLQ: A Journal of Lesbian and Gay Studies* 11:2, 205–35.

Leander, K. (2005), 'Reflections on Sweden's Measures against Men's Violence against Women', *Social Policy and Society* 5:1, 115–25.

Lowman, J. (2000), 'Violence and the Outlaw Status of (Street) Prostitution in Canada', *Violence Against Women* 6:9, 987–1011.

Monto, M.A. and S. Garcia (2001), 'Recidivism among the Customers of Female Street Prostitutes: Do Intervention Programs Help?', *Western Criminology Review* 3:2.

Nussbaum, M. (1998), 'Whether from Reason or Prejudice: Taking Money for Bodily Services', *Journal of Legal Studies* 27:2, 693–724.

Nussbaum, M.C. (2004), *Hiding from Humanity: Disgust, Shame and the Law* (Princeton, NJ: Princeton University Press).

Outshoorn, J. (ed.) (2004), *The Politics of Prostitution: Women's Movements, Democratic States, and the Globalisation of Sex Commerce* (Cambridge: Cambridge University Press).

Pawson, R. (2002), 'Evidence and Policy and Naming and Shaming', *Policy Studies* 23:3/4, 211–30.

Phoenix, J. and S. Oerton (2005), *Illicit and Illegal: Sex, Regulation and Social Control* (Cullompton: Willan).

Pitcher, J., R. Campbell, P. Hubbard, M. O'Neill and J. Scoular (2006), *Living and Working in Areas of Street Sex Work: From Conflict to Coexistence* (Abingdon: The Policy Press).

Prasad, M. (1999), 'The Morality of Market Exchange: Love, Money and Contractual Justice', *Sociological Perspectives* 42:2, 181–215.

Sagar, T. (2007), 'Tackling On-Street Sex Work: Anti Social Behaviour Orders, Sex Workers and Inclusive Inter-Agency Initiatives', *Criminology and Criminal Justice* 7:2, 153–68.

Sanders, T. (2008), *Paying for Pleasure: Men Who Buy Sex* (Cullompton: Willan).

Sanders , T. and R. Campbell (2007), 'What's Criminal about Indoor Sex Work?' in K. Williams, P. Birch, G. Letherby and M. Cain (eds), *Sex as Crime* (Cullompton: Willan).

Scoular, J. (2004), 'Criminalising "Punters": Evaluating the Swedish Position on Prostitution', *Journal of Social Welfare and Family Law* 26:2, 195–210.

Scourfield, J. and M. Drakeford (2002), 'New Labour and "the Problem of Men"', *Critical Social Policy* 22:4, 619–40.

Soothill, K. and T. Sanders (2004), 'Calling the Tune? Some Observations on *Paying the Price: A Consultation Paper on Prostitution*', *Journal of Forensic Psychiatry and Psychology* 15:4, 642–59.

Svanstrom, Y. (2004), 'Criminalising the John: A Swedish Gender Model?' in J. Outshoorn (ed.), *The Politics of Prostitution* (Cambridge: Cambridge University Press).

Ward, H., C.H. Mercer, K. Wellings, K. Fenton, B. Erens, A. Copas and A.M. Johnson (2005), 'Who Pays for Sex? An Analysis of the Increasing Prevalence of Female Commercial Sex Contacts among Men in Britain', *Journal of Sexually Transmitted Infections* 81:6, 467–71.

Weizter, R. (2007), 'The Social Construction of Sex Trafficking: Ideology and Institutionalization of a Moral Crusade', *Politics and Society* 35:3, 447–75.

Wortley, S., B. Fischer and C. Webster (2002), 'Vice Lessons: A Survey of Prostitution Offenders Enrolled in the Toronto John School Diversion Program', *Canadian Journal of Criminology* 44:4, 369–402.

Chapter 11

The Consumer, the Consumed and the Commodity: Women and Sex Buyers Talk about Objectification in Prostitution

Madeleine Coy

Introduction

This chapter explores the supply/demand dynamic in prostitution in terms of psycho-social dimensions, based on empirical research with young women who sell, and men who pay for, sex. Notions of objectification and commodification feature in constructions of commercial sex from both perspectives. The aim here is to highlight that 'the way in which the objectification involved is not simply to do with how the customer thinks of the prostitute, but how the prostitute thinks of herself' (Marshall 1999, 145). Conceptually, the analysis draws upon Nussbaum's (1995) characteristics of objectification to explore commercial sex transactions, and discusses the wider socio-cultural context of the mainstreaming and increasing normalisation of the sex industry.

This analysis is underpinned by my perspective as a feminist researcher with a background in residential and outreach work with sexually exploited girls and young women (aged 12–17 years), and adult women in prostitution. The chapter draws on the wealth of feminist theory and research highlighting the harms of prostitution and links with other forms of violence against women (Barry 1979; Farley 2003, 2004; Jeffreys 1997). Using this analytical framework, and my experience of providing support to women, I hold the perspective that prostitution constitutes not only a significant barrier to gender equality but also a form of violence against women. As Shrage comments:

> Because of the cultural context in which prostitution operates, it epitomises and perpetuates pernicious patriarchal beliefs and values and, therefore, is both damaging to the women who sell sex and, as an organised social practice, to all women (Shrage 1989, 352).

Holding this perspective carries with it a responsibility to find ways to enable women to exit selling sex and develop effective interventions that prevent women and girls from being coerced in entering, or continuing in, prostitution and that challenge the legitimacy of the global sex industry. Despite concerns that this may lead to a pragmatic *cul-de-sac*, there are a number of ways in which the development of policy can take into account what I refer to as the psycho-social dimensions of prostitution. For instance, these include challenging the 'normalisation message' of contemporary commercial sex through education, awareness raising and prevention campaigns (Coy, Horvath and Kelly 2007). This chapter interrogates the roles of sexualised culture and consumerism in sustaining and normalising the sex industry. In doing so, it owes debts to decades of feminist analyses of how attitudes and beliefs enable other forms of violence against women to continue with impunity, which – far from remaining theoretical plateaus – have led to legislative, policy and practice progress that have made a significant difference to women's lives and safety.

Commonalities between different positions on prostitution are often overlooked in favour of emphasising divisions. However in terms of immediate, short-term practicality, there is often shared ground, including decriminalisation of women who sell sex and expunging criminal records that prevent women from finding alternative employment. There is also broad agreement on specific measures to address factors and manifestations of vulnerability, such as provision of safe housing, access to drugs treatment, health care and other forms of support that should be available when needed rather than subject to waiting lists and inadequate resources. Where my perspective, informed by working and conducting research that is discussed in this chapter, takes a different approach is a matter of long-term, gendered social vision. On this basis, I do not support regulation of the sex industry and instead endorse approaches that aim to eliminate prostitution along with other forms of violence against women.

Multiple Methodologies

The chapter draws on strands of data from two research projects on the sex industry – life story narratives and arts work with women involved in prostitution (Coy 2007a) and semi-structured interviews with men who pay for sex (Coy, Horvath and Kelly 2007). They were not undertaken simultaneously, or even in relation to one another, but provide complementary vantage points.

The ethnographic research with women who sell sex was conducted as a doctoral study on the links between young women's experiences of local authority care and their entry routes into prostitution. Building on my experience of working with sexually exploited young women in care, and the limited existing literature (O'Neill et al. 1995; O'Neill 2001; Friedberg 2000), the research sought to explore young women's psycho-social constructions as shaped by their material circumstances. Using a feminist participatory action research approach, it combined life story interviews with arts workshops[1] (O'Neill 2001) on the theme of the relationship with the self and the body in prostitution. The theme of disrupted sense of identity and (dis)embodiment emerged from the young women's life story narratives as a significant element of their entry into prostitution, and the arts workshops enabled women to visually (re)present this experience using digital photography (Coy 2007b).

1 The arts workshops were a joint project with a local youth arts team, and led by an arts worker with experience of working with women in prostitution. Final images were exhibited at a local art gallery during 2004.

Throughout the period of the research I was employed as an outreach worker in a health promotion project for women in the sex industry. The negotiation of these two roles of researcher and outreach worker is discussed fully elsewhere (Coy 2006), but worth noting here is the privileged access to the women's everyday lived experience. External researchers with women in prostitution are able only to access women's 'face value' actions and motivations. Even in ethnographic studies, the researcher is present as a time-limited figure, located outside the relationships between women who sell sex and the support project. However, my daily contact with women in a relationship of rapport and trust enabled a deeper engagement and, critically, an awareness of surrounding issues with which women may need support and intervention (Coy 2006). In the findings and analysis, then, women's narratives of their emotional and psycho-social ontology are embedded in a wider knowledge of their personal and social histories and milieux. This chapter, therefore, draws not just on what women said, but how it was juxtaposed within their everyday expressions of embodied identity.

The 14 women who participated in the life story interviews were aged between 17 and 33 years, and all had backgrounds of local authority care. At the time of the research, some women were selling on the street and some indoors, although all had initially begun to sell sex on the street when aged between 11 and 17 years. Half were coerced into prostitution by older men and half drifted into selling sex through peer association and involvement in the street 'prostitution subculture' (Hakkinen 1999). Only one of the women cited a need to sustain a drug habit as an initial motivation, but all 14 had at some point used heroin and/or crack cocaine. In their personal histories, there were high levels of sexual and physical abuse in childhood and in intimate partner relationships. This prevalence of abuse and the abusive dimensions of their routes into prostitution during adolescence may inflect their sense of objectification differently to women who begin selling sex under varying personal circumstances.

The arts work was a collaborative project with a local youth arts team, running parallel to the life story interviews. Over 40 women participated to varying degrees in the creation of the final 11 images, ranging from women involved in street prostitution with multiple vulnerabilities, to women selling sex indoors who framed this as a non-problematic entrepreneurial activity. The chapter draws on representations of the commercial sex exchange from both these research strands and demonstrates that a sense of objectification is compounded by personal and social disadvantage – but ultimately also transcends them. Across the various commercial sex settings, women who participated in the arts project expressed elements of violation and objectification. These accounts and experiences are not suggested to be representative of all women who sell sex, but are used as heuristic devices to illustrate harmful psycho-social dimensions of the prostitution transaction.

The research with men who pay for sex was conducted by the Child and Woman Abuse Studies Unit (CWASU), commissioned by a project in East London (Coy, Horvath and Kelly 2007). A total of 137 men were recruited through newspaper advertisements. Semi-structured interviews were completed by telephone, collecting demographic data and responses about men's motivations and decision-making processes when paying for sex. Specifically, they were asked: what were the reasons they paid for sex; what they got out of it; if anything made them feel nervous; and what, if anything, would deter them from buying sex (see Coy, Horvath and Kelly 2007 for the full questionnaire). They were also asked what they thought of women who sell sex, and their preferences. Their responses ranged from opinions about the individual women that they paid for sex to attitudes reflecting broader notions about female sexuality and prostitution. The data was coded using a coding dictionary developed for the study, entered and analysed using SPSS. The interviews were also transcribed and analysed using grounded theory (Glaser and Strauss 1967). The final report explores sex buyers' preferences about women they buy sex from, what type of acts they typically pay for, use of pornography and attitudes towards women who sell sex. An analytic framework for understanding the accounts of sex buyers was developed from the data that suggests that, under an umbrella of male entitlement, men who buy sex are 'boasting' and/or 'consuming' and/or 'confessing' (Coy, Horvath and Kelly 2007).

Exploring Objectification

The sexual objectification of women in prostitution and pornography is well-documented in some strands of feminist theory and research (Dworkin 1981; Mackinnon 1987; Barry 1979; Jeffreys 1997; Farley 2003, 2004). Ethnographic research highlights the complexity of women's lived experience of prostitution – that commercial sex encompasses both feelings of vulnerability and victimisation and a sense of agency and autonomy for some women (Phoenix 1999; O'Neill 2001; Coy 2007a). The voices of women in this chapter demonstrate that prostitution as a practice of gender inequality does not preclude individual women from feeling personal power. However, this is typically based on accepting and celebrating a sexualised selfhood, embedded in gender orders of male domination (Miriam 2005).

An attempt to explore the historical roots of the notion of women as commodities is presented by Rubin (1975). Drawing on Levi-Strauss, she identifies the historical process of gift exchange (where women are the exchanged and men the exchangers) as an outcome of patriarchal gender orders. Core structural features of the exchange are hegemonic heterosexuality, the association of power with phallic masculinity and the gendered division of labour. The longevity of the exchange of women therefore has genesis in, and is supported by, the substantive socio-economic inequality between men and women (Rubin 1975). Applied to a contemporary context, this gendered asymmetry of men as buyers and women as sellers in prostitution remains. Thus, 'men have been [and are] sexual subjects – exchangers – and women sexual semi-objects' (Rubin 1975, 176).

Margaret Radin (1996) discusses 'universal commodification' as an analytic concept, where all property and attributes can be exchanged for money. When attributes are traded as commodities, they are reduced to their economic value, interchangeable, and subject to the contractual nature of free markets. However, she considers that certain elements of personhood are incommensurable and, therefore, 'contested commodities'. Social contexts are important in determining what we should think of as a contested commodity, as defining a commodity in conditions of subordination and inequality means that the basis of the exchange is oppressive (Radin 1996). Developing Radin's discussion of commodification and prostitution in these terms, objectification operates harmfully as gendered subordination by framing women and women's bodies 'as means of lesser personhood' (1996, 157). As she suggests, 'objectification comes about through commodification when our cultural rhetoric conceives of certain attributes of the persons as commodities that can be bought and sold' (1996, 156). Andrea Dworkin (2000, 30 – cited in Papadaki 2007) suggests 'objectification occurs when a human being ... is made less than human, turned into a thing or commodity, bought or sold. When objectification occurs, a person is depersonalised.' In the same vein, Bartky (1990, 26) defines sexual objectification as:

> when her sexual parts or sexual functions are separated out from the rest of her personality and reduced to the status of mere instruments or else regarded as if they were capable of representing her.

For Papadaki (2007, 340), these various analyses draw on Kantian notions of objectification based on 'treating a person as an object (a mere sexual tool), in a way that leads to the reduction of the individual in question to the status of a thing for us ... [and] constitutes a serious harm to an individuals' humanity'. Although there are debates about the value of Kantian thought to feminism, the strands of feminist theory on which this chapter draws share the above perspective of objectification as harmful.

The detailed analysis is primarily based on the notions of objectification that draw on Martha Nussbaum's philosophical exploration of how people are constituted as objects. She identifies seven elements of the concept of objectification, defined as 'seven ways to treat a person as a thing' (1995, 256). Marshall (1999) applies two of these to prostitution – fungibility (objects being interchangeable with others of same type) and denial of subjectivity (experiences and feelings of 'object' not recognised). I add a third of her elements in this chapter – instrumentality (where objectifiers treat the object as a tool of their purpose) (Nussbaum 1995, 257).[2] Using these analytic notions enables the dynamic of how commercial sex is viewed, constructed and enacted by sex buyers to be explored. Although Nussbaum links objectification with inequality, she does not argue that it is intrinsically harmful to individual humanity (Papadaki 2007). Following my perspective outlined earlier, I use Nussbaum's notion to illustrate the dynamics of objectification within prostitution, and conceptualise them as constitutive of harm to women. I use the term 'harm' here to refer to the destructive physical, sexual and psychological/emotional impact of selling sex that is well documented in research (Farley 2004). This is supported by existing research literature and some of the accounts of women and sex buyers in this chapter. Harm arises from objectification in prostitution as:

2 Nussbaum (1995, 257) has a further element of objectification on ownership defined as 'the objectifier defines the object as something that is owned or bought by another, bought or sold etc.'. This definition of ownership may be too prescriptive for situations of the majority of women involved in prostitution, but may be useful to conceptualise the trafficking of women for the purposes of sexual exploitation.

> objectification is improper treatment of persons because it makes them means not ends (that is, treats them as available means with all other objects). As means, objects may be bought and sold in markets to achieve satisfaction of persons' needs and desires … (Radin 1996, 156).

The recent positioning of the sex industry as legitimated 'business' shapes the ways in which women internalise aspects of the ontology of prostitution and experience themselves as commodified objects. Marshall (1999) suggests that framing prostitution as a commercial service involves a degree of objectification since it does not require interpersonal mutuality – men pay for their sexual pleasure not a mutually pleasurable experience. This echoes Månsson's (2004, 8) suggestion that the discourse of consumerism in relation to the sex industry creates 'an essentially mercantile vision of sexuality, where sex is comparable to a consumer product rather than an intimate relationship'.

The following section explores the accounts of sex buyers as they perceive women within the commercial sex transaction as commodities in terms of instrumentality, fungibility and denial of subjectivity. The sexualisation of contemporary society is referred to in men's accounts, and discussed in detail in later sections.

Sex Buyers

The men who were interviewed were demographically diverse. Just over a third (35.7 per cent) were in a relationship, a further 16.1 per cent married and 88.4 per cent in employment. The age range was 19–64 years, with the highest concentration (40 per cent) of the buyers in the study aged between 20 and 29 years, and with 14 different ethnicities represented. Far from being deviant 'peculiar men' (Månsson 2004), the respondents cut across a range of ages, ethnicities and socio-economic groups. This suggests a potential normalisation of buying sex amongst generations of men, albeit concentrated in younger men, and a shared denominator of masculinity as a constitutive and supportive attitude (Coy, Horvath and Kelly 2007).

The majority reported buying sex in off street settings (67.9 per cent), a quarter in both street and indoor settings (25.5 per cent) and 6.6 per cent solely on the street.

Seeking Sexual Instruments

The most common sexual acts that men reported paying for were vaginal and oral intercourse (73 per cent). Contrary to stereotypical preconceptions, men were not seeking 'kinky' or specialist acts that they struggled to find elsewhere, but were paying for conventional heterosexual practices (Coy, Horvath and Kelly 2007). This raises a question about how men view the instrumental purpose of sexual intercourse, and women's bodies, both within and outside of commercialised sex. Some men explicitly articulated viewing women in prostitution as interchangeable instruments for satisfying their sexual requirements:

> I don't really have any feelings about them at all – I don't dislike them, overall I'm indifferent to the women I see.

One man described his view of women who sell sex explicitly in terms of instrumentality (Marshall 1999; Nussbaum 1995):

> It [paying for sex] serves a purpose, it's non-committal. It's a psychological thing, no ties, available when I want it and where I want. This is the key.

This framing illustrates the ability of sex buyers to exercise their will and entitlement to sexual release in their terms. Another response (echoed by several men) about the outcome of buying sex and the power of command over a woman's body that the transaction affords him, elaborates on this:

> You can do anything you want for twenty minutes – everything and anything for forty quid.

For these buyers, women are substantively present but subjectively absent in the exchange, as commercial sex enables them to exercise an entirely self-focused sexual behaviour. This suggests that some men are seeking a literally objectified, disembodied sexual release. As such, the value of women who sell sex remains with only their sexual availability (Månsson 2004). The most malignant expression of viewing women as instrumental sexual objects was in the ways that men were derogatory about women and framed them not just as 'other' but also as (worth)'less':

> A prostitute is a piece of meat.
>
> I don't have to ask or think 'No, is that too dirty for her?' or – like I don't really have to be as respectful as if it was my girlfriend or my wife or partner.
>
> I like going with a dirty bird, I know that's wrong but that's what I like.

One man described his instrumental use of women in prostitution even when he suspected that they were coerced into selling sex:

> A couple of places I visited, it was Slovenian and Polish girls and I wondered whether they were kind of being forced into it. But I never discussed it with them because I went there just for sex. Although I did wonder whether they were being forced into it (cited in Coy, Horvath and Kelly 2007, 24).

Instrumentality is also evident from the way some men spoke about commercial sex being a more favourable option to masturbation:

> When I get the urge, I want to relieve the tension … Instead of masturbating myself I get relieved.

Some men referred to the importance of 'feeling like a man' as an outcome of paying for sex. Therefore, sex buyers are enabled to 'exhibit [their] masculinity by contracting for use of woman's body' (Pateman 1988, 200). This suggests, as Chen (2003, 5) has noted about male sex buyers in Taiwan, that 'physical sexual needs are not the first concern; instead it is how to have sex in masculine ways that makes seeking prostitutes desirable.' The consumerist market enables men to frame this instrumentality in a very practical sense akin to other decisions that make life more comfortable:

> It's like paying for a cab instead of walking.

Where prostitution is located as 'consumerism', women who sell sex become objects in a commercial-market-based sense: commodities that can be bought and evaluated (Coy, Horvath and Kelly 2007). Evaluations are a core part of websites established as information sharing forums where sex buyers rate women for other potential buyers' perusal before purchase (Earle and Sharpe 2007). Women's subjectivity is absent when what is sought is an outlet for sexual release which requires no more than any woman's body (O'Connell Davidson 1998). This reflects the instrumentality of Nussbaum's (1995) analysis where she identifies the object as a way for the protagonists' purposes to be met. Some sex buyers clearly perceive the function of women as to facilitate their sexual gratification (Coy, Horvath and Kelly 2007). As Nussbaum clarifies, if women are viewed as 'a set of bodily parts that are useful tools for one's pleasure, and the powerful urge to secure one's own sexual satisfaction will ensure that instrumentalisation (and therefore denial of autonomy and of subjectivity) [will] continue' (1995, 267).

Denial of Subjectivity

Integral to these perceptions of women and commercial sex is a sense that women's selfhood is irrelevant. This was evident when men reported that what they got from paying for sex was a convenience on their terms, where they had no responsibility to the feelings of women:

> I don't really need to have sex, but it provides me with that sort of availability – obviously as long as I have the money available to pay. There's no obligation put on me to have a relationship with a person, they're available, therefore at your disposal.

For many men, it is precisely the lack of emotional connections or 'no hassle' that makes commercial sex attractive (see also Månsson 2004; McKeganey and Barnard 1996).

What is revealing amongst the men who expressed guilt and ambivalence about buying sex was a recognition that commercial sex did not provide them with emotional connections that they (tacitly) recognised that they were seeking. Thus, buying sex depended on objectifying women in a way that made some men feel dissatisfied and even uncomfortable:

> The only thing with paying for sex is you can't actually have a good relationship with a woman, it's just bang bang really, nothing – there's no feeling in it.
>
> It leaves you feeling nasty, but you can't always be bothered to go through the relationship business with a woman so you take the easy way out and buy sex.

A few men emphasised that they thought of women who sell sex as 'ordinary people' and a minority stated that it was important that they developed an emotional connection with women they were paying. These men implicitly recognised the inhumanity and depersonalisation of objectification, and whilst they can use and benefit from it in the short term, they see it is unrewarding and dissatisfying. Their guilt and ambivalence indicates that they experience a psycho-social expectation to take pleasure in commercial sex that is contradicted by the actuality of buying sex.

Fungibility/Interchangeable Objects

The ways in which some of (even many of) the men conceptualised women as commodities are also apparent in their descriptions of exercising consumer choice in the commercial sex transaction (Coy, Horvath and Kelly 2007). Some men reported feeling indifferent to which woman they paid for sex, frequently using phrases such as 'I'm not fussy' or 'I'm pretty indiscriminate'. Women are therefore objectified by fungibility (Nussbaum 1995) when sex buyers view them as *interchangeable* instruments – where *any* woman will fulfil the purposes of the commercial sex encounter:

> I just try anything really.

At the same time, some men viewed their ability to choose women as an integral element of commercialised sex – 'When I've seen a girl I can choose which one to take' (Coy, Horvath and Kelly 2007):

> It's what you fancy on the day. Many times I've gone [to the massage parlour], not see what I like, and not had nothing that day. Because I won't go for the sake of having sex, the woman has to be what you want to go with that day, and if it's not what turns you on let's just forget it.

Just over 10 per cent of respondents (n=15) reported having no preferences in the women they sought for paid sex, demonstrating that for many there was no sense of individuality, just a desire for functional sexual instruments (Nussbaum 1995). Preferences for 'types' of women ranged from specifying age brackets (the most common being for women in their twenties) to ethnicity (either women as exotic Other or women from their own ethnic background) or a basic requirement that they found the woman attractive. A few descriptions of preferences were finely nuanced, with combinations of body shape, age, ethnicity, breast size, height and hair length mentioned. What was interesting about all of these responses was that all the men who expressed preferences talked only about physical attributes and aesthetics. None of the respondents made any references to women's personality or identity.

Preference or no preference can be understood as two sides of the same coin; women are interchangeable and, therefore, defined solely as sexually satisfying orifices, or they are viewed as a range of largely interchangeable options that are commodified by the market exchange, where aesthetic preference may be exercised but individuality remains irrelevant. This has been referred to as the 'McDonaldised context' where women are picked from a line up of available options for consumption (Brents and Hausbeck 2007). Whichever position men take, they are exercising a 'self focussed, consumer-oriented conception of sexuality' (Busch et al. 2002, 1097).

Sexualised Culture: A Context for the Normalisation of Consuming Sex

The emerging body of research on sex buyers and responses illustrated above indicate that motivations offered for buying sex are multiple (O'Neill 2001), but rely on a naturalised discourse of the male sexual urge/need (Hollway 1984) or, as we have termed it, a sense of entitlement (Coy, Horvath and Kelly 2007). In this discourse, male entitlement to sexual access to women is presumed and protected, prostitution accepted as a public service that prevents 'innocent' women from being sexually assaulted. In contrast, some studies have identified men's desire for intimacy and emotional relationships as a rationale for buying sex (Soothill and Sanders 2005; Kinnell 2006). However, only a minority of men in our research cited this reason and they also reported feeling disappointed by the capacity of the supply/demand interaction to fulfil this desire. These findings highlight the need for further research that explores motivations in respect of the diversity of the base of sex buyers. The accounts of the men who participated in our study and international research (Marttila 2003; Månsson 2004) suggest that framing the purchase of sex as a commercial service akin to other forms of leisure activity has provided a further legitimation. In both of these justificatory frameworks, sex for money is awarded an inevitable ahistorical status, while women who sell sex are Othered, located outside of meaningful parameters of respectable womanhood.

Conceptualising prostitution as a consumer service shifts the emphasis from the interpersonal interaction to the benefits for seller and buyer in a similar way to other market economic transactions. In this model, men's sexual needs and women's financial needs are met in an exchange that is based on mutual reciprocity (O'Connell Davidson 1998; Brewis and Linstead 2000). This was a strong theme in some of the sex buyers' accounts. Almost three quarters (71 per cent) of respondents (n=98) talked about paying for sex in terms of 'consumerism' (Bauman 2007). These men talked about the cost of buying sex and the quality of the service (Coy, Horvath and Kelly 2007). Where men view commercial sex in this context, as Månsson (2004) has termed it, 'shopping for sex', gendered power relations are clearly visible – the sex industry is a 'market for men' (O'Neill 2001).

The globalisation of the sex industry and developments in technology have created 'new forms of contact between buyer and seller' that have 'increased the availability of sex for sale' (Månsson 2004, 3). The influences of these new forms of contact on sex buyer's constructions were apparent in the men's decision-making processes and also reflect shifts in the organisation of prostitution. Buying sex on the street was largely framed as 'seedy' and 'dodgy', with frequent references to 'junkies', but buying sex indoors or ordering women over the internet was normalised – legal, so therefore socially legitimate. This attitude reflects a growing respectability attached to some sectors of the sex industry that Brents and Hausbeck (2007) suggests is likely to increase as commercial sex businesses adopt similar marketing strategies to mainstream businesses.

The socio-cultural context of commercial sex can be traced through accounts of sex buyers. For instance, the motif of sexualised imagery of women within mainstream advertising and music videos cultivates an everyday association of women as sexualised (Kelly 2005). Buyers demonstrated an ability to link their activities with this representation of glamour and enjoyment of hyper-sexual behaviour, which in some cases enabled them to overcome ambivalence:

> [It's] just a cultural thing, isn't it, where everything is sexualised and certain things are portrayed as normal, and, you know, they're probably not!
>
> I just think it's like we live in a consumer society. And I think that's become a bit of a commodity now, really ... Just the whole sex thing. Because the internet's there and magazines are there and you've got images all the time (cited in Coy, Horvath and Kelly 2007).

This construction of prostitution as a legitimate service industry should be explored since 'prostitutes themselves are the commodity that is consumed' (Brewis and Linstead 2000, 84). However, the current focus on consumerism obscures this by reframing the 'product' being bought and evaluated as a sexual service rather than women's self/body (Pateman 1988; O'Connell Davidson 1998).

The next section turns to analysis of how women who sell sex describe objectification, (dis)embodiment and (lack of) subjectivity in commercial sex.

Women who Sell Sex

Women's experience of being an object in the commercial sex exchange is well documented in research (Farley 2004; Hoigard and Finstad 1992; McKeganey and Barnard 1996; O'Neill 2001; Phoenix 1999). Although this is nuanced by personal circumstances, the *theme* of objectification is traced in this section through the ways in which women talked about their sense of self and descriptions of their role in the ontology of prostitution in life stories and arts workshops.

Becoming an Object

The process of identifying self as sex object in young women's routes into prostitution from local authority care demonstrates how women identify their self and socially situate themselves. Elsewhere, I have detailed a conceptual framework (Coy 2007a, 2007b) that links the four stages of identity development and stages of involvement in the sex industry, identified by women in their life story narratives. This framework provides a way to understand how young women drift into/are coerced into, and maintain their involvement in, prostitution. It traces a trajectory of young women's paths into prostitution, based on layers of analysis of the psycho-social development and positioning. This chapter focuses on the layer of sex object status and draws out parallels and tensions with the accounts of sex buyers. Briefly, the conceptual framework of young women's lived experience is as follows:

- *Abused Child* – refers to the experiences of sexual and physical abuse and feelings of abandonment, but also the abusive dimension of involvement in prostitution during adolescence.

- *Sex Object* – both sexual abuse and professional intervention that focuses on sexual behaviour promote the primacy of self = sex object status. Women develop a sexualised sense of self and associate their value with sexual availability.
- *Survivor* – the sense of belonging found in street communities and ability to generate an income provides young women with a feeling of autonomy. Prostitution is therefore a pragmatic 'choice' within limited socio-economic and psycho-social circumstances.
- *Profession Prostitute* (O'Neill 1996; Phoenix 1999) – young women develop an identity and role based on embracing their sexualised perception of self embodied identity. This sense of value and purpose is reinforced by a position of 'somebody' in the prostitution subculture (Hakkinen 1999).

In the sex object layer, women begin to experience themselves as sexualised and develop a sense of their personhood based on the way that others perceive and respond to them. To draw a straightforward correlation between childhood sexual abuse and subsequent adolescent and/or adult prostitution oversimplifies the complex ways in which abuse and sexualisation embed 'the exchange value of the female sexed body' (Wesely 2002, 1186) in the young women's psycho-social terms of reference. However, the women linked experiences of abuse to selling sex through the sense of the body being sexually used by others and survival strategies, such as dissociation. Three quarters of the women experienced sexual abuse in childhood from a wide range of perpetrators, echoing US and UK research on childhood/adolescent experiences of women in prostitution (Farley 2004; O'Neill et al. 1995). The common theme of women's narratives relating to abuse was, ultimately, a lack of opportunity for recovery, and consequent disruption of a robust, embodied sense of self. In this way, the objectification and commodification – for Wesely (2002), the exchange value – that are apparent in the commercial sex exchange are familiar processes:

> I lost my virginity when I was 10 … I was raped when I was 12, no one believed me … I met these two guys, I was made to work, they said they will beat me so I did it. I was like 15, 15½, coming up 16, dead skinny, blond hair, tall. Punters loved it. It was scary at first but after a couple of weeks I'd just got used to it (Stacey, 25).

Stacey's life story narrative featured physical and sexual abuse from family members and peers. Like many other women who participated in the research, it is clear that the formative events of her life led to the development of what Maria Epele (2001, 165) has termed 'estrangement of bodily experiences'. That this enabled prostitution to seem meaningful in accordance with how they viewed themselves, or an activity they became quickly accustomed to, tells us much about how commercial sex exchanges depend on the objectification of the female body.

The Objectified Body

(Dis)embodiment in prostitution is at the core of the women's experiences and requires specific exploration as the power of command over women's bodies is essentially what sex buyers pay for (Pateman 1988). O'Connell Davidson (1998) suggests that this power of command over the body that punters buy in the commercial sex transaction is not merely physical but also symbolic. That is, the body is bought for the purposes of specific functions, but ownership also transfers from the woman to the buyer, who assumes belonging of the body within the parameters of agreed contractual boundaries. One woman who participated in the arts workshops articulated this when she depicted her body in a series of photographs – legs, arms, torso, head – and placed a price tag on each one.[3] This sense of her body in parts, that had been bought after negotiation as to their worth, represented at a concrete level her own theorising of objectification through her sense of ontological fragmentation.

Although the term 'sexual services' is frequently used in both marketing and analysis of commercial sex, it obscures how the delivery of these services necessitates the use of the body. Even acts that do not involve penetration of the body – such as hand relief – still require touch and contact, and some buyers ask for additional visual stimulation such as exposure of breasts. The centrality of how women conceptualise their (dis)embodiment is also linked to how they locate the body as objectified:

> I hate my body, it doesn't belong to me anymore, not since everyone got their fingers on it (Hannah, 21).

> I'm not ashamed of my body or anything … it doesn't really matter about my body, so many thousands of people have seen it already … I wouldn't say I have any respect for it (Dee, 26).

For two of the women, prostitution provided a context in which they sought to reclaim and resituate their bodies, following childhood sexual abuse, in ways that they perceived as positive:

> Working gave me confidence, more confidence than I'd ever had. When I was a teenager I was very, conscientious of my body, hated sex. But with punters, I felt 10 feet high … I don't know what it was, but I used to go to work with all my stuff in my bag, all stockings and suspenders and make up, go out with not a scrap on my face, and get to work and get ready and go out feeling 10 feet high, like I was some kind of sex god that all these men wanted and I could just flaunt it …. And I suppose that's still the way I look at it (JC, 33).

> I think it's the way I look. I used to be really big, and it was like people were against me. Now it's like, I look good, and people, especially punters, notice me. So I'm noticing myself a bit more. I don't really like myself, but that's something I've got to start doing, liking myself (Christina, 21).

These accounts explicitly illustrate the personal/structural distinction of agency in prostitution, where women are able to feel personally powerful by embracing a key

3 This image did not make it into the exhibition as the young woman drifted out of contact with the outreach project and was not able to give approval to the final image.

socially constructed norm of female sexual behaviour/availability. For Christina and JC, selling sex takes them from being no one to being someone; from invisibility to others to existence in the eyes of others. They describe a sense of self as a subject that is based on objectification through women as interchangeable, sexualised beings (Nussbaum 1995). In other words, for JC and Christina, selling sex represents an opportunity to reposition the body image as useful and valued, without challenging the ways in which the women define themselves by their sexualised bodies and are reduced to their bodies. By situating their sense of self as an object for purchase that represents their worth, they are able to avoid feelings of bodily alienation and celebrate being valued as a sexualised commodity.

In the arts work, *MyBody MySelf: Getting Under the Skin*, exploring the relationship with self and body in prostitution, women created images about rape, sexual abuse, drug use, the ontology of selling sex and self harm. The images revealed that the emotional legacies associated with violence – shame, guilt, hating the body, blame and alienation – are identical to those women reveal when discussing the ontology of commercial sex encounters. These (dis)embodied impacts and meanings contribute to how women viewed the wider dynamics of interactions with sex buyers and their own social location.

Being an Object

Some women recognised that selling sex was predicated upon fulfilling buyers' needs and thus, to varying degrees, sublimating themselves. In this way, they identified that they were both instrumental in serving men's sexual desires and also interchangeable in Nussbaum's (1995) notion of objectification:

> One thing I've learned through all that time, you're never in control … you're lying down on the bed, you could be missionary, you could be lying down frontward, anything … I mean you're there to be what they want, whatever that is (Dee, 26).

> People don't realise the skills it takes. You know, to make them [sex buyers] come back to you. They don't care who you are as long they get their rocks off (Sue, 33).

> I always felt dirty …. They just want a hole. I mean, some of them are nice to you and that, but some don't even talk to you, they just want to come (Jackie, 19).

Here, women explicitly minimise their own selfhood, as sex buyers seek to fulfil their own sexual purposes. This diminishes their capacity to assert their own subjectivity as their needs, wants and, for some women, ability to determine what happens, are sublimated. They also recognise how they are constructed as transposable where any woman can fulfil the functions of the encounter for buyers. Where women recognise that they are rarely defining the terms of the encounter, men as sex buyers retain a privileged status – not just a sense of entitlement, but also the power to choose and reflect (Coy, Horvath and Kelly 2007) – that women who sell sex build into their sense of self.

Managing Object Status

In women's ontology of selling sex, awareness of objectification is also functional: by behaving like an object that is required to not experience emotion or sexual pleasure, they are able to effectively dissociate from the encounter. Women described distancing strategies such as zoning of the body into acceptable 'for sale' boundaries, refusing intimate practices such as kissing and using condoms as psychological barriers (see also Hoigard and Finstad 1992; Phoenix 1999; Sanders 2002). Dissociation is almost universally documented in research literature on the sex industry, to the point that Farley (2004, 1106) notes that 'dissociation is a job requirement for surviving prostitution'. Echoing this, women talked about dissociation as predicated on the psycho-social protection of object status. The following accounts illustrate the necessity of dissociating from what buyers are doing to their bodies:

> It ain't sex is it, just lying back and thinking of England while they do their thing (Stacey, 25).

> At first it made me feel degraded, but now I just switch off. Pretend I'm not there (Christina, 21).

Such techniques are not always successful – maintaining the distinction between 'real me' and 'work me' is not always effective, the realities of commercial sex impact on the sense of self and ownership of the body (Hoigard and Finstad 1992). Thus the processes of compartmentalisation that women develop have permeable boundaries and feelings of guilt, shame, worthlessness inflicted by selling sex carry over from 'work' life to 'private' life:

> I hate my body … I don't have sex with my husband anymore … (Tammy).

Dissociation demonstrates an explicit recognition that women's subjectivity is typically absent for sex buyers seeking instrumental sexual release. In order to manage commercial sex encounters effectively, women are required to operationalise objectification in their practices of self in ways that reflect how they are viewed and constituted by sex buyers.

Conclusions

> Prostitution is not the mutual, pleasurable exchange of the use of bodies, but the unilateral use of a woman's body by man in exchange of money (Pateman 1988, 199).

The experiences of both women who sell and men who buy sex demonstrate that the psycho-social dimensions are significant, and embedded in socio-cultural gender norms. The accounts detailed in this chapter strengthen the evidence base of harm in relation to prostitution by highlighting aspects of objectification in commercial sex that perpetuate views of women who sell sex as depersonalised, which are, in turn, frequently, and destructively, internalised by women.

Accounts from men who pay for sex demonstrate that they locate women as objects in the commercial sex exchange through viewing women as instruments for their sexual release: 'fungible' and interchangeable (Nussbaum 1995). This necessitates a denial of women's individuality and selfhood that also constitutes women as objects (Nussbaum 1995). Expressions of this vary from seeing women as reduced to sexual body parts (Bartky 1990) to a self-oriented view of sexual satisfaction that occludes mutuality. For those men for whom intimate mutuality is their desire, prostitution constitutes an illusion (Coy, Horvath and Kelly 2007).

The lived experience of selling sex for women is predicated on managing this sense of being 'just a hole for men to use' (Tammy, 32). Most of the women in this study describe a sense of self/ownership of the body where the process of selling sex replicates abusive experiences, and ultimately means they 'are forced to see themselves as objects … reinforcing and reminding women of their inferior status' (Wesely 2002, 1183).

Contemporary mainstreaming of sexualised consumption constructs prostitution as a socially legitimate industry and form of entertainment that promotes an instrumental view of sex. Women are presented as McDonaldised consumer products (Brents and Hausbeck 2007), in mainstream advertising and entertainment, notions of objectification are obscured and entitlement to access women's bodies as commodities is protected and promoted.

References

Barry, K. (1979), *Female Sexual Slavery* (New York: New York University Press).

Bartky, S. (1990), *Femininity and Domination* (London: Routledge).

Bauman, Z. (2007), *Consuming Life* (Cambridge: Polity).

Brents, B. and K. Hausbeck (2007), 'Marketing Sex: US Legal Brothels and Late Capitalist Consumption', *Sexualities* 10:64, 425–39.

Brewis, J. and S. Linstead (2000), '"The Worst Thing is the Screwing" (1): Consumption and the Management of Identity in Sex Work', *Gender, Work and Organization* 7:2, 84–97.

Busch, N.B., H. Bell, N. Hotaling and M. Monto (2002), 'Male Customers of Prostituted Women: Exploring Perceptions of Entitlement to Power and Control and Implications for Violent Behaviour toward Women', *Violence Against Women* 8:9, 1093–112.

Chen, M.H. (2003), 'Contradictory Male Sexual Desires: Masculinity, Lifestyles and Sexuality Among Prostitutes' Clients in Taiwan', paper presented at British Sociological Association Annual Conference, University of York, 14 April 2003.

Coy, M. (2006), 'This Morning I'm a Researcher, this Afternoon I'm an Outreach Worker: Ethical Dilemmas in Practitioner Research', *International Journal of Social Research Theory and Methodology* 9:5, 419–32.

Coy, M. (2007a), 'Between the Self and the Other: Women's Experiences of Routes into Prostitution from Local Authority Care', unpublished doctoral thesis, Loughborough University, March 2007.

Coy, M. (2007b), 'Young Women, Local authority Care and Selling Sex', *British Journal of Social Work*, advanced access published 14 August 2007, <http://bjsw.oxfordjournals.org/ >.

Coy, M., M. Horvath and L. Kelly (2007), '"It's Just Like Going to the Supermarket": Men Buying Sex in East London', London: Child and Woman Abuse Studies Unit, London Metropolitan University.

Dworkin, A. (1981), *Pornography: Men Possessing Women* (London: The Women's Press).

Dworkin, A. (2000), 'Against the Male Flood: Censorship, Pornography, and Equality' in D. Cornell (ed.), *Feminism and Pornography* (Oxford: Oxford University Press), 19–38.

Earle, S. and K. Sharpe (2007), 'Intimacy, Pleasure and the Men Who Pay for Sex' in G. Letherby, P. Birch, M. Cain and K. Williams (eds), *Sex as Crime* (Cullompton: Willan).

Epele, M.E. (2001), 'Excess, Scarcity and Desire among Drug-Using Sex Workers', *Body and Society* 7:2/3, 161–79.

Farley, M. (2003), 'Prostitution and the Invisibility of Harm', *Women and Therapy* 26:3/4, 247–80.

Farley, M. (2004), 'Bad for the Body, Bad for the Heart: Prostitution Harms Women Even if Legalized or Decriminalized', *Violence Against Women* 10:10, 1087–125.

Friedberg, M. (2000), 'Damaged Children to Throwaway Women: From Care to Prostitution' in J. Radford, M. Friedberg and L. Harne (eds), *Women, Violence and Strategies for Action* (Buckingham: Open University Press).

Glaser, B. and A. Strauss (1967), *The Discovery of Grounded Theory: Strategies for Qualitative Research* (Chicago, IL: Aldine).

Hakkinen, A. (1999), 'Clients of Prostitutes: An Historical Perspective on Finland' in L. Keller and M. Jyrkinen (eds), *Who's Buying: The Clients of Prostitution* (Helsinki: Council for Equality, Ministry of Social Affairs and Health).

Hoigard, C. and L. Finstad (1992), *Backstreets: Prostitution, Money and Love* (Cambridge: Polity).

Hollway, W. (1984), 'Gender Difference and the Production of Subjectivity' in J. Henriques, W. Hollway, C. Urwing, C. Venn and V. Walkerdine (eds), *Changing the Subject* (London: Methuen).

Jeffreys, S. (1997), *The Idea of Prostitution* (North Melbourne: Spinifex).

Kelly, L. (2005), 'Trafficking in the Framework of Global Economy', paper presented at the European Women's Lobby Seminar 'Trafficking in Women for Sexual Exploitation: Who Is Responsible?' London, 14 October 2005.

Kinnell, H. (2006), 'Clients of Female Sex Workers' in R. Campbell and M. O'Neill (eds), *Sex Work Now* (Cullompton: Willan Publishing).

MacKinnon, C. (1987), *Feminism Unmodified: Discourses on Life and Law* (Cambridge, MA: Harvard University Press).

Månsson, S. (2004), 'Men's Practices in Prostitution and Their Implications for Social Work' in S. Månsson and C. Proveyer (eds), *Social Work in Cuba and Sweden: Achievements and Prospects* (Göteborg/Havanna: Department of Social Work/Department of Sociology).

Marshall, S.E. (1999), 'Bodyshopping: The Case of Prostitution', *Journal of Applied Philosophy* 16:2, 139–50.

Marttila, A. (2003), 'Consuming Sex: Finnish Male Clients and Russian and Baltic Prostitution', paper presented at 'Gender and Power in the New Europe', the 5th European Feminist Research Conference, Lund University, Sweden, 20–24 August 2003.

McKeganey, N.P. and M.A. Barnard (1996), *Sex Work on the Streets, Prostitutes and Their Clients* (Buckingham: Open University Press).

Miriam, K. (2005), 'Stopping the Traffic in Women: Power, Agency and Abolition in Feminist Debates over Sex-Trafficking', *Journal of Social Philosophy* 36:1, 1–17.

Nussbaum, M. (1995), 'Objectification', *Philosophy and Public Affairs* 24:4, 249–91.

O'Connell Davidson, J. (1998), *Prostitution, Power and Freedom* (Cambridge: Polity).

O'Neill, M. (1996), 'Prostitution, Feminism and Critical Praxis: Profession Prostitute', *The Austrian Journal of Sociology*, special edition on Work and Society (Winter).

O'Neill, M. (2001), *Prostitution and Feminism: Towards a Politics of Feeling* (Cambridge: Polity).

O'Neill, M. et al. (1995), 'Juvenile Prostitution: The Experience of Young Women in Residential Care', *Childright* 113 (December).

Papadaki, E. (2007), 'Sexual Objectification: From Kant to Contemporary Feminism', *Contemporary Political Theory* 6, 330–48.

Pateman, C. (1988), *The Sexual Contract* (Cambridge: Polity).

Phoenix, J. (1999), *Making Sense of Prostitution* (Cambridge: Polity).

Radin, M. (1996), *Contested Commodities: The Trouble with Trade in Sex, Children, Body Parts and Other Things* (Cambridge, MA: Harvard University Press).

Rubin, G. (1975), 'The Traffic in Women: Notes on the Political Economy of Sex' in R. Reiter (ed.), *Toward an Anthropology of Women* (New York and London: Monthly Review Press).

Sanders, T. (2002), 'The Condom as Psychological Barrier: Female Sex Workers and Emotional Management', *Feminism and Psychology* 12, 561–6.

Shrage, L. (1989), 'Should Feminists Oppose Prostitution?', *Ethics* 99, 347–61.

Soothill, K. and T. Sanders (2005), 'The Geographical Mobility, Preferences and Pleasures of Prolific Punters: A Demonstration Study of the Activities of Prostitutes' Clients', *Sociological Research Online* 10:1, available at <http://www.socresonline.org.uk/10/1/soothill.html>.

Wesely, J. (2002), 'Growing Up Sexualised: Issues of Power and Violence in the Lives of Exotic Dancers', *Violence Against Women* 8:10, 1182–207.

Index